Currencies and Cultures

Currencies and Cultures:

The Impact of Culture on Economic Policies and the Foundations of Money

By

Noel Mark Noël

Cambridge Scholars
Publishing

Currencies and Cultures:
The Impact of Culture on Economic Policies and the Foundations of Money

By Noel Mark Noël

This book first published 2019

Cambridge Scholars Publishing

Lady Stephenson Library, Newcastle upon Tyne, NE6 2PA, UK

British Library Cataloguing in Publication Data
A catalogue record for this book is available from the British Library

ISBN (10): 1-5275-2649-6
ISBN (13): 978-1-5275-2649-5

Dedicated to my three Janes and son, Nicholas

TABLE OF CONTENTS

ACKNOWLEDGMENTS

It is a pleasure to thank those who made this book possible. The author is indebted to the patience of my wife and family for the long hours I was away from home in the development of this book. Grateful appreciation is given to my wife Jane for her support with the artwork and helpful formatting advice and skills. Gratitude is expressed to Peggy Sweeney for her professional editorial comments and assistance. I'm beholden to my fellow faculty colleagues for their professional perspectives and extra work absent from my administrative duties and missed faculty meetings. I wish to thank our campus librarian, Diane Fulkerson for her uncanny ability to find historical references and a shared interest in business history. I am indebted to those professors who taught me to critically reason and think who most benefits in a business transaction. A respectful acknowledge Drs. Nessim Hanna, John McNamara, Wilson Brown, and Chester Wasson, among others.

Of course, none of this would occur without my parents who taught me the basics of work, money, and taxes. I wish to thank my mother for escorting me as a teenager to the Federal Reserve Bank of Chicago and depositing my savings in U.S. Treasuries before my enlistment in the military. Having written this book, I can now fully appreciate and understand how capital and wealth is created. Thanks, Mom!

"The Best Way to teach kids about taxes is by eating 30% of their ice cream."
— Bill Murray comedian

LIST OF FIGURES AND ACKNOWLEDGEMENTS

List of chapter figures for illustrations, charts, maps, and photographs with credits, acknowledgements, and attributions to copyright holders. Every effort has been made to contact the copyright holders and provide rightful attribution for their works as requested. The author and publisher will be happy to make good in future editions any errors or omission brought to their attention.

U.S. Copyright law does not appear to contain any provision dealing with the ownership of copyright in currency (and it is possible that currency would be considered a non-copyrightable work under 17 USC 101 and 105). 18 USC 504 (Printing and Filming of United States and Foreign Obligations & Securities) allows the filming of real currency and sourced in the public domain.

The basic legal tenet is that if a photographer is attempting to create an exact photographic copy of a work of art or coin that is in the public domain then it is not covered by copyright in the USA and member OECD countries. www.coinsoftime.com/Articles/Copyright_of_Coin_ Photographs.html

Front Cover: Photographs of coins are from the author's personal collection with photos courtesy of JanesSunCoastWorks@comcast.net.

INTRODUCTION

CURRENCIES AND CULTURES

Keywords: *cui bono; economic history; Cliometrics; moral relativism*

"The only thing new in the world is the history you don't know."
President Harry Truman

Various historians have written about history from the view of the eye of the beholder. This book presents a pragmatic and factual account grounded in *following the money*. The Romans question everyday transactions by way of a common Latin phrase *cui bono* literally meaning *to whose profit?* —a protocol followed throughout researching the sources for this book. The author hopes to take the traveler on a different journey through time by connecting currencies and their economic policies and foundations with various cultures and civilizations. Hopefully, surprising twists and turns will bring the reader into a deeper appreciation of currencies, money, and the documented human and cultural behaviors behind them.

The interdisciplinary study of economic history, sometimes called the "*new economic history*" goes by the formal name of *Cliometrics.* Clio is the personified lyre-playing muse of history and poetry in Greek mythology. A view through the lens of cliometrics provides a quantitative set of fact-based econometric tools including historical methods, economic theory, statistical tools, demographics, labor data, financial, institutional, and business case studies. Modern cliometric studies bring an assortment of historical facts and interdisciplinary insights together to form an added human dimension to economic history. As the noted 20th-century philosopher George Santayana wrote: "*Those who cannot remember the past are condemned to repeat it.*" Similarly, Albert Einstein noted: *"Insanity is trying the same thing over and over and expecting a different result."* A more holistic approach to history may help us understand our cultural behavior and avoid being condemned to repeat its mistakes.

Economic history, as a discrete academic discipline, began in the 1930's with a dispute between the London School of Economics (LSE) and the

University of Cambridge. Cambridge viewed economic history as inseparable from the general study of history across disciplines and consigned it to the history departments commonly housed today in most colleges of the liberal arts. The study of history is frequently criticized based on *moral relativism,* as historical narratives vary according to each author's interpretation and are thus unreliable or circumspect. LSE, on the contrary, housed the study of economic history within the school's business program and international relations department. They currently support economic and geopolitical history courses, a focused research agenda, a dedicated faculty, and department chair separate from the discipline of mainstream history departments. The result is that the sciences of today are often void of their own history. Cliometrics, however, is still not widely adopted in most business programs, nor disseminated to the public at large, although business faculty often embrace business case studies as a favored pedagogical instructional method.

Modern scientists in archeology and anthropology have adopted a transdisciplinary reassessment of the origins of civilizations and cultures to study what makes them successful—or not successful. Scientists once commonly held the belief that all civilizations arose from rudimentary farming, agriculture, and animal husbandry. More recently, however, archeologists and anthropologists have begun to rethink this assumption by way of cliometric studies. It is now frequently accepted that the fundamental foundation of any civilization or culture is centered on barter, trade, and exchange—along with a division or a specialization of labor.* The nature and character of how these human behaviors evolved provide a unique cultural signature of their economic success or failure.

Human behavior is inherently insatiable with an outsized consumer desire for just about everything imaginable. Some may call this greed while others goodwill. We, humans, have the option to either take what we want, steal, murder and wage war—or we can be civilized and barter, trade, and negotiate for it. Germany and Japan once waged global war to forcibly take resources from their neighbors—only to lose the war and become great and prosperous industrial powers based on barter, trade, and exchange. Their people and culture learned how to create specific goods and services for others who were willing to reciprocate in a similar manner. Barter, trade, and exchange underlie the fundamental human incentive to design and develop things that others want and for others to respond in-kind.

The earliest humans learned to live with each other by producing goods that others wanted. Fashioning an arrowhead takes time and skill to create leading to a specialization of labor. The same holds true for a baker, a cheesemaker, or a fisherman. The 18th century economist Adam Smith described the process as a *division of labor* by those who use their skills to produce something they can trade. It was this very desire to exchange goods and services that motivated the earliest humans to specialize and fashion agriculture, farming, and animal husbandry into products that others wanted. Commerce is, therefore, the prime motivator behind most human endeavors.

Throughout history, daily transactions have led to slow, prolonged and time-consuming negotiations between the buyer and seller. Some unsuccessful cultures discouraged and even nullified this process. The Neanderthals, from what we know of them, failed miserably in their ability to trade, as did many autocratic societies that are now consigned to the trash heap of history.

The economic signature of a successful culture is based on how it can best expedite and advance the barter and trade process. Transactions are built on trust inculcated and defined by the unique signature of a culture's values, norms, and beliefs. Trust becomes the defining moral and cultural characteristic based on the widely held beliefs by its people. Successful cultures make policies to advance these behaviors and strengthen the economic foundations of their money. The social fabric of a culture rests on the degree of trust built behind its currency. Likewise, the currency and supportive economic policies mirror the level of trust within the culture.

The author will take you on a journey to explore how cultures have come to expedite and advance the process of barter, trade, and exchange. How we humans have come to adopt and use various currencies helps explain many of the cultural differences in our values, norms, and beliefs—and provide insights into who we are and the policies we make for ourselves. Recognition of our past provides insights into today's challenges brought on by globalization and the new arrival of digital cryptocurrencies and block-chain technologies. The modern application of economic history into how various cultures have exploited their wealth will ultimately reveal *cui bono* or *to whose profit?*

* For a spirited presentation that the basis of human behavior was first grounded on commerce and trade: Ridley, M. (2010). *The rational optimist: How prosperity evolves.* Harper

CHAPTER ONE

THE BIZARRE WORLD OF CURRENCIES AND CULTURES

Keywords: exonumia; Rai-stones; knife money; manilla (slave trade money); digital cash

> "He had heard people speak contemptuously of money: he wondered if they had ever tried to do without it."
>
> —W. Somerset Maugham, *Of Human Bondage. 1915*

Money is one of the most misunderstood, overlooked, essential, and taken for granted human schemes used in our everyday lives. We count on it as our primary means of value and exchange. We possess it, hold it, spend it, save it, and hoard it thinking that its value is permanent and unchanging. We use it to let others know how important we are and how smart we are to own it and hold onto it. We like to believe that the money we possess is sound and trustworthy. But money is only as sound and trustworthy as the culture is principled, honest, and uncorrupted.

The concept of *"money"* seems extremely simple and straightforward. When "money" is defined as a type of *"currency,"* however, its value becomes more complicated. The world's most bizarre and unusual currencies have their roots in some form of intrinsic value. Other than coins and paper money as official legal tender, unsanctioned items are referred to as "*exonumia.*" These are highly prized personal items either hoarded or used sparingly for trade or gifts. Their perceived value, subjectively judged at that moment in time, becomes an effective mechanism for trade and exchange. Anthropologists and archaeologists have recently come to agree that many human species and cultures have perished based on their inability to engage in barter and exchange. [1] Barter or trade is an arduous method of negotiation, while exchange needs a commonly accepted form of currency to expedite the transaction based on a value that is widely recognized as consistent, stable, and uniform.

The alternative to a negotiated exchange is simply to plunder and steal what is desired. For example, anthropological evidence suggests that the Neanderthals, who became extinct around 40,000 years ago, failed as a result of living in small groups that were sparsely dispersed leading to inbreeding and congenital mutations. Their encampments, which included hand-made tools found within a mile of their dwellings, suggest a lack of engagement with others. There was no indication of decorated shells, jewelry, or items of creative artistry that may have been evidence of trade. Their self-imposed isolation and lack of any barter or exchange with others outside of their small tribal group are recognized as the likely cause of their demise. Their culture failed to advance them into an inclusive network of human beings trading and exchanging goods among themselves and with others. [1]

Human nature is never completely satisfied; perhaps that is why so many of us remain awkwardly unhappy even when we are otherwise comfortable and wealthy. Prosperous cultures are driven by the insatiable desire of humans for "more." Culture teaches us how to get *more* through the barter and exchange of goods and services, and that process is built upon commonly accepted norms and values. Adam Smith, the Scottish moral philosopher, and pioneer in political economy published his classic work "*An Inquiry into the Nature and Causes of the Wealth of Nations*" in 1776. He postulated that the wealth of a nation is built on trade, driven by a specialization of labor among those seeking an exchange.

Humans who repeat a task usually learn to do it better the next time. A vintner will likely need to exchange his wine for cheese, and the cheesemaker is likely to trade the baker for bread. People who specialize in a trade or profession eventually become better at it while some will become noted experts. The geological resources of a region or country further drive others to negotiate an exchange for goods unique to that area. Olive oil from Spain, for example, may be exchanged for cheese from Holland. This "black hand" of exchange behavior, as Smith would call it, was something far different from the dominating political and religious institutions that preceded this new institution called an *"economy."* Recognized as the first economist, Adam Smith added a new institutional dimension to how we define ourselves and our culture based on trade and exchange.

Rai Stones or Stone Money

People from all parts of the globe have used different items to facilitate barter and exchange resulting in some strange currencies. The famed economist Milton Friedman based his University of Chicago master's thesis on Rai Stones; a currency used until the 19th century on the Islands of Yap and Guam. Located in Micronesia, Rai, or stone-money are large round disks carved out of limestone. Each stone had a hole in the middle to allow the physical movement of the larger stones, some as large as 12 feet in diameter and weighing up to four metric tons. The smaller ones (7-8 centimeters) were traded or worn as jewelry. The Island of Yap had a long established and stable population of 5,000 to 6,000 residents, and the ownership of the stones was based on oral history and trust. Using one of these stones to buy an item was as easy as saying that it no longer belonged to you, but that it was now owned by the person to whom you gave it. Larger transactions were often marked in chalk on the larger stones and placed in the center of the village for all to see. No physical movement of the larger stones was necessary as everyone knew where they were located, marked, and to whom they belonged. [2]

The people of Yap and Guam were happy with their reliable and stable currency which remained a means of efficient exchange among themselves. Their economy came to an untimely end when the Irish-American David O'Keefe was shipwrecked off the Island of Yap in 1871. O'Keefe was warmly nursed back to health by the natives and, in return, he convinced them to trade their dried coconut meat for iron tools from the surrounding islands. When the natives used the iron tools to carve more Rai stones, severe inflation followed as the newly produced stones were considered more valuable and prized than the older ones. Trade with Rai-stones finally stopped in the 19th century, as the occupying Japanese expropriated the stones and used them for construction and military fortifications. *His Majesty O'Keefe,* a 1954 adventure film starring Burt Lancaster, is entertainingly based on these events.

Milton Friedman used Rai-stones as a cultural lesson in economics. He compared the exchange of these stones with the transfer of gold between the governments of France and the U.S. during the heat of the global monetary crisis of 1933. France had requested that the U.S. government pay all its debts in gold just before the U.S. was due to abandoning the existing gold standard. Instead of shipping the gold back to France, however, it was simply moved from one vault in New York into another vault close-by that was identified as owned by France. The exchange, which was made public and deemed newsworthy, was said to have contributed to the financial panic of 1933. [2]

Figure 1-1 *Stone Money of Yap, Western Caroline Islands 1904 by William Henry Furness III*

Milton Friedman summarized this as a monetary example along with *"numerous additional ones—that illustrate how important is myth and unquestioned beliefs in monetary matters. Our own money, the money we have grown up with, the system under which it is controlled, these appear real and rational to us. The money of other countries often seems to us like paper or worthless metal, even when the purchasing power of individual unit is high."* [3]

Salt Currency

The word s*alary* stems from the Latin word "*salarium*" meaning *salt*. The early Romans paid their soldiers an allowance of salt, and *salarium* came to be a term for military pay. A soldier's salary was cut if he was "*not worth his salt,*" a common expression still used to this day. It was not until 396 B.C. that the first Roman soldiers were paid with coins. The long-delayed adoption of coinage is a phenomenon unique to the Romans, as coins were already in widespread use by other cultures. Salt is not only a food preservative, but a necessity as all humans and animals require some amount of salt to survive. Difficult to find in some places, as it was in Rome, salt was highly valued for trade and used as a common currency.

Slabs of rock salt were used as a form of coinage in what is now modern-day Ethiopia. The coins were made of dried salt, cast into slabs ten inches long by two inches thick, and easily broken into smaller sizes to make an exchange. As early as the 6th century B.C., the Moorish merchants commonly traded salt for gold at the same value per measure or weight! Ancient "s*alt roads*" were historic and heavily traveled trade routes over which salt was transported to regions in vital need of it. Trade in salt existed in the early Bronze Age and spread throughout the archaic world. The historic Roman road "*Via Salaria*" ran from the Adriatic coast to Rome and is considered by some to be the road that built Rome. [4]

Knife Money

Many cultures around the world used weapons as a currency. Archeologists have uncovered large amounts of arrowheads which they believe were used as currency to facilitate barter. What is fairly unique is the Chinese "*knife money*" of the Zhou dynasty from around 600 B.C. Knives were fashioned and inscribed with numbers and single words such as "*goat*" or "*fish*" to determine their value.

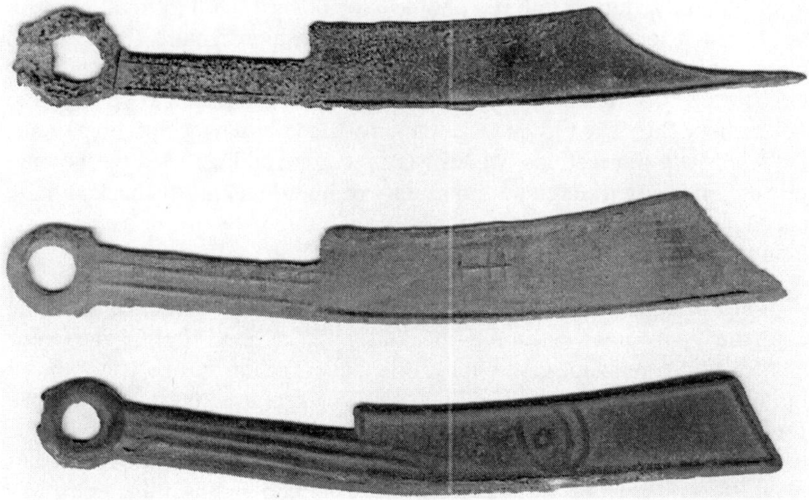

Figure 1-2 *Chinese knife money*

Manilla or Slave Trade Money

Currencies have been tied to all manner of items. Currency, or what is in *circulation,* has only recently been thought of as banknotes and coins. Forms of early currencies reflected the intrinsic value of items used as personal ornamentation, long before they were considered for use as a means of exchange for barter and trade. The early Phoenicians, based in what is now Syria and Lebanon, were thought to be the originators of a valued form of "*penannular*" (almost ring-like) money which they likely copied from the ancient Egyptians.

Penannular money is crafted ornamentation, originally bracelets and armlets, that evolved for use in trade as a more stable and constant representation of value. The Phoenicians were considered the greatest maritime traders of the Mediterranean from 3200 B.C. to 300 B.C. They deplored the inefficient, archaic, tedious and time-consuming effort required by bartering for trade. It took what seemed forever to determine: *Exactly how much is that goat in trade for wine or cheese?* They were quick to accept common items as recognized benchmarks of personal value to expedite the barter and trade process.

Phoenicia in classical Greek means "*land of purple*" in reference to the Phoenicians' export of valuable and highly prized purple murex-shell dye. The Tyrian dye turns cloth red and develops over time into royal crimson hues, which today remain a highly alluring fashion feature. True Tyrian purple paint currently exceeds $3,500 a gram. The Phoenicians' seafaring expeditions recorded their trade with the ancient Egyptians as early as the 14th century B.C. The Egyptians commonly used written receipts on papyrus for their daily transactions, which were recorded and certified by the high priests. The trusted religious community of high-level priests backed these accounts with precious metals, stones, grains, and foodstuffs as a sign of the Pharaoh's wealth over the state.

The ancient Egyptians were late in human history to introduce their first coin, the "*Nefer-nub*" (meaning fine gold) minted circa 360 B.C. The Greek General Ptolemy, who served under Alexander the Great, likely introduced the first coinage to Egypt. The Pharaoh Teos first used these coins to pay for Greek mercenaries in his service to battle the Persians. Finding no value in papyrus receipts, and before the minting of gold coins, the Phoenicians would accept metals for trade, especially common and useful jewelry like bracelets and armbands.

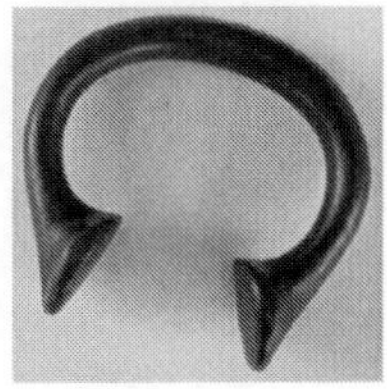

Figure 1-3 *Egyptian gold coin or the "Nefer-nub" (fine gold). Coinage was introduced to Egypt by Pharaoh Ptolemy I Soter (a general of Alexander the Great and founder of the Hellenistic state of Egypt) circa the beginning of the Ptolemy dynasty 323 B.C. The coin featured the head of Queen Arsinoe II (first daughter of Ptolemy I Soter) and was stuck under the rule of her husband and brother Ptolemy II. 8.42 grams 14-15 mm.* Figure 1-4 *Manilla slave token circa 1850s, sizes varied.*

Before the introduction of coinage, one general purpose currency that was widely used throughout ancient Egypt and Africa and into the late 1940s was the *manilla*. "*Manilla"* is derived from the Spanish word *"manella"* or bracelet and was commonly used as a medium to buy and sell slaves. Manillas were usually horseshoe-shaped jewelry clasps, with flattened ends facing each other, and likely originated in the ancient southeast Nigerian coastal cities. The Africans had names for a wide variety of manillas based on their metal content, and even the quality of the sound they made when struck. Gold manillas were regarded as adornments or jewelry and used for external trade with other distant tribes. Copper manillas were primarily crafted and produced for internal exchange among the local tribes. [5]

Copper is still regarded as the "*red gold*" of Africa and was initially mined and traded across the Sahara. It was first transported over the Silk Roads by merchants from Arabia to as far as Northern Europe and China, and often traded in the form of copper manillas. Many of the smaller copper manillas were used as a currency, while larger ones were worn as bracelets, anklets, hairpins, head jewelry, and as a show of wealth. Crafted metal clips were widely used to fasten cloth robes, capes, and fashioned as hair adornments.

The early Portuguese explorers were the first Europeans to adopt the local custom of copper bracelets and leg-bands as the common means of trade and exchange along the west coast of Africa. Portugal was then under Islamic rule and later united with Spain to form the Iberian Peninsula Union from 1580 to 1640. The Portuguese were the first to develop deep-water craft, and with the newly invented compass, were able to set sail and navigate across the ocean rather than follow the safety of the coastline. They found the navigation of the Indian Ocean child's play. [6] The Portuguese were known to have landed in the seaport of Calabar, Nigeria in 1505. These early traders purchased ivory tusks, peppers, spices, palm oil, and slaves by exchanging currency *bracelets* acceptable to the Africans. Eventually, the manilla currency became known as slave trade money and was widely used by Europeans to purchase slaves. [7]

Later, Dutch traders "*…bought slaves against payment in rough grey copper armlets which had to be very well made, otherwise the natives rejected them by the hundred.*" [8] A slave sold for about 12 to 15 brass manillas in the 1490s but correspondingly less if the manillas were solely of copper. In 1522 a female slave aged 16 in Benin cost about 50 manillas. Later, smaller pattern "*popo manillas*" which were too small to wear as bracelets, were mass produced in Birmingham England solely for the slave trade. The price of a slave, expressed in manillas, varied considerably according to time, place, and the quality of the manilla being offered.[9]

In Nigeria, the Native Currency Proclamation of 1902 prohibited the import of manillas except with a permit from the High Commissioner. The law encouraged the use of coined money pegged to the British pound, and to replace the image of the manilla as a slave currency. However, manillas were still in regular use and constituted an administrative problem until the late 1940s. The largest ethnic group in Africa, the Igbo tribe, still use them to this day. At Wukari in Nigeria, a deep-bowl of corn is considered equal to one large manilla, and a cup-shaped receptacle filled with salt is worth one small manilla. Manillas were considered legal tender as they floated in value against British and French West African currencies. The palm-oil trading companies often manipulate the value of the manilla to their advantage during the market season. [9]

Over time, humans have tried to use different items of personal value as money, from beaver pelts in North America, parmesan cheese in Italy, and tea bricks in Mongolia. Many commodities in short supply and high demand have been used to facilitate trade and barter of goods and services. Whether it be Ria-stones, salt, knife money, or manillas, they once had their place in human history, but eventually became obsolete.

Cigarettes

We shouldn't be complacent in thinking that these strange currencies only existed in history. The *funny money* of history has been reenacted even in modern times. Following Germany's defeat in World War I, the Treaty of Versailles forced Germany to pay considerable reparations to the victorious Allies. Germany simply went off the gold-backed *Goldmark* and converted it to a fiat *Papiermark* to finance the payments. By the end of 1923, it took one trillion *Papiermarks* to buy one single *Goldmark*! Prudent German middle-class savers were punished as all of their savings lost value. Again in 1945, Germany's defeat saw an end to the gold-backed *Reichsmark*. Three years elapsed before the Deutschemark was officially introduced in June 1948. During the three-year interim, the de facto currency was American cigarettes: primarily of prized value were Pell Mell and Lucky Strike brands. Both were used as currency for commonly traded goods, while more expensive items, gifts, and favors were paid in cognac.[10]

Even today cigarettes serve as an international currency in some parts of the world. Prisoners in many penitentiaries and reformatories use cigarettes or postage stamps as common currencies. Giving and sharing cigarettes is customary in China as cigarettes play a routine role in Asian culture. Although all forms of corruption are officially banned, nothing gets done unless those in power are presented with gifts for favors. Cartons of *Good Cat* brand cigarettes have become the customary currency that is used to bribe officials for favors in China.[11] Please, don't tell the Chairman!

Red Gold – Copper & Bronze Currency

Copper, found pure in nature, was the first metal to be used by humans. Neolithic artifacts of raw hammered copper, discovered in items made by native Indians in the Great Lakes region of the U.S., dating back to 8,000 B.C. The technology which led to furnace-like pottery kilns, circa 4,000 B.C., provided the higher temperatures necessary for the smelting and refining of copper. Anthropologists, therefore, link the excavation of pottery to the ability of a culture to smelt copper. The addition of other metals, by early 3500 B.C., was used to harden copper into bronze.

Copper in the early Roman era was largely mined on the Mediterranean island of Cyprus. The word for Cyprus is corrupted from "*cuprum*" from which we now get the English word copper. Copper, silver, and gold are in Group 11 of the periodic table and share certain attributes which make them valuable to humans. Copper is bright red-orange, mixes well with other metals at relatively low temperatures, and is found in abundance. The price of copper has been historically unstable, as demand for it correlates to fluctuating economic conditions. It is used in the building trades, electric wire, plumbing, electronics, and even jewelry.[12] "*Red gold*" was considered as a precious metal for use in an exchange transaction.[13]

Large quantities of copper were discovered in Sweden about 1,000 years ago in a place named Stora Kopparberg or the Great Copper Mountain. The Falun Mine produced over two-thirds of Europe's copper needs up until the 18th century. Copper smelting started with local farmers, who chopped down trees and started large fires alongside the mountain. Eventually, the dangerous task of digging into the mountain led to the certification of licensed miners as the first professionally recognized occupation. King Olof Skotkonung was very impressed by his miners as they made Sweden wealthy by trading copper with other nations. The miners unionized in A.D. 1288, and the King gladly granted the free-miners shares and ownership control as an incentive for them to increase production. Later, in A.D. 1347, King Magnus IV granted a corporate charter.

Today the company is named Stora Enso and continues as a privately held Swedish company with some 27,000 employees. It owns half as much territory as Belgium and operates primarily as a forest and paper products company.[14] Stora Enso is believed by many experts to be the oldest continuously operating corporation in the world. Copper can be credited with giving the world its first chartered corporation and the first ownership shares to its laborers.

In the 17th and 18th century Sweden, owing to its numerous high-quality copper mines, was one of the great empires in Europe. Queen Christina of Sweden (A.D. 1632 to 1654) initially offered paper-based money backed by copper. The official proclamation incentivized overproduction, resulting in the loss of value for both the copper and the paper money it backed. The Queen then issued copper in lumps as large as fifteen kilograms (33 pounds) to serve as hard currency. Unwieldy as it was, this first copper-based monetary system worked for a while until the world copper price slumped from overproduction. Baron von Görtzhe, a Swedish central banker, saw this as an opportunity to issue a copper-based coin currency. The copper coins were easy to counterfeit and became so abundant that they depreciated rapidly towards their raw metal value, spreading the belief that the copper coins would soon be unacceptable as a form of payment of taxes. Görtz was blamed for this failure and was subsequently beheaded as punishment, greatly pleasing the Swedish people.[15]

Gold: The Big Brother of Copper

Gold, like copper, occurs purely in nature. Humans have used it as a show of status in jewelry and other art forms since the beginning of recorded time. This colorful, shiny yellow metal is durable, corrosion-resistant, conducts electricity, and is widely used and valued for industry. It never deteriorates and lasts indefinitely. Gold crafted artifacts were first found in present-day Israel with many items dating back to the 4th millennium B.C. Hieroglyphs from 2600 B.C. describe Egyptian gold as more "plentiful than dirt" among the wealthy and social elite. Egyptian gold was mined in the Nubian mountains and panned downstream of the Nile River as it flowed from the highlands of central Africa to the Mediterranean Sea.

Pure gold coins are a relatively new invention, with the first ones appearing about 550 B.C. Today an estimated 50% of gold is used in jewelry, 40% as investments and 10% by industry. It is estimated that for every ounce of gold, miners will dig up and haul away 30 tons of rock. The rock then requires a tedious and hazardous process to extract and refine it. Gold primarily remains valuable due to its scarcity. The gold standard, as a stable monetary system, was successfully implemented among nations for more than several hundred years. The existence of such a small amount of gold provides a benchmark for the value of any currency by which it is officially backed.[16]

Figures from the Thomson Reuters' Annual Gold Survey are used by investors to track the daily value of gold. This real-time report accounts for all the gold that has ever been mined. This includes all the above-ground gold stored in Fort Knox and the New York Federal Reserve, all central banks around the globe, all jewelry, coinage, and everything else that is gold. Gold is measured in *tonnes*, with one metric tonne equal to 1.10231 U.S. tons—often called a short ton. An American short ton of 2,240 pounds equals one metric tonne or 1,000 kilograms. The global quantity of gold currently weighs in at 183,600 tonnes. (The gold tomb of Tutankhamen's coffin contains 1.5 tonnes). Given a spot price of about $1,300 (January, 2019) per troy ounce, 183,600 metric tonnes at 32,150.75 troy ounces of gold per tonne, would today yield a value of $7,673,741,010,000 or about $7.6 trillion.[18]

If you have gold for your wedding ring or watch, it may have been mined by the Romans over 2,000 years ago. The United States Government Gold Reserve reports 261,498,926 troy ounces of gold, mostly in deep storage in Denver CO, Fort Knox KY, and West Point NY. The U.S. has the largest of all government reserves with some 8,133.5 metric tonnes or 2.1 percent of all sovereign countries' holdings worldwide. United States gold production was estimated to be just 200 tons in 2015. U.S. government's ownership of gold is followed by Germany's 3,381 tonnes, Italy's 2,451, France's 2,435, China's 1,693, Russia's 1,317 and Switzerland's 1,040.[19]

Figure 1-5 *Trustworthy estimates conclude that all the existing gold in the world if cast into a square cube, would measure 20.7 meters or 67.9 feet on each side—the equivalent of a single six-story square building!* [17] *The United States is the largest sovereign holder of gold but holds only four percent of the global total – the size of a small retail store in a six-story building.*

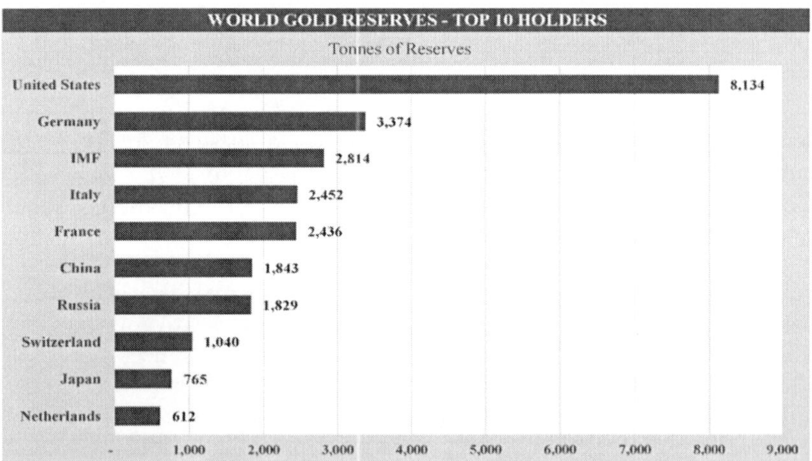

Figure 1-6 *Chart of the top ten largest gold reserves 2018 Data Source: World Gold Council.*

Two of the largest holdings of gold today can be found in New York and London. The largest known stockpile is buried deep in the bedrock of Manhattan by the Federal Reserve Bank of New York. However, only 2% to 5% is owned by the U.S. government while the remainder is owned by foreign countries. If Germany wants to pay Russia for something in gold, it calls the U.S. Federal Reserve and has the bars physically moved to the Russian vault for a small transaction fee. Few such transactions now occur, however, as gold is no longer officially recognized as a government-backed currency used for exchange.[20]

The New York Mercantile Exchange's commodities division trades a variety of metals, including gold, silver, copper, and platinum, which are stored in vaults throughout New York. This cache is used to back futures contracts through its commercial trading venue. The world's largest stash of silver is housed in London, not because the British government uses the pound sterling as a currency, but because J.P. Morgan Bank keeps tons of silver as collateral to back Barclays IShares silver (SLV) exchange-traded fund.

Historically the United States issued paper currency backed by both gold and silver. However, due to the inflationary costs of the Vietnam War, the War on Poverty, and other fiscal entitlements and spending, President Nixon repealed the Bretton Woods Agreement in August 1971 which had tied all the world's currencies to the dollar. The United States and most European governments at the time posted little sovereign debt. If a government issued too much currency over that of its fiscal productivity, it would clearly be seen as inflationary. In 1971, the U.S. went off of the gold standard and entered the world of fiat money as it refused to address its fiscal problems. Fiat is Latin for *"let it be done"* as in a government decree or edict. The U.S. government, through the Federal Reserve Bank, now sells paper dollars–not backed by gold but by decree. Globally, since 1971, other governments have followed the U.S.'s lead in determining the value of their fiat currencies, and national debt loads for all counties have spiraled upwards. The Swiss franc was changed to a fiat currency on May 1, 2000—the last currency that was backed by a gold standard.

Most central banks, however, still maintain their sovereign gold holdings as they figure into the Special Drawing Rights (SDR) assigned by the International Monetary Fund (IMF) to a basket of key international currencies which is reviewed by the IMF every five years. To supplement a shortfall in preferred foreign exchange reserve assets, the SDR was created in 1969 to deal with the lack of a common gold standard. SDRs are technically not a currency, but instead, represent a claim to currency held by IMF member countries for which they may be exchanged. Effective October 1, 2016, the IMF decided that the Renminbi (Chinese yuan) would be added to the basket of SDRs. Currently, the basket now consists of the following five currencies: the U.S. dollar 41.73%, Euro 30.93%, Chinese renminbi 10.92%, Japanese yen 8.33%, and the British pound 8.09%.[21]

The Federal Reserve Economic Data (FRED) estimates the M2 Money Stock (liquid instruments of cash, checking deposits, mutual funds, and other no-interest time deposits, or near cash deposits that can be quickly converted into cash within two days) is reported to be $13,060,900,000,000 or 13 trillion dollars as of September 2016. In 1971, the M2 money stock totaled only 611 billion dollars representing an increase of nearly 22 times in just 45 years. The United States government reports gold holdings of 8,133.5 metric tonnes with 32,150 troy ounces per tonne. Dividing the M2 currency of $13 trillion by 261 million troy ounces of U.S. gold reserves results in an astonishing $49,808 per troy ounce of gold today–significantly more than the $35 per ounce gold standard in 1971.[22]

The Silver Standard

In the early 1500s, King Ferdinand of Spain proclaimed the priorities for his conquistadors as they set sail for the New World. "*Get gold,*" he told them, "*humanely if possible, but at all costs, get gold!*"[23] Not only did the new civilizations they encountered possess gold, but they also held vast amounts of silver. Silver is often produced as a plentiful by-product of gold mining. Compared to gold, the price of silver can be notoriously volatile. Although silver coinage was in widespread use throughout the centuries, it was the Spanish discovery of enormous silver deposits in Potosi, Bolivia, and Lima, Peru in the 16th century that established a new international silver standard. The repercussion of this would have enormous consequences on trade, war, and conquests as well as currency markets worldwide.

The great Spanish treasure fleet, founded primarily on silver and some lesser gold shipments, was a convoy system of ships governed for over two centuries by the Spanish Empire (1566 - 1790) linking Spain to its territories in the new world. Spain at that time controlled the seas and required, by law, return trade with its colonies to be assigned to only one port in Seville. Seville became the official Spanish port where import taxes were collected to replenish the King's treasury. Spanish cargo fleets transported lumber, agricultural goods, spices, and tobacco, however, the prized commodities were gold and silver confiscated by the conquistadors.

By the end of the 16th century, Spain was the richest country in Europe, based on its inordinate access to silver. The Spanish "*piece of eight*" coin became the basis for an international silver standard that lasted nearly four hundred years and would compete with gold as a currency of preference. The import of ever larger quantities of silver to Europe began a process of inflation which began to destabilize the long-held ancient Roman silver-to-gold ratio of 12 or 12 ½ ounces of silver to every one ounce of gold.[24] In 1792 the ratio was fixed in the United States by law at 15:1. By 1803, France had reset the ratio of silver to gold at 15 ½ to 1. The discovery of silver at the Comstock Lode in Nevada in 1849 would force the United States to rethink the link of silver to gold altogether. More recently, large discoveries of silver have destabilized the historic silver to gold ratio. Today, although volatile, the value of silver to gold is more on the order of 81 to 1.

Since the 1800s, silver has been discovered in regions all over the globe. Only 20 percent of silver production comes from silver mining. Most of it is a by-product of mining for other metals, such as copper, lead, zinc, and gold. Global silver production is estimated to increase by 26,000 tons (2016) annually, or about 5 percent, with the three largest silver producers being Mexico (5,400), China (4,000) and Peru (2,500).[25] Other than use as a currency, silver has numerous industrial and medical applications.

Electronic Cash

A debit card is a plastic payment card that is used for cash transactions. Unlike that of a credit card, the money is immediately withdrawn from the user's bank account. Early forms of electronic transfer funds using debit or charge cards were first issued by the Western Union Company and later by some oil companies for exclusive transactions. Bank consortiums soon evolved into a *revolving credit* financial system in which a card issued by a third-party bank was accepted by a number of various merchants, as opposed to merchant-issued charge cards accepted by an exclusive trade group of merchants. The first universal credit card was introduced in 1950 by the Diners' Club, Inc., to be used in a variety of establishments, followed by the travel and entertainment card issued by the American Express Company in 1958. Bank of America convinced its vast network of merchants to accept its card under the brand name of VISA in 1976, and Citibank branded its card as MasterCard. Credit cards became a widely accepted and effective way for customers to make purchases without having access to their local banking institutions or carrying large amounts of cash. Countless variations on the concept of revolving credit include affinity cards, corporate user cards, brokerage accounts, and various merchant cards. Regulations and social norms among countries reflect the acceptance of different types of currency transactions, with Japan remaining a very traditional cash-oriented society, while the convenience of credit cards is most preferred in the United States.[26]

Merchants that accept transactions by way of credit cards must pay interchange fees and merchant discount fees to the card companies. These merchant transaction fees amount to 1 to 4 percent on the total sale price, along with a variable charge for each transaction called a merchant discount rate. In some cases, merchants are barred by contract from passing these fees directly to the customers who use credit cards. The result is that merchants are obligated to charge all customers (including those who do not use credit cards) higher prices to cover credit card transaction fees. Some countries allow their merchants to offer discounts to customers who use cash.

The merchant's fee is a percentage of the sale price and has a disproportionate effect on the profitability of businesses that are dependent on credit card transactions. In 2008, credit card companies in the U.S. collected a total of $48 billion, or an average of $427 per family with a typical rate fee of about 2 percent per transaction.[27] As a comparison, Alexander Hamilton in 1792 set the price of an ounce of gold at $19.39 in exchange for the convenience of a paper twenty-dollar bill, or a 3 percent bank transaction fee.

The first widely accepted cash machine was installed by Barclays Bank of London on June 27, 1967. [27] The idea was borrowed from a chocolate bar dispenser and evolved into a sophisticated method for banks to dispense money and later accept deposits. The automatic teller machines (ATMs) or bank machines (ABMs) soon developed into interbank networks known as ATM consortia, which enabled ATM transactions to be performed among members of the network. Member banks pay a slight fee to the consortium as do customers who do not have membership in the bank network.

Digital Cash and Cryptocurrency

E-commerce or the electronic transfer of funds requires a third party to *pull* information from both the merchants' and customers' bank accounts, all of which require a fee to complete the transaction. This type of transaction is open to fraud as it is only as secure as its weakest link—whether it be the merchant, customer, bank or fund payment system.

A cryptocurrency is a *push* style peer-to-peer payment system that takes place between users directly without an intermediary, other than a currency exchange which may charge less than .05 percent of the transaction. *DigiCash* was first to demonstrate a digital cash transaction in 1994.[28] Bitcoin successfully overcame security hurdles with the release of open-source MIT-licensed software based on *blockchain* technology in 2009. The security provided by the blockchain technology is assured through the decentralized computational power required to validate the phenomenal blocks of code attached to match the exchange between the buyer and seller for each transaction. Blockchain technology is now widely used in many forms of trade other than just currency transactions. A cryptocurrency is cash in digital code that can be carried on a flash drive or simply transferred over the global internet. Since the system works without a central repository or single administrator, the U.S. Treasury categorizes all types of cryptocurrencies as a decentralized virtual currency.[29]

Bitcoin currently has the largest market penetration of all the new competing cryptocurrencies. Instead of the interchange fees of the charge-card processors, merchants who accept bitcoin pay zero to less than one percent transaction fee. Consumer research estimates that a third of all users abandon an online transaction when they reach the cumbersome step of keying in a 16-digit credit card number, along with personal information that may be open to fraud. Bitcoin, as well as other cryptocurrencies, are now accepted as payment by many merchants and can be exchanged through global based currency exchanges.

Cryptocurrencies are meant to facilitate an immediate exchange transaction and not for safe long-term keeping. In comparison, an internet purchase of stock through a mutual fund may charge several percent for the transaction, versus that of personally investing in an internet electronic traded fund or ETF, which would charge 1/18,000 of a percent for the digital cash transaction.

The Nugget

Whether it be: Rai Stones from the Islands of Yap and Guam, slave trade Manillas, or modern-day cryptocurrencies—the preferred medium of exchange presents a significant insight into the functioning of a culture. As a culture evolves and becomes more sophisticated and complex—so mirrors that of its currency.

CHAPTER TWO

CIVILIZATIONS & CULTURES: THE FOUNDATIONS OF WEALTH

Keywords: cradle of civilization; Mesopotamia; Egypt; China; Indus Valley; Norte Chico; Mesoamerica

> "The greatest advances of civilization, whether in architecture or painting, in science and literature, in industry or agriculture, have never come from centralized government."
>
> Milton Friedman, 20th-century economist

Scientists in anthropology and archaeology, armed with new scientific innovations and genetic techniques, are reassessing the origins of the earliest of human civilizations. A civilization is identified when evidence supports that it evolved independently and formed its own set of languages, traditions, social structure, values, and norms. A civilization provides the catalyst for the formation and evolution of associated cultures under its signature umbrella. The earliest indicators of the emergence of civilizations occurred in the final stages of the Neolithic era when advances in agriculture and trade led to rapid urbanization fundamentally changing human existence. Scientists have identified six great civilizations which have influenced, to varying degrees and levels of success, the modern cultures of today. Each provides insights into their use of money and economic mindset.

Although the concept is still open to much debate and discovery, each *cradle of civilization* comprises interconnected cultures, subcultures, and societies with distinct and separate stages of economic development.[1, 2, 3] Scholars have identified four geographically "old world" civilizations that meet their criteria. They include *Mesopotamia, Egypt, the Indus Valley,* and *China*, while the "new world" housed the civilizations of the *Norte Chico* and *Mesoamerica*. These six civilizations are the predecessors which influenced the emergence of many cultures. The differences that characterize these highly diverse civilizations provide a window to view the foundations of their economic heritage and cultural progeny.

Scientists believe that we modern Homo sapiens evolved about 300,000 years ago, while the earliest civilizations arose only within the last 6,500 to 10,000 years. [4] Six cradles of civilization are documented as they transitioned from the Neolithic Stone Age into agrarian cultures.[5, 6] The *Fertile Crescent* (~3000 to 500 B.C.) is a region that provided the foundation for two of the earliest known civilizations, those of *Mesopotamia* and *Ancient Egypt.* Both civilizations overlapped within the same period and shared close geographic proximity to support a regional concept. The early adoption of horses and the introduction of horsepower advanced human prosperity throughout the Fertile Crescent, which gave it a substantial advantage over other developing civilizations. Horses originated in the Ural Mountains in what is now northern Russia. Remains of the earliest domesticated horses were discovered entombed with chariots in eastern European cultures. "Horsepower" was an innovation rapidly adopted by the people of Mesopotamia and Egypt circa 2100 B.C.[7]

Mesopotamia lies to the east of the Fertile Crescent, between the Tigris and Euphrates rivers, in what is now Turkey and Iraq. This area was first inhabited by the Sumerians and Akkadians circa 3500 B.C., long before the beginning of written history.[8] The diversity of cultures connected with this area expanded over time to include areas within the Levantine coast of the Mediterranean Sea, Syria, Jordan, Israel, Palestine, and Lebanon, along with portions of Turkey and Iran. Many of these cultures would later coalesce into the Persian Empire around the 6th century B.C. Mesopotamians were the first to worship one monotheistic god through the religion of Zoroastrianism: a predecessor to other major world religions. Scholars consider the Mesopotamian civilization to be the cultural foundation for the Hebrews, the ancient Greeks, Romans, and onward to modern-day Western Civilization.

Ancient Egypt historically coincided with Mesopotamia within the region of the Fertile Crescent, although it remained more culturally and geographically isolated. The surrounding vast deserts provided isolation and protection from neighboring incursions. The lush environment of the Nile Valley, and the predictable flooding cycle of the Nile River, allowed agriculture to flourish. Now located in the modern country of Egypt, this civilization reached its pinnacle of world power during the New Kingdom. Radiocarbon dating places the exact beginning between B.C. 1570 and B.C. 1544.

The ancient Egyptian civilization experienced over 175 pharaohs, from the first declared Pharaoh, Narmar (3150 B.C.), to its last Pharaoh, Cleopatra (30 B.C.). Ancient Egypt was built upon an elaborate system of religious beliefs and an authoritative administrative bureaucracy, while Mesopotamia harbored more self-reliance and autonomy based on a free flow of barter and trade. Mesopotamian and Egyptian civilizations were often engaged in wars, as well as in reciprocal barter and trade, both of which accelerated the development of the Fertile Crescent.

The cultures spawned within the Fertile Crescent were dependent on agriculture and hand-crafted goods. Commercial trade between them developed along well-documented trade routes which featured prominently in their economic development and rising prosperity. The open waterways flowing through Mesopotamia made it an ideal marketplace for commerce to evolve. The network of trade routes, later to become known as the Silk Road, connected vast territories from Egypt to China, India, and Central Asia. Early items of trade included grains, cooking oil, pottery, jewelry, and baskets. Mesopotamians acquired gold from Egyptian traders while pearls and ivory were obtained from Indian merchants. [9]

Paper money or coins did not exist until much later. The common method of exchange was based on weights of barley for local trade, personal items or exonumia, and raw silver, tin, and other metals for more distant transactions. Barley is a heavy grain that can be counted and used on weighing scales to set exchange values for common goods throughout ancient Mesopotamia. Traders could borrow barley from a barley banker to use as a commodity currency. The term “shekel” originated from the early Hebrew word for a weight of barley, and the shekel is now the currency of the State of Israel. Interest rates on loans of barley (up to 33 percent) were substantially higher than on silver (20 percent).[10] Conversely the ancient Egyptian government centralized their wheat harvests and meticulously recorded the acquisitions on papyrus. By order of the Pharaoh, commercial transactions took place under the guarded scrutiny of the government appointed priests who appropriated much of what was produced.

The *Indus Valley Civilization* encompassed an expansive territory that currently includes Pakistan, Afghanistan, and northwest India, which flourished in the basin of the Indus River. It is also known as the Harappan Civilization, after Harappa, the first of the sites to be excavated in the 1920s. The Indus script is still un-deciphered, and much remains to be learned about this newly discovered ancient civilization.[11]

Figure 2-1 Left. *Silver Half Shekel circa 66-70 A.D. Obverse "Shekel of Israel/ Year 3.'Reverse "Jerusalem the Holy" from the First Jewish-Roman War. The coin served as the medium of payment for the temple tax in Jerusalem. Source: Classical Numismatic Group, Inc. Http:///www.cngcoins.com* Figure 2-2 Right. *The Cleopatra bronze coin drachma of infamous Cleopatra VII Philapator, last of the Ptolemies and Pharaohs circa 50-31 B.C. Obverse: Draped bust with hair in a bun. Reverse: Eagle standing left of a thunderbolt.*

The ancient *Asian or Chinese civilization* was founded upon a system of family lineage or dynasties. The Shang dynasty, in 1766 B.C., provided the earliest known body of Chinese writing. The distinctive character of this civilization is attributed to the two great rivers—the Yellow River to the north and the Yangtze to the south.[12, 13] Shell money was widely used as it was found abundantly in the Indian Ocean. The glossy porcelain-like cowry shells were first used for ornamentation and evolved into a form of currency for trading. Knife money, handcrafted of various shapes of iron and limited in scope, was also used to make commercial exchange transactions.

The first circular coinage of this civilization had a square hole in the center apparently to tie the coins together. It was made from iron and other non-precious metals and was introduced circa 350 B.C. The coinage originated as fiat money based on the discretion of the government or dynasty du jour.[14] The value of such coinage would change with every dynasty leading to antique coins of dubious worth.

Silver coinage was not introduced into this region until the late 15th century beginning with the establishment of trade by way of the Spanish conquest of the Philippines. The silver "Dragon" coins, sometimes known as *Dragon dollars* were only later adopted and issued by China, Japan, and Korea for general circulation in their own countries. The Dragon coinage was based on the Spanish introduction of the popular silver *Spanish Piece of Eight* or *Spanish dollar*. The lack of precious metal coinage largely stunted the development of the Asian economies as they lacked a standard and stable measure of value to speed commercial and trade transactions.

In A.D. 1600, after a long period of internal strife and constant warfare, the Japanese warlord Tokugawa Ieyasu united Japan under one government.

The Tokugawa era provided the island nation relative peace and prosperity by creating a clockwork system of continuity and feudalism which closed the country off to the outside world. Its economy existed largely on barter with the government taking 30 to 80 percent of the harvests leaving farmers only subsistence for a living. The currency was a hodgepodge of non-precious metal coins and paper notes occasionally being debased by official decree. Paper monies included rice notes, umbrella notes, string notes, and potter's wheel notes, among others.

The Tokugawa era of a medieval society persisted until 1886, anachronistically, up to the middle to the industrialized nineteenth century. The great transfiguration occurred when Commodore Matthew Perry sailed into Tokyo Bay in 1853. With a mere eight ships, and at gunpoint, extracted a free-trade treaty from the Japanese government. By 1876, within only several decades, the Meiji government adopted a Western-style banking system and introduced a nationwide Japanese currency based on a gold and silver standard of one yen to one U.S. dollar. [16] Japan's economy blossomed.

Figure 2-3 Left *Ancient Chinese iron coins with square holes that can be strung together.* Figure 2-4 Right *Korean Silver Dragon, 1905*

Two great civilizations arose in the new world era of pre-Columbian America long before the arrival of the Spanish in 1521. The earliest is the *Norte Chico* civilization which flourished from 3200 B.C. to its period of decline circa 1800 B.C. The Norte Chico were located along the Pacific coastline in present-day Peru, home to the later well-known Inca Empire. The citadel of Machu Picchu in Peru, often referred to as the "Lost City of the Incas" was abandoned in A.D. 1450 soon after it was built. The great pre-Columbian *Mesoamerican* civilization was a mosaic of the early cultures of Central America best known by the more recent Aztec and Mayan cultures. Both civilizations were inclusive of many different cultures, subcultures, and tribes. Their civilizations peaked well before the era of the Portuguese and Spanish conquests and colonization.

The indigenous llama was widely used for meat and as a domesticated pack animal since the Pre-Columbian era. While the Mesoamerican and Norte Chico civilizations did know of the wheel and basic metallurgy, neither of these technologies became culturally important. Norte Chico's differences as a civilization are notably striking as a total lack of ceramics persisted throughout the period. British Broadcasting Corporation observed that Norte Chico's people would have roasted their various crops as there was no pottery in which to boil them.[16] The lack of pottery was accompanied by a lack of archaeologically apparent art. A BBC special feature noted: *"In the Norte Chico we see almost no visual arts. No sculpture, no carving or bas-relief, almost no painting or drawing—the interiors are completely bare. What we do see are these huge (burial) mounds—and textiles."* [17, 18]

The later Aztecs, of the post-classic Mesoamerican period from A.D. 1300 to 1521, occasionally used cocoa beans as a currency, which varied in success and stability considering the diverse size and quality of the beans. No mention of a standard currency to replace barter and trade can be found in the historical literature for either of these civilizations. Scholars now believe that it was the autocratic structure of these societies, based on demands and dictates from authoritarian rulers, that inhibited and suppressed the individuals' initiative to trade and exchange goods more efficiently.

Some cultures expanded while others lay dormant or exist only as mere remnants of once great civilizations. The heritage of every culture is germane to the birthplace of its civilization and its inherited characteristics. The origins of civilization have considerable implications for the successes or failures of their economic policies and their position in today's world economy. Successful cultures evolve and re-invent themselves over time to adapt to their changing environment, while autocratic dynasties often remain stagnant and resist innovation. Western culture has successfully managed to transition and redefine itself with new cultural identities such as Greco-Roman, the Renaissance, the Enlightenment, the First, Second, and Third Industrial Revolutions, and up to the present Western inspired Technological Revolution. Presently the West encompasses an unclear and undefined geographical area, as globalization has spread Western ideas so widely that all modern cultures are influenced by Western culture.

The Dawn of Money

The Lydians, descendants of the Mesopotamian civilization in western Asia Minor, are noted as the first culture to introduce a form of gold and silver coinage in 650 B.C. They were geographically centered along the commercial trade routes of the Fertile Crescent and are recognized by scholars as the first culture to establish permanent retail sites. They adopted and shared many of the cultural values and beliefs of their neighbor the ancient Greeks and are associated with pre-Hellenistic culture as described by Homer. The Lydians worshiped the Olympian gods and contributed to the mythology by way of their King Croesus. The expression "as rich as Croesus" (pronounced KREE-sus) is said to have come from the legendary hoarding of gold by King Midas.[19] The ancient Greeks quickly adopted the Lydian concept of money and portrayed in their coinage the images of their sacred and favorite Olympian gods. The Romans would later embrace and convert to all things Greek.

Figure 2-5 Left *A Roman Republic silver denarius Mars god of war coin circa 182 A.D. which was widely popular among the soldiers. (19mm, 3.65 gm) The reverse is nude Mars walking to the right. The obverse features Emperor Commodus.* Figure 2-6 Right. *A Greek tetradrachm silver owl coin which features the Greek goddess Athena circa 512 to 50 B.C. Hephaestus was widely favored as the god of the males while Athena was most revered as the goddess by the females.*

The ancient Greek culture was first to transform precious metal coins into a sacred and religious context. The Greeks were very religious and devout people who worshipped the family of the twelve Olympian gods. Today we dismiss their religious ideas as just Greek mythology. However, their beliefs were revered and venerated by the ancient Greeks. Their gods and beliefs were replicated by the later Romans who simply renamed and adopted them into their Roman culture. The Olympics Games were first initiated in the 8th century B.C., as a religious celebration of these ancient gods. Greek mythology has since served as a basis of lore and legends for Western civilization.

The male Greeks most admired and idolized the Olympian god Hephaestus, who served as the blacksmith to the gods and was highly revered in the manufacturing and industrial centers of Greece. Zeus had cast him out of Mount Olympus due to a physical deformity (likely acquired from his metalsmithing). However, he was the only god to be allowed to return and thus became the favorite male role model for the ancient Greeks.

The Temple of Hephaestus, still located at the base of the Acropolis, is where gold and silver coins were first minted to pay for the construction of Athens during the "Golden Age of Pericles" (495-429 B.C.)

According to mythology, Hephaestus was the metalsmith who crafted the golden thrones for each of the Olympian Gods. Each throne had different folkloric ideals and principles important to the traditions of Greek culture. Hera's Throne (Goddess of marriage), Demeter's Throne (Goddess of agriculture) Aphrodite's Throne (Goddess of love and beauty), Apollo's Throne (God of the sun and music) all served as foundations for societal values, traditions, and norms.[20] Their images were often portrayed on their coinage.

Gold and precious metals have served as both a system of monetary worth and a method to convey important cultural values and beliefs since the beginnings of Western civilization. Alexander the Great, for example, strategically portrayed the Goddess Athena and himself on gold and silver coinage while advancing his global conquests. The cultural tradition continues with the official motto of the United States "*In God We Trust*" printed on all U.S. currency along with that of the founding fathers and admired presidents.

Defining Culture and Nation Building

"A nation's culture resides in the hearts and the soul of its people."
Mahatma Gandhi

Culture is a central concept in anthropology and is defined as the social behavior and norms found in human societies. It provides a structure for knowledge transmitted by human members of society from one generation to the next. Human knowledge shapes culture and that knowledge mirrors society's cultural institutions. During the Stone Age, people fashioned rocks and bones into crude arrowheads. Over time, innovations in materials and enhanced skills, advanced from one generation to another, continuously building upon what had been previously learned. Arrowheads led to spears, spears to bows, bows to longbows and compound bows, leading to present-day archery as a competitive sport and recreation—even into an art form. Similarly, a modern cordless computer mouse is about the same size as an arrowhead, but it evolved over generations of continuous human inventions and advances in technologies. It would be impossible today for one person to create a cordless computer mouse without building upon the knowledge of past discoveries and accomplishments.

Cultural institutions are formal organizations that uphold and support the learned values of its members. What is most important and valued by society are considered the *values* of that culture. We think of culture as found in places like museums, libraries, churches, and art galleries—as these institutions serve to confirm and promote culture. However, the primary functions of these institutions often go unnoticed, neglected, or taken for granted. The existence and interaction of social institutions reflect and reinforce the values of culture as they are essential to the concept of self-identity and nation-building. For example, the economic right to the private ownership of property, only valued in some societies, is supported through the political, legal, and other social structures providing social order for that value. The United States Constitution defines many of the nation's cultural values in its Bill of Rights, which establishes specific protections of individual liberty and justice and places restrictions on the powers of government. The protections and continuity of these stated values are reinforced by cultural institutions.

Highly successful institutions and organizations actively monitor their environment and review changes in society that may directly affect their planned activities. "*Environmental scanning*" is a strategic tool or model, often taught in business schools and used to examine the impact of culture on some economic endeavor. It is an important first step in a documented and evolving business plan. Monitoring the environment provides new managerial insights into products and business ventures by scanning for disruptive technologies or societal changes that can affect the business plan.

One early business model is PEST analysis (political, economic, social, and technological) which is used as a framework to examine cultural institutions for a possible impact on a business decision. Business analysts use this model to understand market growth or decline, business positioning, and the potential or direction of future operations. Popular in the United Kingdom is the PESTLE business framework that includes legal and environmental factors in a given cultural setting. An evaluation of the internal *strengths* and *weaknesses* of an organization, and the external *opportunities* and *threats* provides a documented *SWOT* analysis that businesses can use to determine and defend their strategic decisions. [21]

Our understanding of modern cultural institutions has expanded along with the number of institutions that need to be monitored. "G2-FREEPT" is a useful mnemonic or metaphor for Geography and Geology, Family, Religion, Economics, Education, Politics, and Technology. The sequence is noteworthy as it tracks a progression of cultural integration and influence in a specific region or country. The study of a culture's primary institutions starts with its physical environment, which includes both its geology and geography designated as G2. Other institutions monitored are the family, its religious beliefs, the economic structure, education, politics, and technology. The mnemonic of G2-FREEPT provides a schema to study the influence of a culture and its economic policies.

G2 - Geography and Geology

> "Geography has made us neighbors. History has made us friends. Economics has made us partners, and necessity has made us allies. Those whom God has so joined together, let no man put asunder."
>
> John F. Kennedy

G2 stands for geography, and its cousin—geology, both refer to a region's location and natural resources. G2 has a substantial impact on human development and the formation of its cultural institutions. Ancient Rome, for example, had few natural resources but a geographic location that sparked its many conquests. The global location and access to natural geological resources provide an early foundation for the cultural development of human institutions.

The subterranean geology of the Wall Street district in New York City, has as much to do with its entrepreneurial achievements as does its Manhattan island location. The institutional backbone of the U.S. economy is built on a geologic foundation of granite only twelve feet below its surface. The granite supports the high-rise office buildings that house a concentration of interrelated businesses. Without the granite floor, "Wall Street" might well be located elsewhere. Moreover, the city of New York remains a hub for global business largely due to its position midway between Europe and the West Coast of the U.S. This ideal location allows financial and distribution transactions to be conducted during the trading day.

Similarly, the U.K.'s role as the center of global finance is largely the result of the adoption of the Greenwich Prime Meridian as the world's established time standard since 1884. The geographic location of the United Kingdom is that of an island nation surrounded by seas and ideally located next to a European land mass. It is the official center of a global time standard which provides it with a substantial financial advantage of spanning both eastern and western hemispheres. It also allows for the more efficient coordination of ocean transport by way of latitude and longitude. The political convention of a time standard became an intangible geographical resource which allows banking and other financial institutions to exploit to their advantage.

Australia and Canada are known for their strong global currencies based on bountiful natural resources and extensive mineral wealth. Their cultural heritage and institutions work in concert to take advantage of these geological gifts of nature. Venezuela was once the economic powerhouse of South America. Its vast oil wealth is estimated to be greater than that of Saudi Arabia. However, the development of its cultural institutions failed to keep pace with the development of its natural resources. Scholars postulate that economic progress throughout Latin America has been hampered by a heritage of authoritarian rule that limits the adoption of an individual work ethic based on a history of autocratic Spanish and Portuguese colonial rule.[22]

The cultural prosperity and complexity of the island nations of the U.K., Japan, and Singapore are a result of their geographic access to the world's oceans and the resultant opportunities for global trade. The U.S.'s status as a global superpower is based not only on its immense natural resources but also on its boundless access to oceans and inland waterways. Its proximity to water has made the U.S. a naval superpower and has provided access to global trade, distribution, and commerce. Its role as an economic superpower is founded on the confluence of its heritage, as well as other supportive and functioning institutions.[23]The dominant global currency of today reflects the foundations and heritage of its cultural institutions. A country may or may not have access to natural wealth, but it is ultimately up to its institutions to raise a culture to a higher level of global prosperity.

Family

> "There is simply nothing so important to a people and its government as how many of them there are, whether the number is growing or declining, how they are distributed as between ages, sexes.... I have often wondered whether the government pays so little attention to these issues for the simple reason that when it does, the government must confirm the fact that the great decisions of the world are made by solitary couples – males and females – and are made in bed to boot."
>
> U.S. Senator Patrick Moynihan Aug 15, 1977, *WSJ*

The family unit plays a central role as a key institution in defining a society's structure and its culture. Anthropologists consider the family to be the principal institution for the socialization of children and the transmission of family values. "*Family values are the moral and ethical principles traditionally upheld and transmitted within the family, as honesty, loyalty, industry, and faith."* [24] The trend in the composition of the family portends much about its culture and economy. A family is a group of people affiliated by blood, legal affinity (marriage) or in co-residence to nurture kinship. A nuclear family consists of two adults and children, while an extended family includes other relatives sharing a living arrangement. Anthropologists and sociologists focus their interest on the changing role of family values based on trends in birth and age categories, divorce rates, single-parent homes, abortions, same-sex marriages, and stages of the family life cycle. Economists primarily focus on trends in the number of households to be able to provide a forecast for goods and services and the overall economic progression. Economic trends are forecasted by analyzing any number of demographic changes that affect the family.

Demographics

Demo is Greek for *people*, and *graphics* is a picture. A demographic picture of a country is often used to provide businesses with economic forecasts. A collection of valuable demographic data can be accessed online from the *World Factbook* produced by the U.S. Central Intelligence Agency.[25] The Gross Domestic Product (GDP) data is provided by the *International Monetary Fund.* [26] Economists forecast financial trends based on the number of households and related economic measures in comparison with other countries. The demographics underlying a family structure provide a unique perspective and view of the direction of its culture and economy. The following chart illustrates large differences in cultural perspective when comparing demographic to economic data.

Country	Population*	Households	Avg. Hsld Size	GDP*	GDP per capita
China	1,373,541,278	457,847,092	3.0 (2012)	$11,218,364	$6,188 (2012)
India	1,266,883,598	263,934,083	4.8 (2011)	$2,618,885	$1,489 (2012)
E. U.	513,949,445	223,456,280	2.3 (2015)	$16,397,979	$32,676 (2012)
United States	323,995,528	124,613,665	2.6 (2014)	$18,569,100	**$49,965** (2012)
Indonesia	205,823,051	52,775,141	3.9 (2010)	$932,259	$3,557 (2012)

Figure 2-7 Demographic Profile Comparisons **Est. July 2016. The chart indicates how the population and its composition of households and average household size*

can have an impact on its economic future. Data source: The World Factbook and International Monetary Fund

A "population pyramid" or the age-sex ratio illustrates the distribution of various age groups in a population and helps visualize a culture's gender and age distribution. The graphic highlights key age groups by gender to compare, forecast, and determine unique business and economic opportunities and tells much about the region and its culture.[27, 28]

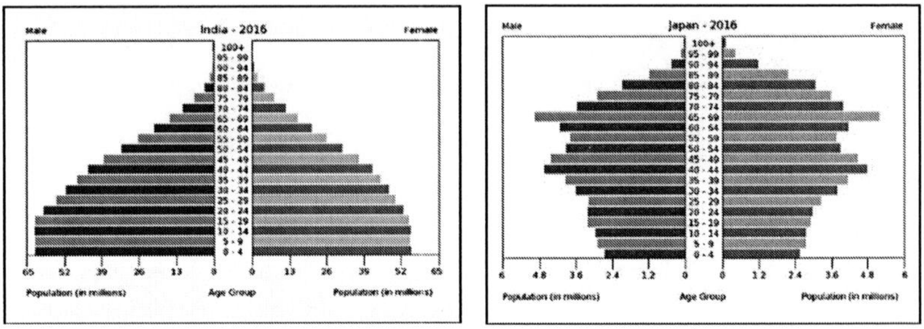

Figure 2-8 Comparison of patterns of population change. *The population pyramid of India (left) indicates a developing economy with a large projected increase in population, Japan's population (right) is declining which may have negative economic implications. The World Factbook 2016 People and Society: Data Source: Central Intelligence Agency.*

Religion

"Science without religion is lame, religion without science is blind."
Albert Einstein

Religion is a set of internal beliefs about the cause, nature, and purpose of the universe. A nation's religion provides useful insights into the economic behavior of its adherents. Religion has a substantial role in defining a society's beliefs, values, traditions—even its diet and cuisine. There are an estimated 4,200 organized religions in the world. While religions may be viewed as monolithic, there are many subsets and offshoots. Christianity has the most adherents, but they belong to a variety of denominations such as Lutheran, Baptist, Evangelical, Pentecostal, and others.

An estimated 73 percent of the world's population is affiliated with just four of the largest religions, namely Christianity (33%), Islam (21%), Hinduism (13%), and Buddhism (6%). Secularism is not an antithesis of religion (as is atheism) but separation of religion from the state, while the agnostics view human reason an incapable of justifying the existence of God. The rise of secularism, which represents those choosing to be non-religious, is a growing trend in Western culture.[29] Religion and religious beliefs form strong attitudes toward economic concerns as they have a direct impact on the consumption of goods, the economic role of women, family economics, the religious organization themselves, and the often-bitter disputes that arise because of religious differences within a culture.[30]

Much of the discord and animosity between religions reside in their underlying beliefs concerning usury. Usurious lending practices have long been condemned, even before specific laws banning the practice were enacted. For example, in "The Divine Comedy" Dante places lenders who charge usurious interest rates into the "Seventh Circle of Hell" a level that ranks even below that for people who have committed suicide. The practice of usury, or the charging of interest of any kind, remains problematic for most of the world's religions.

Condemnations of usury are found in many religious texts from Buddhism, Judaism, Christianity, and Islam. The Hebrew Torah contains over one-hundred references dealing with economic transactions (including that of usury), more than the instructions concerning diet and food. Historically in Christian societies, and still in many Islamic societies today, charging any interest at all is considered usury. Over time, cultures and nations have passed laws to regulate interest rates. These laws can vary even within a country. The State of Alabama, for example, caps the interest rate on loans at 8 percent, while the State of Florida allows an interest rate of 18 percent on loans under $500,000 and 25 percent over that amount.[31]The Jewish religion has largely been blamed and accused, often by other religions, based on their practice of charging interest on money without creating value for both parties.

Economics

The study of economics includes the overall structure and philosophy of an economic system and the operating monetary and fiscal benchmarks used to describe its overall development. Economic theory spans the gamut from the acceptance of free market principles to the degree of centralization in economic decision-making. No country has a totally free market orientation. However, there are numerous examples of centralized economic systems from Marxism, socialism, communism, and various forms of dictatorships. How well the economic system functions and operates can be observed by its economic and monetary outcomes. Numerous economic theories abound—from the utopian to the impractical—as to how our economic lives should be governed. However, the ideal goal of economics is to ultimately improve the living conditions in everyone's everyday lives. [32]

The *Index of Economic Freedom* provides an annual ranking of the degree of economic freedom for each of the world's nations. *The Heritage Foundation* and *The Wall Street Journal* created the program and used an approach similar to the classical free market theory of Adam Smith that "*basic institutions that protect the liberty of individuals to pursue their economic interests result in greater prosperity for the larger society.*" [33] The *Index* provides an interactive program for online comparisons based on the selection of ten different measures of economic freedom.

Two of the most widely used tools that impact a nation's economic activity are monetary and fiscal policy. Monetary policy is primarily concerned with the management of interest rates and the total supply of money in circulation administered by the central banks. Fiscal policy is the collective term for numerous tax and spending actions of governments. In the United States, the Executive and Legislative Branches determine the fiscal policy, while the monetary policy is controlled by the Federal Reserve.[34] Nations with a free market orientation use both structured monetary and fiscal policy to guide their economy, while authoritarian regimes simply dictate political policy.

Education

"An investment in knowledge pays the best interest."

Benjamin Franklin

Education transmits the present-day culture and traditions to new generations. It includes the process of transmitting skills, ideas, and attitudes, as well as training disciplines. In developed countries, education usually refers to formal training as key benchmarks, such as years in school or graduation rates, which indicate much about a society. High rates of education are essential for countries to achieve high levels of economic growth.[35] A variety of *best in education rankings* exists on various measures such as I.Q scores, Nobel Prizes by country, teacher ratios, math scores, etc. The results of these measures often vary based on which students are sampled and the survey methodology. China rates high on math scores for example, but it is unlikely that the results include the 30 percent of the population that remains outside of the educational system. The assessment and measure of a culture's educational achievements often ignore the impact of the culture's cohesiveness, its subcultures, and societies. Japan's cultural close-knit family values regarding education, for example, have a far greater influence on educational attainment than does the pedagogy by itself.

Politics

"Power tends to corrupt, and absolute power corrupts absolutely."
Lord Acton 1887

Politics is derived from the Greek definition meaning "*affairs of the cities*" and is practiced on a wide range of social levels. It is commonly accepted that politics is about power.[36] The degree of individual freedom a person possesses spans the political spectrum from an authoritarian state rule to an individual's libertarian freedom. Plato, in *The Republic*, relates his discussions with Socrates about the differences between morality and justice in the formation and function of government. He identified the stages and structures that governments form. The stages evolve from a democracy (rule by the majority) into a plutocracy (ruled by the wealthy), an oligarchy (the ruling class), an aristocracy (ruled by the nobility), and ultimately into that of either a republic (elected representatives of the people) or a tyranny (by authoritarian or totalitarian regimes). Authoritarian regimes tell their people what they can do while totalitarian regimes tell their people what to think. All nations and cultures adhere to some form of government that Plato first identified in 380 B.C.

A country's political sovereignty is comprised of rules and regulations which become its legal system. The misuse of power gives way to political corruption, which may include extortion, cronyism, nepotism, patronage, graft, embezzlement, and a surprising number of words specific to politics. A state of unrestrained political corruption is known as a *kleptocracy*, literally meaning "rule by thieves." *Transparency International* is a non-profit organization whose purpose is to combat corruption. It publishes online the *Global Corruption Barometer* and *the Corruption Perceptions Index (CPI)* providing a "very strong and significant inverse relationship" between corruption and gross domestic product per capita.[37]

Technology

"Technology is nothing. What's important is that you have faith in people, that they're basically good and smart, and if you give them tools, they'll do wonderful things with them."
Apple Inc. founder Steve Jobs

Innovation is based on a human desire to find new ideas, devices, or methods that lead to better uses and solutions for various sectors of technology. The simplest form of technology is the creation and use of basic tools that lead to new knowledge of techniques and processes. The first stage of technology is research and development or R&D, known in Europe as research and technology development (RTD). There exists a positive correlation between a firm's research and development to its productivity and that this correlation is much stronger in high-tech firms than in low-tech firms.[38]

Governments also fund and support research and development. Comparisons of international R&D statistics, however, are hampered by the lack of R&D-specific exchange rates based on different assumptions about the value of the currencies involved. *"For example, China's R&D expenditures in 2010 (as reported to the OECD) were $178 billion in PPP (Purchasing Power Parity) terms but only $104 billion using MER (Market Exchange Rates)."* [39] The nugget: R&D expenditures for private industry can be readily evaluated while reports on government spending widely lack transparency and measured outcomes and can't be trusted.

Advances in technology include such factors as time and money spent on research and development, automation, technology incentives, and the rate of technological change are often difficult to identify and report. They can determine barriers to entry, minimum efficient production levels, and influence outsourcing decisions. Furthermore, technological shifts can affect costs, quality, and lead to socially disruptive innovation. Other cultural factors, however, may hinder the acceptance of new technology. For example, without changes to U.S. anti-trust laws in 1982, smartphones could not have been invented by Steve Jobs of Apple Inc. fame. Some countries have yet to support smartphones, leading to what is known as a "technology gap" between countries and cultures. Many repressive governments have placed restrictions on the use of technology as it may conflict with cherished cultural institutions.

The Nugget

Cultures, however different, evolve as they accumulate knowledge. The building blocks of knowledge are the cultural institutions that provide a pathway to learning from one generation to another. A culture's medium of exchange—their currency—mirrors the accumulated knowledge, values, and the sophistication of their cultural institutions. Culture and currency are indeed, intertwined.

CHAPTER THREE

ATHENA: GODDESS OF WISDOM & WAR

Keywords: drachma; tetradrachm; the Lydian Lion; the Athenian ‘owl’; Alexander the Great

> “Money is like a sixth sense–and you can't make use of the other five without it.”
>
> William Somerset Maugham, British playwright

The Greek mythological goddess Athena played a remarkable role in the founding of Western civilization where she was immortalized in the coinage of Greece–the drachma. Her likeness on currencies spanned more than ten centuries. President Theodore Roosevelt was so obsessed with making the U.S. dollar look like the Greek drachma that in 1908 he commissioned various gold and silver coins that depicted Athena holding olive branches.[1] So as not to be accused of placing a pagan goddess on the U.S. coinage, she was renamed the Walking Lady Liberty coin. The ancient drachma evolved into the first stable, valued, and widely distributed international currency—the tetradrachm. The beginning and evolution of Western civilization from its early roots in philosophy, democracy, and science can be traced back to this Athenian coin.[2]

Figure 3-1 *Athenian tetradrachm Attribution: www.ancientcoin traders.com.*
Figure 3-2 *Walking Liberty Half Dollar 1921 (CC By-SA-3.0).*

According to myth, Athena was the goddess of wisdom and war, although an unlikely combination of powers given today's moral code, it made perfect sense to the ancient Greeks. Athena's mother was Metris, goddess of prudence and the first wife of Zeus. Mother Earth told Zeus that if Metris bore him a child, it would grow up to have more power than Zeus. Since Zeus didn't like that idea, he played a trick on Metris by getting her to change herself into a fly, after which he inhaled and swallowed her whole. Ever after, Metris was lodged in Zeus's head and directed him from there. As it happened, Metris was pregnant with a baby girl which caused Zeus to experience pounding headaches. Hoping to ease his misery, he took an ax to his head, split it open, and out sprang Athena fully grown.[3] The Romans would later adopt the Olympian family as their own and renamed Zeus as Jupiter, and Athena as Minerva.

From these mythical beginnings, Athena became the virgin patroness of Athens. The Greeks built the Parthenon on the Acropolis and named it in her honor: Athena Parthenos (the virgin). She was venerated by having her portrait on the drachma which circulated as a currency continuously from 510 to 38 B.C. and sporadically afterward. Many Greek cities and colonies had heraldic drachms imprinted with distinct images and symbols of their cities. However, it was the Athenian tetradrachm featuring the goddess Athena which became the most widely used currency throughout the ancient Greek world. It was valued at four drachms or about the weekly wage of a citizen soldier. The coinage spread Greek culture (and the Olympian folklore) throughout and far beyond the Mediterranean due to its revered religious and cult-like mythology.

One of the significant advantages of Athens was its Laurium silver mines located close to the city-state and under the direct control of the Senate. The mines and port city served as the chief revenue sources for the Athenian state. Laurium silver was largely known for its silvery-white charm and was prized more than the drachmas of the other city-states. Revenue from the Laurium mines financed the golden age of Greece and, under the leadership of Pericles (495-429 B.C.), was used to build the Temple of Hephaestus—the mythical god of metalworking. The Romans would later rename him Vulcan. The Temple was built at the base of the Acropolis and used to mint silver ore into coins. The Senate paid craftsmen with drachmas to build the Parthenon and other construction projects providing a quantity of currency to support an expanding economy.

The mining of silver ores started in the 15th century B.C. It would reach its zenith between the 7th and 5th centuries B.C. when a coin-based monetary economy began to replace barter and trade. Silver ore was mainly extracted through opencast mining until the beginning of the 5th century B.C. when continuous underground mining became more productive. The Laurium silver mines are estimated to have had 2,000 deep mine shafts worked by 10,000 to 30,000 miners. The ore was extracted with the use of low-cost laborers and indebted slaves.

The Delian League, which consisted of a loose association of 150 to 173 Greek city-states, was formed to defend against the incursions of the Persian Empire. Each city-state panned or mined silver and gold to mint its drachm coins. They were fiercely independent, reflecting the dawn of democratic ideals and a lifestyle open to the sea for trading and conquest. Greece is a mountainous country with many city-states located close to a river valley or a seaport which influenced the Greeks to become master mariners and seafaring traders. The constricted geological nature of the mountainous land and hard soil lent itself to be managed by small landowners. The geography was ideal for the production of wine, olive oil, pottery, and the breeding of sheep and goats, all of which were used for barter and trade across the Aegean Sea. [4, 5]

The Lydian Lion

The first metallic coinage of value is considered by many numismatists to be *"Lydian Lion trite"* first minted circa 610-550 B.C. The Lion is considered the *"Adam of coins"* as all coinage used today is considered the progeny of the Lydian Lion.[6] It was cast in electrum, a natural compound of gold and silver, along with some minor impurities of copper or tin for hardness. Our word for electricity is derived from the Latin word *"electrum"* which comes from the Phoenician term for *"shining light"* in reference to the glimmer or sparkle of light seen off the water of the sea. The first coins were cast of ores from the mines of the city of Ephesus (Lydia) in the ancient region of Anatolia, an important commercial center in the Aegean region.

Anatolia, now western Turkey, was then populated by a Hellenistic culture largely influenced by the Greeks but with their distinct rites and rituals. Several treasure troves of the Lion coinage have been found beneath the Temple of Artemis, considered the preeminent site of the Seven Wonders of the Ancient World. The Temple's name was taken from the Greek goddess Artemis, the twin sister of the god Apollo, both of whom were considered the most physically beautiful and handsome of the Olympian gods. The Temple was a likely vacation spot close to the Aegean beaches and housed travelers and tourists. Ephesus is now a historical site which many Christians and Muslims believe is the home of Mary Levi, the virgin mother of Jesus.

Ephesus was a city-state located close to the Greek colonies of Asia Minor and the ancient trading routes that extended from India to northern Europe. According to the Hellenistic Lydians, it was here that King Midas turned everything he touched to gold. Midas was believed to live upstream of the Pactolus River near Ephesus where he was believed to bathe to rid himself of gold dust. The Lydians panned for the gold downstream using sheepskins to sift and collect gold specks from the silt of the Pactolus River—giving rise to the legend of the Golden Fleece. The Golden Fleece symbolized authority and kingship as recounted by Homer in his chronicle of the travels of Jason and his band of Argonauts.[7]

Figure 3-3 *Lydian electrum trite (4.71g, 13x10x4 mm). This coin type or token was made of a gold and silver alloy and considered the world's first minted coin in Sardis, Lydia, Asia Minor (present-day Turkey), B.C. 610-546. Many trites were found in the vicinity of the Temple of Artemis. (GNU Free Documentation License). Classical Numismatic Group, Inc. http://www.cngcoins.com*

The Lydians were on land what the Phoenicians were by sea. They are recognized as the first commercial land-based merchants having established the main trade conduit between Persia and Greece including the ancient trade routes from India to northern Europe. They were the first culture to mint coins and the first to establish permanent retail shop locations. Primarily, merchants and commercial traders, they were motivated by a need for an exchange method to replace barter and trade: hence the innovation of the Lydian Lion coin. This innovation has led scholars to believe that they created the first free market, transitioning from an agricultural barter economy to an early commercial monetary and urban economy. Historians and numismatists argue as to the value of a Lydian

Lion coin during the time it circulated, as it ranged from one sheep or three amphorae of wine and later to eleven sheep or ten goats. [7]

Many of the Greek city-states eagerly adopted the idea of precious metallic coinage as an easy and efficient way to conduct trade, versus the time-consuming effort of barter and trade. By the end of the sixth century, every city-state had its coinage all variants of the drachma.

Figure 3-4 Left *Ancient Greek drachmas from the City-State of Ephesus with a bee* Right *Gela with a man-headed bull. (OTRS) (GNU Free Documentation License).*

The Athenian tetradrachm was a silver coin equivalent to four drachmas and replaced the earlier heraldic versions of the other city-state drachmas. Historians estimate that the value of a drachma at the height of ancient Greece, during the 5th and 4th centuries, was equal to the daily wage for a skilled worker or citizen soldier, known as hoplites.[8] A tetradrachm would likely be a week's payout to a productive worker or soldier. The transition to Athenian coinage took place shortly after the Battle of Salamis in 480 B.C. The Greeks won both naval and land battles over the overt incursions by the Persian King Xerxes. King Philip II, the king of Macedonia, would later win control over Athens and consolidate many of the Greek city-states, thereby spreading the use of the Athenian stamped tetradrachm coinage. The kingdom of Macedonia was centered in the northeastern Greek peninsula and comprised the largest and most fertile agricultural region at the time, as well as the largest gold mines in antiquity. Economically, it was sufficiently wealthy on its own to support the conquest of the other Greek city-states.

The tetradrachm, known to many as the Athenian "owl" was the most prized of city-state coinage and favored by King Philip. The coin's obverse features the image of Athena, which evolved through the ages into many variations of her appearance, including the gradual transition into the likeness of Alexander the Great. The reverse often featured an owl with olive branches. The owl's wide-open eyes symbolized all-seeing foresight and knowledge. Numismatists note that the head of the owl was often split open during a transaction to verify the metallic content and thus authenticity of the coin. Many recovered coins were also split into various fractions to make change. Archeologists occasionally uncover droves of such coinage often buried under the remains of ancient temples.[8]

Figure 3-5 Left *Athenian tetradrachm circa 465 B.C.* Figure 3-6 Right *Classical Hellenistic design circa 350 B.C. The AOE translates to "of the Athenians." Attribution: Classical Numismatic Group, Inc. http://www.cngcoins.com*

The Athenian Meaning of Wisdom and War

King Philip II's son, Alexander the Great, assumed his father's throne and inherited a strong united Greece and an experienced army. Tutored in his youth by the philosopher Aristotle, Alexander and his classmates undertook his father's quest to conquer Persia (now Iran). Alexander left Greece in 334 B.C. with an estimated infantry of 30,000 foot soldiers and 5,000 cavalry. He crossed Hellespont (known today as the Dardanelles) into Asia, never to return to Greece. His unprecedented military campaigns expanded the Greek coinage into the first truly international currency. By the age of thirty, Alexander had created one of the largest empires in the ancient world, extending from Greece to Egypt, Persia to Asia Minor, and into northwest India. He was never defeated in battle and is considered one of history's most successful military commanders. In a series of decisive battles, Alexander broke the power of Persia's Achaemenes Empire. His legacy resulted in the spread of Greek culture and initiated the Classical Greek period. His name is memorialized worldwide in the names of twenty cities, from Alexandria, Virginia to Alexandria, Egypt. Military academies still teach his tactics, not just of battle, but of winning the support and hearts of the people.[9]

Alexander's strategy for success was brilliant, yet simple. He blockaded a city by using his navy to patrol the port and his army to restrict entrance and exit. Scouts would search for the city's wealth while his army would confiscate any gold or silver often in the form of jewelry and artworks. Precious metals served mainly as a show of wealth and power for the exclusive use of the elite but lacked broad monetary value useful for expanding trade and exchange. Alexander's troops would mint the booty into tetradrachms, thereby becoming a self-supporting sustainable army.

His soldiers were paid with tetradrachms considered to be valued at four days' worth of conquest or work, or an arduous week's wages. Only those who proved their worth were compensated directly with the coins. The soldiers purchased needed supplies and services from the local inhabitants, who now had a stable and widely accepted currency forming the first monetary coin-based economy. This is what many today consider to be *trickle-down* economic theory. Alexander was welcomed by many tribes and cultures who disliked their current state of authoritarian rule and subsequent impoverishment. Many were very receptive to his inclusive economic policy of introducing coinage as a means of exchange and trade. Alexander triumphed over despotic rulers with a well-paid, incentivized, and loyal army often supported by the people he came to rule.[10]

The Athenian coins later adopted the image and likeness of Alexander himself. The Greeks were reluctant to show a person's face on any coin as they considered it hubris, arrogant, and pretentious. Alexander's prodigious conquests overcame any objections. His image soon replaced that of Athena on the obverse of the coin, as her likeness was relegated to the reverse of the coin which depicts her sitting on a wooden throne.

Alexander was first to recognize that coins could be used as advertising and political propaganda. The Romans would later take political advertising on coins to new heights. Gold tetradrachms were preferred for large state or commercial transactions and are called "staters" by numismatists, while the silver coins were commonly used for local tender. Archeologists have uncovered 26 official mints following the path of Alexander's conquests at the height of his empire. The Greek tetradrachms became the first international currency which communicated the power of the Athenian culture and the monetary beginnings of Western civilization.

Figure 3-7 *Images of Alexander the Great on tetradrachms.* Right *Alexander the Great in the guise of Heracles and Zeus seated. (CC By-SA-3.0)*

Alexander the Great died at the age of thirty-three in the city of Babylon (now central Iraq) of either malaria or another infectious disease. Following his death, a series of civil wars tore apart his empire. Three of his surviving generals known as the Diadochi carved out kingdoms for themselves. The action marked the transition from Classical Greek to the Hellenistic period. Without a strong military presence, the drachma had no reference of value nor standard worth, and the conquered lands returned to their previous archaic impoverished past. The power vacuum allowed the era of the Roman culture to advance based on the foundations of the Greek experience.[11]

Epilogue

Roxana, the first wife of Alexander, bore him a son he never met named Alexander IV. Roxana was thought to have his other two wives murdered, only to have her and her son assassinated by Alexander's family and childhood friend Cassander. His sister, Cleopatra of Macedon, became the queen of the Greek Epirotes (the northwest of Greece) only to be assassinated before she could marry Alexander's best friend, classmate, and favored General—Ptolemy.

General Ptolemy had gained his knowledge of the burial customs of ancient Egypt during the many conquests under Alexander. Ptolemy shrewdly carried the body of Alexander for burial from Babylon to that of the namesake city he had founded: Alexandria, Egypt. The recognition and ceremony following the Egyptian burial custom garnered the respect and admiration of the Egyptian people who bestowed Ptolemy the title of "Pharaoh" in 305 B.C. and the conferred Greek title of Ptolemy Soter I (Ptolemy the Wise).

The Ptolemaic dynasty ruled Egypt for the next three centuries, only to succumb to the Romans in 30 B.C. An ancestor of Ptolemy was the Queen and Pharaoh Cleopatra VII Philopator, famously known as Cleopatra, who married Julius Caesar and bore him a son. Later she married Marc Antony. Their defeat by Octavian at the naval Battle of Actium in 32 B.C. ended over 3,000 years of rule by over 170 Egyptian pharaohs. Egypt and North Africa would continually pay the Roman Empire tribute with agricultural commodities and gold from its prolific Nubian mines. Egypt became the main economic and agricultural lifeline to the city of Rome and later to the Roman Empire.

Geopolitics and the Cultural Legacy of Greece

Greece gave the Western world its first cultural identity as exemplified by its coinage–the first truly international currency. The ancient Greeks expanded the study of geopolitics as presented in Thucydides' *History of the Peloponnesian War* (431-404 B.C.), which is considered the seminal work on international relations and the earliest scholarly work of history. The geography of Greece also played a foundational role in it becoming the superpower of its age when the Mediterranean was the center of human civilization.[12]

Geographically, Greece is largely a mountainous country located at the crossroads of Europe, Asia, and Africa. It includes some 6,000 islands of various sizes, with the largest share of coastline in the Mediterranean basin. Nearly all of the fiercely independent city-states were isolated by mountains with small river valleys. Their geography restricted them to local agricultural production along with highly defensible ports open to the sea. The ancient Greeks became a skilled seafaring people and traders with access to all the Mediterranean, Ionian, and Aegean Seas. However, the costs and maintenance of a navy and army required access to large amounts of capital. Today, the Greek economy is in disarray, largely due to the high costs of maintaining central governmental control over a vast region of mostly isolated islands and mountainous terrain.

Ancient Greece was considered a moderately wealthy state based on its maritime ability. Innovation in shipbuilding, especially by the Athenian polis, was based on improvements to their trireme naval vessels. The trireme was a warship with three levels of rowers to allow for increased speed and striking power. The warship was developed from the two-level pentekonters which carried goods for trade as well as infantry for war.

These were large ships even by today's standards. They ranged in size from 20 oared mariners to more than 100 oarsmen, but most often it was the 50 oared pentekonter that traded goods across the Aegean Sea and far beyond.[11] Trireme ships were used by the early explorers to reach new lands and to spread trade and the Greek culture far across the Mediterranean. Greek societies were able to flourish, especially because of the new trade possibilities with advanced cultures such as Egypt. Athenians were skilled in shipbuilding and had the most advanced naval force. Archeologists estimate that the Athenians constructed 200 trireme ships which were pivotal in the decisive conquest of the Persian forces of Xerxes at the Battle of Salamis in 480 B.C. The construction of the fleet was financed primarily with the silver from the rich Laurium mines.[13]

Ancient geopolitics, based upon the control of the Aegean Sea, continues to this day. Piraeus, the port of Athens, is currently one of the top ten ports in global commerce. Greek companies reportedly own almost 20% of the global fleet of merchant ships as well as more than half of the European Union's fleet. The industry makes up 7.5% of the Greek economy and currently employs around 200,000 people.[14]

The legacy of Greece was strongly embraced by the post-Renaissance European elite, who saw themselves as the spiritual heirs of Greece. Will Durant, a noted American philosopher, wrote in 1939 that *"excepting machinery, there is hardly anything secular in our culture that does not come from Greece... and there is nothing in Greek civilization that doesn't illuminate our own"*.[15] The acclaimed commentator Marianna de Marzi also observed the extent to which Classical Greek thought has influenced the progression of Western civilization, writing: "*The profundity of the knowledge gained through this period in history; in art, mathematics, music and more, is incomparable to almost any other chapter in human inquiry.*" The foundations of a hard currency and the democratic ideals of ancient Greek culture may well be the underlying inspiration and logic behind the advancement of Western civilization.

Figure 3-8 *Ancient Athenian owl image on a modern Greece euro. (CC By-SA-3.0)*

The Nugget

The tetradrachms of Alexander the Great freed the common people from their tyrannical oppressors and advanced the values of early Western civilization. He paid his soldiers well, and they, in turn, used the money to pay their local workers and supporters. Wealth was released in the distribution of gold and silver coinage to expedite trade and commerce, and in doing so, created an international coinage that replaced barter. Alexander knew how to win friends and influence people! He did it with—the money.

CHAPTER FOUR

LATIFUNDIA, ROME, & THE ECONOMICS BEHIND THE ROMAN REPUBLIC

Keywords: Vestal Virgins; Temple of Juno Moneta; Marian reforms; Punic Wars; silver denarius

> "To be ignorant of what occurred before you were born is to remain always a child."
>
> Marcus Cicero: Roman consul, historian, orator, statesman.

Ancient Rome is a time capsule cemented into the foundation of Western civilization. Its seven kings, 479 Republic consuls, and over 225 Roman emperors shaped nearly two thousand years of history. The ancient Greeks and early Romans introduced and advanced a large part of the modern world's cultural values, norms, and beliefs. Their political and social structure paved the way for the birth of modern Christianity and Western civilization and seeded the global progress and evolution of today's human condition. How the Roman culture came to accept and use money provides an insightful story into the early evolution of the economic history of Western civilization.

What we know about the Roman Empire primarily comes to us by way of the English historian Edward Gibbon's six-volume epic *"The History of the Decline and Fall of the Roman Empire"* first published in 1776 and completed in 1789. Gibbon's approach primarily focused on the political and social history given the resources of his day. Current methods used by historians to investigate specific topics are known as "historiography" which include published resources, scientific techniques, and theoretical approaches. The ascent of academic history, beginning in the nineteenth century, opened the door to a wider range of cultural perspectives. It also presented a highly debated question: "*To what extent are historians influenced by their colleagues and their loyalties?*" [1]

Gibbon's saw the decline of the Roman Empire in large part due to the gradual loss of civic virtue among its citizens.[2] However, a more insightful story can be told by viewing their economic policies and the foundations of their money and wealth. The over two-thousand-year history of Roman culture can be viewed based on how the Romans utilized land, labor, and capital by following the *money*.

The territorial control of land has been a fundamental force in the rise and fall of empires throughout history as well as the cause of a great number of the world's conflicts and wars since civilization began. Land and labor are two prerequisites for igniting the spark of economic development. Labor can come cheap while land is finite and has unique geographic constraints and resources.

Prosperous cultures have organized both land and labor into collective wealth. Contrarily, less successful cultures are consigned into the dustbin of history due to the unfortunate consequences of landlords in conflict with their laborers, and laborers without any rights to the land. Large parcels of land ownership historically gave rise to various political and social structures. Likewise, workers must organize and offer a fair price for their labor to make the land continually productive to their owners.

Only later in Roman history did the third leg of economic development evolve in the form of a stable currency that provided laborers with a means to determine their labors' value. Today we accept this as a common fact, but it was not always so. Workers without a currency are confined as prisoners without a means of payment or exchange. Laborers are essentially treated as slaves or serfs as their landlords often see them of little value. While human lifespans largely constrain land ownership and labor, capital wealth can be easily stored, accumulated and transferred across time and generations.

The lifespan of Western civilization advanced when currencies were added to the volatile recipe of land and labor. A review of the economic history and cultural transformations of ancient Rome provides a roadmap of economic lessons learned and of wrong roads taken.

Latifundia

Latifundia originated from the consolidation of land ownership over time and family generations beginning in the late 3rd and early 2nd centuries B.C. The process originated as a Roman phenomenon termed "*latifundia*" meaning "spacious estates." Before the rise of privately-owned Greek and Roman properties, all land was collectively owned. The notion of an individual claiming a parcel of land as his exclusive possession was unthinkable! Western civilization often takes private land ownership for granted but it is undoubtedly a prized cultural value. However, much of our modern globe is still dominated by governments and cultural practices that largely restrict their citizens' legal rights to land and land ownership.

Latifundia evolved as a naturally occurring human process. Suppose 1,000 acres of privately owned land is evenly divided by 100 families into sustainable farms of 10 acres each. Typically, ten families would acquire control in as little as five generations, while only two families would obtain full control of all the land in a short seven generations. The reasons are many. Some family farms are more prosperous than others, and some families die out or move away. Whatever the reason, throughout history privately held land, has consolidated over time into the hands of fewer owners. Consider the present-day consolidated ownership of shopping malls or the oligopolies of large industrialized conglomerates.

The term *latifundia* is synonymous with modern terms used for the governance of large estates: Russia's *pomiestny*, Poland's *magnate estate*, and Spanish and Latin America's *hacienda* system, including the *Antebellum* plantations of the American South.[3] Large land holdings confer considerable social and political power to their owners and thereby strongly influence the socioeconomic structure of a culture. How the owners value and manage their land and labor becomes a fundamental geopolitical and economic paradox—juxtaposing the realities of a centralized autocracy with the ideals of decentralized democracy.

The first privately owned and extensively cultivated parcels of land were characteristic of the coastal areas of Southern Italy, originally dominated by Greek colonies. The Romans called this area of Sicily and the foot of Italy's boot "*Magna Graecia,*" or Latin for "Great Greece." The land was abundant, fertile, productive, and extensively populated due to its Mediterranean climate and open access to the sea. The *latifundista* were the landlords that monopolized large tracts of land and gradually became a governing plutocracy, or a society governed by the wealthy.

Before the concept of private land ownership, Egypt's fertile Nile delta, for example, was governed by the ruling Pharaohs and a religious system of collective land use. Scholars cite the present-day disparity that exists between many Latin American countries and their North American counterparts, as due to the Spanish crown's having granted vast tracts of land and control over the indigenous labor to a small number of autocratic colonizers and conquistadors. Contrarily, the North American colonies had no such landed privileges and a long history of private land ownership dating back to A.D. 1215 and the English Magna Carta.

Land ownership evolved and adapted according to the complex economic and political dynamics that characterize a culture during a given period. Scholars conclude that it is the interaction of the geologic environment with the geopolitical structure that produces *latifundism*.[4] The historical confluence of land ownership and private labor initially gave rise to the unique cultural norms, beliefs, and values of both ancient Greece and Rome.

Ancient Greece systematically restricted the land size to small family farms, and no large privately-owned landholdings existed. Extensive tracts of land were held by rulers, appointed ministers, or temple authorities, suggesting religious or communal governance. The privately held Greek family farm averaged little more than four acres (or 1.6 hectares) and was geographically confined by the hilly character of the land and hard compacted soil. The small farms lead to the intense use of labor and cultivation uniquely suited to produce wine, pottery, crafts, cheese, and the husbandry of small animals. Geology and geography set the stage for the development of its democratic ideals. Contrarily, the expansion of large privately-owned estates on the Italian Peninsula gradually led to absentee landlords, often resulting in neglect and agricultural oversight. The farms were either left in the hands of previous tenant owners, other trusted Roman citizens, or increasingly worked by imported slaves.[5]

The Roman statesman Cato the Elder, in his book "*De Agricultura*" or "On Farming" in 160 B.C., described the techniques of farm ownership and management. Cato saw the then medium-sized 200 iugera (0.65 to an acre, or 130 acres) farm, as being managed by a Roman bailiff or magistrate with a permanent staff of 11 peasants or slaves.[6] Wealthy Roman latifundista wielded considerable political power and were the patriarchs of their time. They also held an economic advantage over the peasant farmer, as they had the means to develop hybrid strains for improving crops and livestock. Additionally, slave labor could be bought and sold according to real-time need, an option that wasn't available to the peasant family owners of small plots of land. The early Roman Republic was largely governed by property-owning citizens. Later, the rise of the Roman Empire's aristocratic state and governed land system gave way to non-land-holding peasants and as a pension to retired soldiers.[7]

The Roman Kingdom: 753 B.C. to 509 B.C.

"In this country, you gotta make the money first. Then when you get the money, you get the power. Then when you get the power, then you get the women."

*T*ony Montana (Al Pacino) *Scarface* (1983 crime film)

Mythology is a collection of stories, often derived from commonly expressed adages, truisms, and proverbs which provide a framework for the development of the values, beliefs, and norms for any given culture. The legendary account of the founding of Rome acquired mystical power as it embodied the nature of the Roman character. It would portray and foretell the decline and fall of Roman culture over the next two millennia.

As the legend has it: Romulus and Remus were twin brothers conceived by Rhea Silvia, the noble daughter of a former king, and fathered by the god Mars. (Mars had raped Rhea in the Temple of Tiber no less!) Seen as a possible threat by the local King Amulius, he ordered them bound and abandoned on the banks of the Tiber River to die. The twins were saved by the god Tiberinus, the Father of the Tiber River, and given to a she-wolf who suckled and raised them in the cave Lupercal the present site of Rome. The twins set out to create the city of Rome on the 21st of April, 753 B.C. only to disagree on the exact hill site, whereby Romulus killed his brother Remus and reigned over Rome as their king for many years.[8]

The chilling tale of two children reared by a she-wolf portends much about the cultural and economic foundations of Rome. The legend of Romulus and Remus provides insights into a Roman culture of struggle, conquest, and domination. Two views exist of an early Roman economy: one based on plunder, extortion, and coercion, and the other founded on protection, security, and stability. All people need some level of security and protection, while a government must be paid for providing it. The perceived inequity between the two viewpoints is determined through the eye of the beholder. A government is paid for by either tributes or taxes. Tributes are paid based on extortion, while taxes are paid for services rendered. The history of ancient Rome provides plenty of support for both viewpoints, along with an understanding of its past environment and culture.

The early Roman Kingdom is characterized by an autocratic and monarchical form of government, which by its very nature, extended its dictatorial ambitions to its neighbors. The kingdom was ruled by a succession of seven kings before becoming a Republic in 509 B.C. Romulus declared himself the *"Pontifex Maximus,"* or Latin for the *"Greatest*

Pontiff," a term unofficially adopted by the later Popes of the Roman Catholic Church. Accordingly, kings would thereafter claim their political and religious authority based on the concept of the "*divinity of the kings"* as first set forth by Romulus. A pontiff was taken to mean a "*great bridge-builder"* as Romulus was the personified connection or bridge between the banks of the Tiber River that flowed through Rome.

Romulus organized the city of Rome based on a strict and extensive social class structure. He first appointed one-hundred of the noblest men in the community to serve as his advisory council or *Senate,* which formed a plutocracy comprised of the wealthiest individuals. *Patricians* (from *pater* meaning father) originally referred to a group of the highest ruling class families of ancient Rome. Today "*patrician"* is a vague term used in many cultures to refer to aristocrats and the bourgeoisie. The social order also included the upper-class "*equites"* or those *having horses* and the lower class "*plebeians"* or commoners.[9] Romulus surrounded himself with twelve "*lictors"* essentially his attendants, bodyguards, and henchmen. The *lictors* were also charged with the protection of the officiated Vestal Virgins, and they would become an integral part of the Roman culture as their occupation emerged into Roman magistrates and lawyers.[10]

By the middle of the 5th century B.C., the lector received an annual salary comparable to that of a highly respected legionary soldier. Romulus also established three divisions of horsemen called *centuries* who were commanded by *centurions.* He would need them all as Romulus was the villain of one of the most notorious and scandalous acts in Roman history, infamously known as the "Rape of the Sabine Women." The event was depicted in their coinage to recall the legendary villainy of ancient Rome.[11, 12]

To provide his citizens with wives, Romulus arranged the mass abduction of young women from neighboring tribes whom he had graciously invited to a Roman festival. The insult sparked the legend of the "Treachery of Tarpeia" whereby the enraged Sabine men, led by their King Titus Tatius Sabine marched on Rome to win back their women. Tarperia, the daughter of the governor (and a Vestal Virgin), had opened the Roman gates in exchange for all the golden bracelets the Sabine soldiers wore on their arms. Disgusted with her greed, they crushed her with their shields and threw her off a high rock which became well-known as the Tarpeian Rock. It remained the place where the Romans threw their most contemptible traitors and criminals to their death.[13, 14]

Figure 4-1 Left *A bronze coin dedicated to the city of Rome by Constantine the Great (A.D. 330-336) to re-affirm Rome as the traditional center of the Empire. Note the legend of Romulus and Remus on the reverse. Constantine removed the Republic's common inscription of SPQR dating back to the use of ROMA on coins before 80 B.C. Later commemorative coins of bronze, silver, and gold were issued by various Emperors after the founding of the first Roman mint in 273 B.C. Bronze coins were first used as Rome had little natural access to gold and silver. (CC By-SA-3.0)*
Figure 4-2 Right *A rare gold sovereign stater which shows a Roman elected consul escorted by two lictors circa mid-first century B.C. The coin's reverse shown on the right depicts an eagle standing on a scepter and holding a wreath. Classical Numismatic Group, Inc. http://www.cngcoins.com*

Figure 4-3 Left *Roman silver denarius coin circa 89 B.C. of King Titurius Sabin. The reverse shows two Roman soldiers running away with Sabine women in their arms.* Figure 4-4 Right *Also minted in 89 B.C. is Tarperia being crushed by Sabine shields. Ultimately the Sabine women intervened, reconciled their differences, and assimilated into the Roman Republic along with their men. Attribution: FORVM Ancient Coins: www.forumancient coins.com*

One remarkable feature of Roman culture was the ability to adopt admired cultural values, norms, and beliefs from those they conquered. Conversely, there was a willingness on the part of other cultures to assimilate the values of their Roman conquerors—or face the consequences. Upon conquering a city or province, Rome offered an olive branch allowing some form of inclusivity, such as access to citizenship with varied rights or privileges. The degree of punishment, and the number of rights granted, depended on the level of their enemies' resistance. The price of conquest was first paid as a demanded tribute and later evolved into a recurring tax for providing continued security.

The early Romans adopted the coinage of the cities they conquered as they lacked a currency of their own. Roman gods and beliefs were copied directly from Greek mythology, as were many Hellenistic customs. The Greek *Zeus* thus became the Roman *Jupiter,* along with other names of the metaphorical figures of ancient Greek mythology. The Romans also learned valuable socio-economic lessons from the Greeks concerning the management of their population. While redundant and under-utilized men on farms were recruited into military service, their women were organized into a community service named the "*Vestal Virgins*."

The Vestal Virgins

The Sabine King Numa Pompilius forcibly replaced Romulus and is credited with the creation of a state-sponsored and financially-supported priestesshood established for women only. The concept was adopted from the Greek custom of assigning women to keep the sacred and essential community temple hearth fires burning. Greek temples, of which there were many, were assigned to provide varied community services. The Romans adopted the concept and named the women *Vestal Virgins* after *Vesta* the Greek goddess of the hearth, home, and family. Consequently, they were admired for their mystical powers and became a powerful and influential force within the Roman Empire. After nearly nine hundred years as an integral cultural institution, the Bystantian Roman Emperor Theodosius extinguished the sacred fire and disbanded the community in A.D. 394. The Vestal Virgins and their pagan temples were replaced by Christian churches.[14]

The Vestals were often committed to the priesthood before puberty and strictly sworn to celibacy for thirty years. They would respectively become students, temple servants, midwives, family counselors, and teachers. Upon retirement, they were given a pension and only then allowed to marry. Inevitably, public trials featuring the scandalous behaviors of fallen Vestals made the news, and most often ended with their death.

The king, serving as the high priest or *Pontifex Maximus,* arranged marriages to suitable Roman citizens who often were retired military veterans or noblemen. Marriage to a former Vestal was a high honor and considered good luck, as well as generating a comfortable pension.[14] Magistrates also assigned girls to be Vestals with the knowledge that the family blood-line would be constrained, if not ended. The practice essentially became a form of birth control and family planning. It also provided an honorable way to preserve and maintain family wealth and not dilute land ownership.

Figure 4-5 Left A silver denarius coin 58 B.C. of the *veiled head of the Vestal Virgin Aemilia (daughter of Marcus Aemilius Lepidus who famously brought Julius Caesar to power and then served as triumvir with Mark Antony and Augustus). The reverse features the ancient Basilica Aemilia located in the center of the Roman forum which served as a shelter for businesses and money exchange. (CC By-SA-3.0)* Figure 4-6 Right *Denarius with Emperor Nero 68-54 B.C. Reverse is Vesta seated in a temple holding a scepter and patera. (CC By-SA-3.0)*

Conquests and Coinage

Numismatics often look at how soldiers were paid to make inferences about the economy.[15] The many successes of the early Roman conquests were made by highly motivated property-owning citizen soldiers (the *legionary*) conscripted by the king. Later, during the Republic, propertied soldiers would elect consuls who would lead them in profitable conquests. Men often volunteered as they were likely under-utilized labor for the family farm. Military service offered adventure along with the spoils of war, as well as, access to slaves to work their farms. The early Roman military received compensation in the form of salt rations. The *legionaries* were rugged, self-sufficient, loyal, and highly trained soldiers. They were equipped with both a sword and a shovel as they became acclaimed for their fighting and engineering prowess. Their loyalty and allegiance, to the state and themselves, were reflected in their favorite pagan god of worship "*Disciplina*" the goddess of self-discipline, frugality, and faithfulness.[16]

Tribute, including gold and silver coins poured into Rome, as the Romans took whatever they wanted by force and plunder. It took over 350 years after the founding of Rome that coinage from the pillage of conquered provinces was first used to pay the Roman legions. Numismatists estimate that foreign coinage was adopted for Roman use in 394 B.C.

The reasons behind Rome's late adoption of coinage were likely both cultural and geological. The early Romans adopted the concept from the Greeks, not as a need, but as part of their fascination with all things Greek. The Romans rarely used coinage among themselves as their word was their sacred bond. By the early 6th century B.C., the Greek city-states widely circulated coinage, while the Romans would only gradually embrace its usage some 300 years later.

The Romans initially introduced bronze coinage by weight as they had little access to other locally sourced metals.[17] Their basic bronze (copper and tin) coin was the "*as*" which weighed one Roman pound (the libra) or 325 grams (.325 kilogram or 11.5 ounces). It was subdivided into ten *asses* (6.81 grams) equal to 1/48 of a libra. This initial subdivision led to the Roman adoption of a decimal system for their workhorse currency the denarius. The abbreviation for the Latin word for libra is "*Lb*" and stood for the balance of scales in the astrological sign of Libra, which evolved into "*libra pondo*" meaning a "pound by weight."[18] These bronze coins are notable as their nomenclature survives both in the British monetary system where the abbreviation for pound sterling is £, and the abbreviation for a pound weight is a lb.

The early Roman patricians had no pressing need for a currency as they would use the *exonumia* of tableware, jewelry, and talisman figurines of their pagan gods to show appreciation, or in exchange for favors with other wealthy citizens or politicians. The Roman "*as*" was viewed as a mere token of exchange for what was plundered, or simply taken from others, as it was not acceptable for the payment of taxes. The Romans would later adopt the coins of the provincial city-states or *polis* as they expanded their empire. Central Italy was not rich in metal ores, and the only access the Romans had to precious metals was through plunder and exploitation of mineral resources by way of conquest.

The last of the seven kings of Rome was Lucius Tarquinius Superbus or Tarquin the Proud. Lucius appropriately nicknamed himself "*Superbus*" which is Latin for "proud, arrogant, and lofty." The Roman naming convention allows for a third title to be chosen as a nickname, which then may become the accepted hereditary family name. King Superbus gained access to the throne after he assassinated his predecessor and then murdered his wife and older brother. His blatant tyranny appalled even the Romans and is said to justify the abolition of the monarchy, in favor of the first republic form of government in 509 B.C. [19] The first republic evolved about the same time as the first democracy in Athens.

The Roman Republic 509 to 27 B.C.

Lucius Junius Brutus led the bloody overthrow of the last Roman king. He then prompted a public oath by the citizens of Rome to never be governed by a king again. Ten prominent patriarchs designed a constitution which shaped the body of written Roman law and established separate branches of government, with a complex sct of checks and balances. The ten patriarchs or *"decemvirate"* formally introduced the Law of the Twelve Tables, which remained as their foundation of constitutional law until the sacking of Rome by the Visigoths in A.D. 410.

The Twelve Tables provide insight into the Republic's mindset and cultural values. The Tables assigned property rights, the custody of the family, and civil rules for social discourse. Two consuls would be elected to the highest office every year, while the Senate had the option to appoint a dictator for up to six months to handle any crisis. Lucius Brutus was elected the first consul of the new Roman Republic, whereupon he had the sad duty of presiding over the trial and execution of his two sons who conspired to reestablish the kingdom.[20] The most important conquests were made during the five centuries of the Roman Republic. Rome came to control large territorial holdings around the Mediterranean Sea in Europe, Africa, and Asia.

The Temple of Juno Moneta

As Consul to the Republic, Marcus Camillus was justly honored with the title of the *Second Founder of Rome* (after Romulus). In honor of victories over the Greek cities and colonies in southern Italy, the people of Rome built the Temple of Juno Moneta over Camillus's house in 428 B.C. The house was on a summit that overlooked the Roman Forum (plaza). Juno, the patron goddess of Rome, is the Roman equivalent of the Greek goddess Hera, the wife of Zeus and the protector of women. She was also worshipped by their neighbors, the Etruscans, who named her Moneta hence: Juno Moneta. The Latin word "*moneta*" came to mean *mint* and is the origin of the English words for *money* and *monetary*. Citizens' records and magistrates' books were deposited in the Temple. The first Roman coins were minted within the city in workshops attached to the Temple in 273 B.C. The goddess Juno Moneta became the personification of money, and temples have since become associated with mints and currencies. [20] Hordes of coinage are often discovered within temples as they likely charged an admittance fee or donation for their services, meals, and lodging.

Legend has it that the oracle Sybil foretold the coming of Christ to Emperor Augustus in the Temple of Juno Moneta. Augustus envisioned the Virgin Mary with the Christ child and built an altar of worship on the spot. He named it the alter in heaven (*ara coeli)*. Years after the official adoption of Christianity, the Roman Catholic Basilica of *Santa Maria in Ara Coeli* or the Basilica of the "*Virgin Mary in Heaven,*" rose around the ancient Temple of Juno Moneta where it stands to this day.[21]

The Roman army defeated the Greeks and their general Pyrrhus of Epirus in 279 B.C., thereby ending a long military campaign with full control over the Greek colonies and cities in southern Italy, along with the rich agricultural lands of the *Magna Graecia* owned by the wealthy latifundista. The Romans were victorious despite having suffered much greater casualties. Such conquests are known today as *pyrrhic* victories. It was in this southern region of Italy that the minting of the first Roman silver coins took place in the form of the Greek style silver didrachm. The coin was stamped with the head of Mars wearing a Corinthian helmet and a horse head with an ear of grain on the reverse. The Roman soldiers highly favored the coin for its symbolic reference to Mars—the pagan god of war. The Hercules/She-wolf didrachm (valued as two drachmas) is thought to be the first silver coin minted within the city of Rome in the Temple of Juno Moneta.[21]

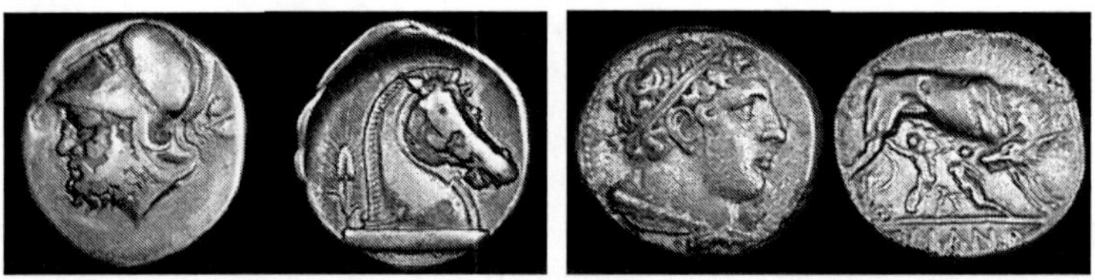

Figure 4-7 Left *The first adopted Roman silver coin 281 B.C. featuring the bearded head of Mars wearing a Corinthian helmet and a horse head on the reverse.* Figure 4-8 Right *The first coin minted in Rome in 269 B.C. with the head of Hercules and the She-wolf suckling the twins. Silver didrachms (6.44 g). (GNU Free Documentation License).*

The native Greek didrachm was replaced in 211 B.C. with the first Roman-inspired coin the *denarius.* The denarius became the backbone of Roman coinage throughout the Republic for more than five hundred years until the great re-coinage act by Emperor Diocletian in A.D. 293. The silver denarius was first struck at 1/72 of a Roman pound (each at 4.55 grams of 95-98 percent silver). The denarius became yet another coin to a complex multi-metallic coinage system. It was equal in exchange for ten pounds of bronze or a Roman bronze "*as*" and valued to a day's pay for skilled labor. The denarius also became day's pay for the Roman soldier who would then need to pay out-of-pocket for his living expenses and his armaments.[21] Other popular denominations were the silver *quinarius* valued at one-half the denarius, and the *sestertius* for one-quarter. The silver d*enarius* is Latin for "containing ten" and set the stage for a coinage based on a decimal system. Historically, it is linked to the British penny and one U.S. cent (colloquially also called a *penny*).[22]

The Roman coin *aureus* is Latin for "golden" and was first founded by Julius Caesar containing 8.18 grams of gold valued at 25 silver denarii. The coin was struck infrequently and seldom used. During Caesar's day, gold was considered an un-Roman like luxury as the Romans had little access to it. Caesar likely used silver and gold appropriated from his military conquests of Gaul, which is perhaps why he was so hated by the Senate and loved by his soldiers. Emperor Augustus' conquests latter increased the popularity of the coin and valued the sestertius at 1/100 of an aureus, or equal to 400 silver denarii, largely inflating the Roman money supply.[23]

Roman emperors over the next three hundred years gradually debased the gold aureus in size and gold content. The denarius would continually be debased in value, re-tariffed in exchange value by order of the state, and during the reign of the Western emperors further reduced in size and purity due to fiscal imprudence. By A.D. 268-270 the denarius had further shrunken to 3.41 grams containing only 2 percent silver. During the era of the Roman Republic, the sestertius was a small silver coin worth ¼ of a denarius. Later during the Western Roman Empire, it was reconfigured as a large brass coin backed only by the authority of Rome. [23]

The debasement of the aureus tracks the decline and fall of the Western Roman Empire. The economic lessons from monetary debasement were well-learned and known. While the currency of the Western Roman Empire and its culture declined, the Eastern Byzantine Empire arose and expanded. The founder of the Byzantine Empire, Constantine the Great, would officially re-set the gold content to 4.55 grams of nearly 24-carat purity. He renamed the coin the *solidus*—where it then remained a stable Roman currency for over 700 years.

Although some silver was mined in southern Italy, it was the gradual Roman annexation and conquest of the eastern Iberian Peninsula (Spain) that brought a treasure trove of silver, lead, iron, and copper to the Roman Republic's economy. By the 2nd century B.C., about 40,000 miners worked in the silver mines of Cartagena in southeastern Spain, yielding a *daily* revenue of 25,000 drachmae (equal to 5,360 ounces of silver).[24] The Greek-style Roman drachma coin weighed 6.1 grams of silver. The coinage was used to pay for the expansion of Rome's infrastructure, military, and overall economic development. The Romans themselves did much of the mining during the early years and later, with the considerable expansion of the mining industry, used foreign slaves, convicts, and exiles to work in the deep and vile mining pits.

Rome's conquest of Carthage (now Tunisia) during the first Punic War in 264 B.C. provided the mint in Rome again with a large supply of silver for coinage. *Punic* is the Latin word for the "*Punicus*" meaning the Carthaginians. The ancestors of the maritime Phoenicians, they expanded settlements along the northern coast of Africa and eastern Spain and became the primary antagonists to Roman rule. Further animosity arose from the Romans' belief, based on archeological evidence, that the *Punicus* ate dogs and sacrificed their children on altars.[25] Their first defeat of the Carthaginians was over the sharing of the island of Sicily and the Iberian Peninsula.

Figure 4-9 Left *An ancient Carthaginian shekel, dated 237 - 227 B.C. Depicted is the face of Heracles with the likely facial features of Hamilcar Barca, father of Hannibal Barca. The reverse is a depiction of a man riding a war elephant. Classical Numismatic Group, Inc. www.cngcoins.com*
Figure 4-10 Right *The helmeted head of General Scipio Africanus, considered the greatest of the Roman Republic's military leaders. On the reverse is Jupiter, Rome's highest god holding thunderbolts and standing between the Roman goddesses Juno Moneta (money) and Minerva (commerce and wisdom). In 211 B.C., during the Second Punic War, the denarius coin was introduced to replace the Greek-style drachma at parity with 4.5 grams silver (18mm), which until then had served as Rome's main silver currency. Classical Numismatic Group, Inc. www.cngcoins.com*

Trade disagreements and the refusal of Carthage to pay tribute to Rome brought the army of Hannibal Barca (and his three dozen war elephants) across the Alps to attack Rome from the north. Hannibal mounted a 17-year siege of central Italy. The countryside around Rome remained loyal and refused to support Hannibal, much to his dismay. The siege was broken by the Roman General Publius Cornelius Scipio Africanus a.k.a. "Scipio, the African" at the Battle of Zama in 202 B.C. Continued antagonism by the Carthaginians, led to the final Third Punic War (149-146 B.C.). Again, Scipio the African returned to stage a three-year siege over Carthage, enslaved 50,000 Carthaginians, and for 17 days (in fitting retribution for the 17-year siege of Rome) systematically sacked, burned, and turned the entire city into rubble until it was utterly destroyed. All the Carthaginian territories became the Roman province of Africa, where they were forced to pay immense tribute to Rome, and General Scipio became an elected consul to the Republic. [26] The lesson: don't fool with Rome and its invincible military.

The Life Blood of the Republic

The Roman latifundista benefited greatly from the large-scale slavery that resulted from the Punic Wars and other Roman conquests between the 2nd and 1st centuries B.C. Roman soldiers, mainly private land-owning farmers, essentially fought to capture replacements to work on their farms. Enslavement was a common fate for both debtors and those defeated in warfare. The ancient Greeks found enslavement a common practice among other cultures and considered it a natural and a sensible way to deal with the payment of debts.[27] The recorded numbers of slaves from Roman conquests: the enslavement of 5,000 Macedonians (197 B.C.); 150,000 Greek Epirotes (167 B.C.); 50,000 Carthaginians (146 B.C.); and such a large number of Sardinians (174 B.C.) that the word "*Sardinian*" became a Latin byword for *cheap slave labor*.[27] Pirates and bandits would soon carry off slaves to Anatolia (Turkey) and sell them by the block in thousands on the island of Delos. The flood of slaves destabilized Rome and the eastern Mediterranean. By 167 B.C. slaves made up about one-third of the city's population.[27, 28]

The early Republic's modest property tax rate of 1 to 3 percent was levied on its Roman citizens in support of the state and the military. Roman citizenship was determined by actual residence within the city of Rome. The tax rate remained stable for well over 300 years. New and sustaining wealth came from the conquest of Spain's silver mines in 167 B.C. and the neighboring provinces for tax collections.[29] The immense flow of tribute and taxes later allowed the state to suspend any tax collections on its citizens living in Rome (a nice benefit).

Tax farmers or "*publicani*" were used to collect the provincial taxes and the official positions were awarded by bids at government auctions. The *publicani* were responsible for converting the collected properties and goods into coinage, provide the payments to the state's treasury, and allowed to keep anything in excess over what was the set bid at auction.

The *publicani* became the bankers, businessmen, and the entrepreneurs of ancient Rome. They provided cash and extended loans to the Roman provinces at rates of 4 percent a month or more. Emperor Augustus ended *tax farming* toward the end of the 1st century B.C. with a direct wealth tax of 1 percent and a flat poll tax (or head tax) on each adult. The collection process essentially switched taxation from being based on property and wealth to being a tax on labor based on income—a controversial practice to this day. Although viewed as fairer and less corrupt, the collected taxable yield varied greatly based on windfall profits from occasional conquests and prosperous economic conditions.[27] However, worsening economic conditions would ultimately lead to ever grim and harsher methods of tax collections in the outer provinces.

Improved sanitation from the constant construction of aqueducts starting in the early years of the Republic, along with the expansion of commercial trade, slowly increased the quality of life. In most cases, the geographically dispersed aqueducts would pay for themselves, as the water would be sluiced around the countryside during construction and used to wash away the topsoil in search of silver and other metals. Aqueducts supplied not only water but also served to supply the watermills for grinding grain, thereby providing for the greatest source of mechanical power in the ancient world.

By the first century A.D., the Romans had begun to exploit the large alluvial gold deposits in Spain. Gold and silver were extracted by a mining technique known as "*hushing*," where aqueducts supplied water to the mine head. The stored water, in huge reservoirs and cisterns, was released to sluice away the overburden and expose the bedrock and any veins of precious metals. The exposed rock was heated by great wood fires and quickly quenched with water. The cracking process claimed any valuable metals. The last step consisted of smelting the ore which left lasting environmental scars that still are plainly evident in Las Medulas, Spain.[30]

The expansion of the money supply provided a major trade stimulus for agricultural goods (wine, oil, salted fish), manufactured items (table pottery, glass, millstones), and luxury goods (silks, spices, architectural marble). Wheat and barley were the main grains for human consumption in the ancient Mediterranean world. However, the thin limestone soil and erratic rainfall around Rome always made the grain harvests vulnerable and variable. Long-distance trade in these commodities was a vibrant business that provided the Roman government with more stable funds from a standard customs tax of 25 percent on goods across frontiers and 5 percent tax on trade within the Roman provinces. The Republic stored its reserves of gold and silver in the Temple of Saturn which housed the Roman treasury or "*aerarium.*" [31]

Wheat and barley were vitally important to the Roman diet. The Romans used the term "*Cura Annonae*" or *"care of the grain supply*" in honor of their goddess Annona. The state-controlled grain dole was distributed from the Temple of Ceres on the Tiber River. Ceres, the goddess of agriculture (the root word for cereal), became a central idol of the pagan Roman culture and evolved into a cult figure for the plebeians in their quest for more entitlements and subsidized food. The lack of enough grain supplies to feed its citizens was the likely motivation for Rome's early conquests of southern Italy. As the Republic grew, there were more mouths to feed. The Roman state took ever more interest in the grain trade to feed both Rome and its armies in the outer provinces.[32]

Gaius Gracchus (154 to 121 B.C) was a Roman populist and champion for the lower social class of common people known as the plebeians. He advocated land reforms and convinced the state to buy ever larger grain supplies for distribution to its citizens for free or at low subsidized prices. He cajoled the state to provide free clothes and equipment to the soldiers, and to shorten the term of military service. The local sourcing of agriculture from Sardinia and Sicily faded in significance during this period, as Egypt and Africa became the primary source of food and coinage from taxation and tribute.

Ship owners were exempted from compulsory military service if they supplied *annonea* to Rome. A typical cargo ship could carry 340 tons of grain, with an estimated 800 to 4000 shiploads delivered directly to the city of Rome. Other vast shipments supplied the legions in the outer provinces. The grain shipments were conducted by free market merchants and traders, while the state sought to stabilize supply and demand at Rome's main distribution point, the Temple of Ceres. Most other goods were freely traded with little government restrictions other than tax collections. [33]

Trade around the Mediterranean had grown from the beginning of the Roman Republic, would peak during the reign of Emperor Augustus, and gradually start its decline for the next 500 years. [34] The archeological chart below illustrates the rise and fall of Rome based on trade and the number of maritime shipwrecks. The shipwrecks and their cargo capacity strongly correlate with both population and trade around the Mediterranean.[34] By the 3rd century A.D., the population of Rome declined to 500,000, or less than a third of what it was when Augustus rose to power.[35, 36]

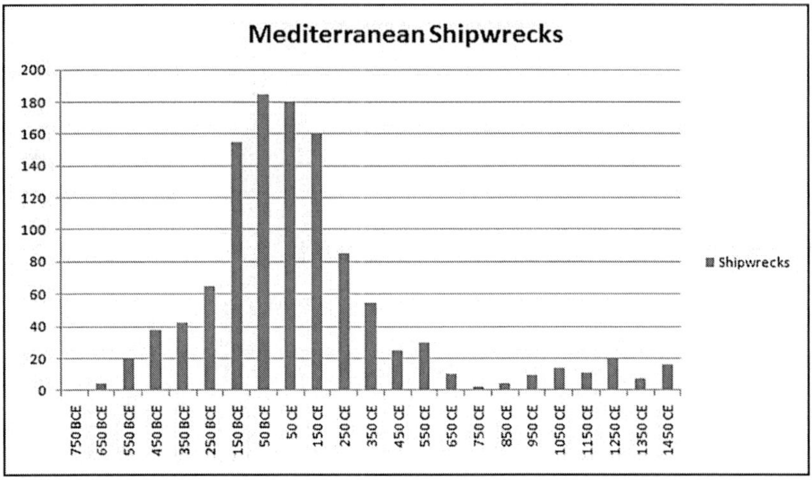

Figure 4-11 Mediterranean Shipwrecks Source: Parker, A.J. 1992 *(GNU Free Documentation License).*

Prelude to the Demise of the Roman Republic

Gaius Marius was a General elected an unprecedented seven times as consul to the Roman Republic from 104 – 86 B.C. He defeated numerous Germanic tribes, became an advocate for the poor and landless "*capite censi*" the largest underserved social class in Rome, and was honored as *the third founder of Rome.* His self-styled "Marian" regulatory reforms largely transformed and reorganized the Roman legions. The reforms set a precedent for recruiting among the landless poor and granted them land upon the successful conclusion of a military campaign by decree of their general, and *not* by the Senate as was the common practice. His reforms solved the many problems of rampant urban strife, homelessness, and unemployment. They also incentivized soldiers to become loyal to their generals—and *not* to the state.

The military reforms of Gaius Marius caused more problems for the Roman Republic than any enemy of Rome ever could. The bought-and-paid-for loyalty of the legions allowed Marius himself to be repeatedly elected consul. Forty years later, Marius's nephew (Julius Caesar) would march on Rome itself. The legions were adversely transformed by the Marian reforms. Historians recognize his reforms as the pivotal step leading in short order to the collapse of the Republic. The legions, now compensated with land and booty at the discretion of their general, affirmed their loyalty to their general rather than to the Senate and the people of Rome.[37]

Before the Marian reforms, the eligibility requirements to become a Roman soldier were strict and exclusive. The social classes of Rome were very hierarchical, and citizenship rights and privileges varied accordingly. There were many classes of non-citizens, with different legal rights, including sundry favors among the slaves. Roman women were citizens who could not vote nor hold political office but were free from military service.

There were three requirements for a Roman soldier. 1: He had to be a tax-payer and therefore a member of the fifth census class or higher. 2: He had to own property worth more than 3500 *sesterces* (~ 875 denarii) in value. 3: He had to supply his own armaments. [38] Paid only a small wage, a legionary on an active campaign, hoped to add to his small wage with the booty of war and the plunder and looting from enemy settlements. The conquered enemy was considered the property of the Senate and for the state to decide their fate. The soldiers received their allowances in cash and booty, but the state deducted a clothing and food tax. However, the Marian reforms rescinded the tax and provided the legionaries with a generous wage of 225 denarii a year. Slaves were divided among the legions for sale which brought in a sizeable supplement to regular pay. Each legionary soldier also received a "*praemia*" (land), upon completion of his term of service, as well as a sizeable sum of retirement money (3,000 denarii in A.D. 5). Farmland awarded to the veteran soldiers also served as a control of the frontier regions and to stabilize rebellious provinces.[38]

General Gaius Julius Caesar and his loyal and legendary 13th Legion conquered Gaul (France), crossed the Rhine, and conducted the first invasion of Britain. The campaign was to exploit Britain's known metal resources, especially lead used widely for waterproofing aqueducts, plumbing, pewter etc.[39] Caesar used Lugdunum (Lyon, France) as his de facto administrative center for the Gallic provinces, a staging ground for further Roman expansion into Germany and an increasingly popular Romanized city. The productive gold, silver, and copper mines of Lugdunum provided Caesar with the coinage necessary to incentivize his soldiers. The Lugdunum branch of the imperial mint was established in 15

B.C. and produced much of the imperial Roman coinage from Emperor Augustus and onward for the next three centuries. The less valuable copper alloy coins that were circulated in Britain came from the Lugdunum mines.[39]

Caesar disregarded the Senate's mandated decrees not to return to Rome and to step down from his military command if he so did. In defiance, he crossed the storied Rubicon River and eventually assumed control over the Roman Senate. Caesar's conquests were enhanced by the loyalty of his 13th Legion not to the state, but to their general. The loyalty to Caesar was largely a result of the Marian reforms, the new military pay incentives, and the social entitlements in favor of the lower and landless classes. Caesar's ability to pay his soldiers in hard gold and silver coinage surely added to his immense popularity among the lower social classes.

Nearly 500 years after the founding of the Republic, General Julius Caesar demanded that the Senate appoint him dictator for life. The resulting civil war impoverished the city of Rome and Caesar had to deal with widespread debt, the repayment of loans, and a crash in real estate values. Caesar ultimately responded by increasing demand for more tribute from the provinces.

Figure 4-12 *A silver denarius issued by Senator Marcus Junius Brutus in 43/42 B.C. The obverse features a portrait of Marcus Brutus. BRVT IMP L PLAET CEST translates to Brutus, Imperator, Lucius Plaetorius Cestianus. Lucius Plaetorius Cestianus was the official concessioner who managed the mint workers who produced the coin. The reverse EID MAR means the "Ides of March" concerning the death of Caesar. The two daggers are meant to indicate that more than one person was involved in the slaying. The cap is a "liberty cap" that was given to slaves on the day of their emancipation from slavery. Marcus Brutus obviously issued the coin making it clear that Caesar's assassins were defending the Republic from the dictator's grasp of kingship. (Public domain).*

To save the Republic, Senator Marcus Junius Brutus staged the famous assassination of the newly proclaimed Dictator Julius Caesar. According to Plutarch, Marcus Brutus and his companions marched through the streets of Rome crying out: *"People of Rome, we are once again free!"* They were met with dead silence as the newly entitled lower classes, with whom Caesar was popular, were enraged that a small group of patriarchs would murder their beloved and generous Caesar. Ironically, this occurred on the first full moon at the start of the Dictator's newly proclaimed Julian calendar: the Ides of March, or March 15, 44 B.C. It marked the end of a Republic ruled by its people—to an Empire ruled by autocratic emperors.[40] Ironically, Marcus Brutus was a descendant of Lucius Junius Brutus, the first Roman consul and founder, dating back to its very beginning of the Roman Republic in 509 B.C.

The Nugget

The early Romans paved their way out of a hardscrabble and an impoverished existence with that of a profound sense of "*pietas*" or respect and dutifulness to their country, family, and friends. They had few resources, no currency for trade, and initially paid their citizen soldiers with salt rations. Regardless, they rejected the corruption and tyranny of their early kings and replaced it with the world's first constitutional Republic. A Republic of laws ensured the citizens' freedoms and their right to the private ownership of land and property. Only later in 394 B.C. did they adopt the use of coins which added fuel to their economy and global expansion.

The adoption of coinage incentivized early Roman culture. As engineers, they built an enormous road network, constructed aqueducts, erected religious and public temples, and organized the social behavior of their society and of those they conquered. The citizens of the Roman Republic built the economic foundations for prosperity and expansion using a mixture of labor, land, and—*money.*

CHAPTER FIVE

THE IMPERIAL ROMAN EMPIRE & ROMAN IMPERIAL COINS

Keywords: Tribute Penny; Five Good Emperors; Roman Imperial Coinage; Gresham's Law; Edict of Maximum Prices

> Jesus, referring to a denarius coin asked, "*Whose is this image and superscription?*" When answered that the likeness was Caesar, He replied; *"Render therefore unto Caesar the things which are Caesar's and unto God the things that are God's."*
>
> *Matthew 22:20-21.*

The rise of Christianity began in the shadow of Roman power. During Christ's time on earth, the popular coin used throughout the Roman Empire was the dime-sized silver denarius which represented roughly a day's labor by a skilled worker, craftsman, or a soldier. Tiberius was the ruling Caesar at that time, and his coin is most often referred to as the "*The Tribute Penny.*" The King James Bible described the Roman denarius as a *penny* by the British monetary system and is colloquially referred to as the U.S. *cent*.

The official Roman Imperial Coin (RIC) was struck from A.D. 15 to A.D. 37 at the Lugdunum mint (modern Lyon, France). General Julius Caesar had seized the Lugdunum mines where he minted the money he used to seize the Republic. The denarius is described on the obverse of the coin as "*Tiberius Caesars, son of the Divine Augustus, Emperor.*" The reverse legend is "*PONTIF MAXIM*" or Pontifex Maximus meaning the *High Priest*. The enthroned female on the reverse of the coin is Livia Drusilla (the mother of Tiberius and the long-time wife of Caesar Augustus). Tiberius Augustus was the official Pontifex Maximus, but the association was probably intended to include his mother as having the same divine powers and religious status.[1]

Perhaps Christ didn't recognize the woman on the reverse side of the *Tribute Penny,* or he would have acknowledged her importance along with that of Caesar. The woman behind her man was Livia Drusilla the first Empress of Rome. (In A.D. 800 Irene of Athens became the only other named Roman Empress.) Revered for her loyalty, devotion, and high moral conduct, she was given a second honorific title of *Julia Augusta*: a moniker conferred on all the wives of the future Roman emperors. Livia, the daughter of Julius Caesar's sister Julia, was married to Augustus (a.k.a. Octavian) for 53 years. She co-ruled the empire and continued to do so under the reign of her son Tiberius until she died at the age of 85. Augustus reasserted Roman control over Egypt and other key provinces with the defeat of Marc Antony and Cleopatra at the Battle of Atrium in 32 B.C. He then persuaded the Senate to reclaim the highest of all religious positions that of *Pontifex Maximus* in 12 B.C. The religious and sacred title of a "deity," once relegated to the College of the Pontiffs by the Roman Republic, was now fully granted to Augustus and shared with his wife, Livia. She was given the sacred right to sit with the Vestal Virgins during public performances and obtained enormous political power as the woman behind her husband and later her son Tiberius Augustus Caesar.

Figure 5-1 Left *The storied "Tribute Penny" features Augustus on the obverse and his mother on the reverse of the coin. The bust of Livia Drusilla is personified as the goddess "Pietas" which is loosely translated to mean: "loyalty, devotion, and respect." Pietas was one of the chief virtues of the Romans for duty to their country, parents and blood relations. Classical Numismatic Group, Inc. www.cngcoins.com*
Figure 5-2 Right *A brass dupondius coin of A.D. 22-23. Pietas is found inscribed on the obverse of many early Roman coins. The value of the brass coin was enforced by a decree of the Senate "Senatus Consulto" or SC. Classical Numismatic Group, Inc. www.cngcoins.com*

Livia Drusilla adroitly advised her husband on political affairs while she turned her attention to spending the royal fortunes that flowed into Rome from Cleopatra's vast treasures following the conquest of Egypt. She received large numbers of clients, commissioned and dedicated public buildings, sponsored charities, and interceded on behalf of provincial emissaries. The new money was lavishly spent during the first twenty years of Augustus Caesar's reign, from 30 to 10 B.C. She made sure Augustus maintained popular support by hosting games, erecting new buildings, and overseeing the restoration of 82 temples in one year alone.

Augustus and Livia oversaw grand new buildings like the Theatre of Apollo, the Horologium (a giant sundial), the great Mausoleum of Augustus, and the Pantheon (later rebuilt by Emperor Hadrian), and repaired the city's water system with the addition of two new aqueducts: the Aqua Julia and Aqua Virgo. Livia directed the economy and helped her husband consolidate power while maintaining the appearance of not doing so. Rome received tribute from Egypt that was so enormous that prices escalated in value and real estate increased dramatically while interest rates correspondingly fell from 12 percent to 4 percent.[2]

The Roman peace or "*Pax Romana*" was accomplished primarily through the previous hard-won conquests of the Roman Republic and the initial triumph over Egypt by the newly appointed Emperor Augustus at the very beginning of the Roman Empire. During the last twenty years of Augustus's reign, however, spending gave way to parsimony and continued for nineteen years during the reign of his son Tiberius. Gold and silver coinage were increasingly being sent abroad to pay for needed imports resulting in a trade deficit, while the per capita circulation of coinage within Imperial Rome slowly decreased over the next forty years. Historians note that a severe economic contraction lasted from 9 B.C. to A.D. 32.[3]

This contraction led to a well-documented economic crisis in A.D. 33. It began with the prosecution of money-lenders who charged illegally high rates of interest which is a common symptom of a contracted currency. Other fiscally motivated public prosecutions and confiscations soon occurred. The newly formed Roman Empire experienced a few boom periods created by new money windfalls from occasional conquests. However, more likely to occur were financial busts when the Emperor's treasury dried up, thereby incurring harsh fiscal penalties, higher taxes, and increased tributes and burdens placed on the provinces.

Gaius Octavius Caesar Augustus was the great-nephew and adopted son of the dictator, Julius Caesar. He was Caesar's closest male relative as was the custom. The British called him *Octavian*, others simply *Augustus.* He adopted his self-named cognomen of *Augustus,* which is Latin for *majestic*. He eventually usurped control and was declared the first Roman Emperor and given the official title of "*Principate*" in 27 B.C. He smartly avoided reintroducing an official monarchy given the historical Roman disdain for kings or monarchs. His new title of "*Princeps'* (or first citizen) implied allegiance to both the Senate and the ideals of the early Republic. However, in reality the emperor was granted whatever authority and desires he so wished. In return, he let the Senate and magistrates bid for their fortunes at the expense of the public. In so doing he gave rise to a growing bureaucracy and incessant corruption.[4] Of the 147 emperors that reigned until the Roman Empire was divided into western and eastern empires by Diocletian in A.D. 284, some would be civic-minded, while many others were despotic and tyrannical. Few emperors would die a natural death as family disputes, and political machinations took their toll on the governance of the Empire. The Empire turned away from the founding principles of the Roman Republic and reverted to the corruption and authoritarian rule of early Rome.

The Five Good Emperors

The *Pax Romana* began with Augustus and Livia and ended in A.D. 180 with Marcus Aurelius: the last of the *Five Good Emperors*. Niccolo Machiavelli, considered the founder of modern political science, observed in A.D. 1503 that all the Roman emperors who succeeded to the throne by birthright (except Titus) were bad, and all of those who succeeded by adoption were good. As soon as the empire fell once again to their heirs by birthright, the ruin of the empire would recommence. The "*Five Good Emperors*" (Nerva, Trajan, Hadrian, Antoninus Pius, and Marcus Aurelius) earned respect and good-will of those around them. They would abide by the rules set forth by the Senate, and the workings of a Republic.[5, 6] Respectively, there was only one good emperor to every twenty-eight despots before the empire was divided in A.D. 284.

Roman society and culture were radically transformed during the first period of the *Principate,* roughly from 27 B.C. to A.D. 180. The new Roman Empire faced multiple natural disasters, beginning in A.D. 79 with the eruption of Mount Vesuvius, followed a year later by a great fire and a devastating plague in Rome, along with the first of the provincial Jewish rebellions. However, despite these setbacks, the empire reached its then maximum territorial extent under Emperor Trajan (A.D. 98-117).

Trajan conquered the frontier provinces of Arabia and Dacia (the modern nation of Romania which is Latin for a *citizen of Rome*). Dacia's valuable gold mines replenished the Roman coffers allowing Trajan to reshape the city of Rome. History remembers Trajan as the great road builder who oversaw the construction of the much-appreciated Roman bathhouses. Nerva (96-98) is admired for his brief attempt to bring back the ideals of the Republic. Hadrian (76-138) is remembered for building Hadrian's Wall, which marked the northern limit of Britannia, as well as the rebuilding of the Pantheon and other temples. He is considered by many to be a humanist in an age of autocratic rule. Antoninus Pius (138-161) continued Roman expansion following in Hadrian's footsteps. Marcus Aurelius (161-180) defeated a revitalized Parthian Empire (ancient Iran and Iraq), shielded the Empire from the threat of the growing German tribes, and was an advocate of Stoicism: the Greek Hellenistic philosophy of informed personal ethics and self-reliance.[7, 8]

Nerva Trajan Hadrian A. Pius Marcus Aurelius

Figure 5-3 *The Five Good Emperors. Photograph of coins from the author's personal collection. Photos courtesy of Janessuncoastworks@comcast.net.*

Bread and Circuses

"Bread and circuses" is a metonymy, or a figure of speech, for the Roman practice of social appeasement. It was an attempt to distract the populace from real public policy issues by providing immediate satisfaction, or what is commonly referred to as instant gratification and entitlements. *Bread and circuses* implied the common people's willful ignorance of their civic duty. The phrase originated by the Roman poet and satirist Juvenal (in A.D. 100) who mocked Roman Emperors and politicians for their efforts to rise to power by giving away free food and entertainment.

Historical records of the A.D. 70s bluntly state that North Africa fed Rome for two-thirds of a year. Egypt, an important source of monetary tribute to Rome, sent enough grain to feed her for the remaining third. During the period of the Republic, most grain and other goods were transported by private merchants and ship owners and distributed to independent retailers for sale to the public. The journey took three stages: the collection of cargo at the harbors within the provinces, the shipment across the open seas, and the transport by barge up the Tiber River to Rome itself. The new authorities of the Roman Empire replaced the private sector and took full control of grain distribution from the Temple of Ceres to the government-sanctioned retailers and bakeries.

Increasingly, the problem of securing enough grain to feed the populace reached alarming proportions. The Empire needed a quarter of a million tons of grain a year to feed the just the city of Rome, in addition to feeding its extensive distant armies, and its many locally governed provinces. Under Julius Caesar, an estimated 320,000 plebeians or commoners, sarcastically called the "*frumentationes*" by the Roman elite, demanded free distribution of grain. Augustus limited it to 200,000 citizens who lived in the city of Rome. He eventually established a permanent post, the "*praefectus annonae*" or *Prefect of the Provisions*, while warning that the creation of such a post would lead to the bureaucratic ruin of the state.[9, 10]

Figure 5-4 *A large brass sestertius coin (valued about one-quarter of a denarius). The obverse features Emperor Nero (A.D. 54-68). The reverse is the goddess Annona (standing) as she holds a cornucopia of food facing the goddess Ceres (seated) holding ears of grain and a torch with a modius (a benchmark weight used to mint coinage) between them and a ship's stern behind. Attribution: Classical Numismatic Group, Inc.www.cncoins.com (GNU Free Documentation License).*

The Roman lifespan had reached only 25 years of age due to a high infant mortality rate, but with infant mortality factored out; the average Roman would see six decades of life. The Roman female would bear 6 to 9 children over her lifetime—if she survived past her childhood or mid-teens.[11]

The population within the city of Rome during the reign of Julius Caesar was estimated to be 750,000. Under Tiberius Augustus, it reached well over one and a quarter million people, about the same as the city of London in 1820; then the largest Western city in the world. Comparably, the second largest city was Alexandria in Egypt. It reached a population of 800,000 during the first century A.D. and became a major trading center and provider of tribute to Rome or Rome's second city. The overall population at the beginning of the Roman Empire was about 45.5 million people. Over the next 150 years the population slowly expanded to a peak of over 61 million—soon followed by a precipitous and historic decline.[11] The Imperial City of Rome eventually ruled over the entire Italian Peninsula and was provided with the tribute of free food, slaves, and homage.[12]

Roman Imperial Coinage

The early Romans of the Republic adopted coinage from over 600 cities and provincial mints as they expanded their empire and collected coins from tribute assessed from those they conquered. Roman *provincial* coins each had unique designs and stories to tell, but were of poorer construction and metallic quality than the official *Imperial* coins of the later Roman Emperors. The large round copper and bronze coins or "*asses*" of the early Republic were so sizeable that their value was largely based on their metal content. The workhorse of the Republic was the silver denarius introduced in 211 B.C., while gold coins were only later introduced by Julius Ceasar. Emperor Augustus reformed the Republic's currency during his reign, as the coinage had consisted of a confusing mix of composite metals of various intrinsic worth, but whose monetary value was now enforced by decree of the Emperor. Augustus officially established the following new denominations at the start of the Roman Empire: [13]

Gold Aureus = 25 Denarii
Silver denarius = 4 Sestertii*
*Aurichalcum **Sestertius = 2 Dupondii*
*Aurichalcum ** Dupondius = 2 Copper Asses*
Copper As = 2 Semis
Copper Semis = 2 Quadrans
Copper Quadrans

**Note: A pure silver denarius was minted at 84 coins to a Roman pound or 3.89 grams each. A denarius was about a day's pay for a skilled worker or craftsman. The gold aureus was minted at 40 to the Roman pound's weight of 322.5 grams. Weights were averages as wide differences between individual coins and mints were commonplace. The debasement of the coins wasn't necessarily planned but simply occurred when the mint's supply of silver was low. Forgeries (or fourees) were minted from copper flans coated with silver—a troubling worry for both the Republic and Empire.*

***Note: The distinction between bronze and brass coins was important to the Romans, who gave the name aurichalcum (meaning "gold-copper") to bronze coins with shiny gold-like appearance when first struck. However, they were not corrosion resistant and soon lost their luster and value, especially in contact with ocean salt air. Aurichalcum was considered by weight to be double the value of copper which gave way to the brass dupondius coin. The dupondius was about the same weight and size, but worth twice the value. (Bronze is mainly copper plus tin and oxidizes more quickly than brass, which is mainly a copper-zinc alloy and holds its luster for a longer period.)*

The new coinage (RIC) remained relatively stable for the next two centuries after Augustus. Nero (A.D. 54-68) was forced to reduce the silver content and debase the denarius by increasing the number of coins minted from 84 to 96 per pound. The coin's devaluation was considered necessary to rebuild the city of Rome after the great fire. However, the debasement of the coinage inflated the currency and market prices rose throughout the empire. History would blame Nero for the fire (and the inflation), but there had been no prior city planning, and Rome was a firetrap of wooden buildings. The cost to rebuild Rome with city planning and extensive masonry work was immense and required funds the state treasury did not have. In response, Nero devalued the currency by reducing the weight of the denarius from 3.85 grams to 3.35 grams. He also reduced the silver content from 99.5% to 93.5%; as the silver weight was reduced from 3.83 grams to 3.4 grams. He further reduced the weight of the gold aureus from 40 per Roman pound to 45, and from 8 grams per coin to 7.2 grams each.[14] Nero was the first emperor to devalue the Roman currency, but he certainly would not be the last. Future devaluations of the currency would rekindle inflation with negative repercussions to the economy and the whole of Roman culture.

Provincial coins could be identified and attributed to various mints based on their style, city emblem, other markings, or the ruler du jour. By the middle of the 3rd century, however, the Roman penchant for bureaucracy had begun to standardize the Empire's coinage with the incorporation of imperial mint marks. It would also endeavor to enforce consistent coin weights and measures through 30 official RIC mints spread across its vast territory. The face coinage of the ruler du jour would often be the only way people would come to know the name of their emperor.

The mint markings provide a windfall of historical information to numismatists; the map locations of each mint provide an astonishing record of the vast extent of the Roman Empire. Any problem with a series of coins (underweight for example) could be traced to the offending mint, and the officials held liable. Mintmarks often included symbols such as dots, crescents, or tree branches with leaves, to indicate when the coin was struck and the craftsman who was responsible. An encyclopedia of such information can be found on various websites.[15]

Figure 5-5 *Roman Coins (OTRS and GNU Free Documentation License).*

The Roman Empire confronts Gresham's Law

Gresham's Law, named after Sir Thomas' Gresham (A.D. 1519-1579) is a monetary principle which states that "*Where legal tender laws exist, bad money drives out good money*." If for example, two coins in circulation (i.e., silver and bronze) and are both officially decreed by law as having a similar face value, the more intrinsically valuable coin will disappear from circulation into private collections or leave the country, while the overvalued coin or currency will flood into public circulation. Ubiquitous and widespread non-precious metal coins, or unregulated fiat paper currency, are good examples of bad money. For example, pre-1965 U.S. quarters have all but disappeared from circulation due to their high silver content. What is seldom mentioned concerning Gresham's Law is that provided the total amount of money in circulation is in *balance* with the needs of the economy, good money and bad money *can* both circulate and coexist. For example, non-silver post-1965 U.S. quarters still are in circulation and have kept their perceived value through good supply management.

The operative word is *balance* which can be accomplished through good fiscal management as opposed to political necessity. According to Gresham's Law, a growing economy needs more money of all kinds, while an economy in decline needs less to keep it from declining further.[16, 17] The flow of money into or out of an economy can be largely adjusted either through published interest rates or simply through the adjustment of government reserves. In a declining economy, a currency *can* remain stable by raising taxes, increasing interest rates, or other fiscal government efforts to maintain the relationship of the currency to the current economic conditions. However, politicians are often loath to respond, as they have their reasons to game the economy. They often ignore the fact that trust among citizens is based upon trust in the currency they use to trade among themselves.[18] The Roman Emperors likely had little understanding of Gresham's Law, nor the ability to assess and quickly respond to local market needs for currency.

The economic lesson behind Gresham's Law is that if the amount of money in circulation is perceived to be greater than the needs within the marketplace, then inflation will begin to occur and eventually cripple the economy. Historians mark the reign of Emperor Septimius Severus (A.D. 193-211) as the moment when the economy and empire started to seriously decline. During his reign, the silver content of the denarius was gradually debased to 56 percent to mint more coins to pay the soldiers.

After Severus, each succeeding emperor needed an ever-larger military to maintain his command. The armies, once servants to the emperor, now became his master, as emperors rose and fell with startling frequency. Generals competed for the emperor's throne and preferred to increase taxes to pay foreign armies to fight for Rome, rather than do so themselves. Emperor Caracalla (212-217) responded to the debased denarius by introducing a new A*ntoninianus* coin at double the value of the debased denarius. The silver content of the new coin was only equal to 1.5 denarii, which spurred inflation as everyone recognized the lower intrinsic value of the new coin and elevated their prices to compensate. By the late 3rd century the Roman coins were made entirely of bronze, as silver was privately hoarded and in short supply.[19]

A compelling demonstration of Gresham's Law, however, was represented by the economic and military chaos which began during the reign of Gordian III (A.D. 238-244) when the purity of the silver content in coins rapidly declined to 48 percent. By the middle of the third century, under the reigns of Valerian I (A.D. 253-260) and Gallienus (A.D. 253-268), the silver content was reduced even further. Claudius II (A.D. 268-270) oversaw the silver content drop to just 2 percent. Due to the reduced silver content, the newer coins not only looked bad but proliferated as fewer were needed in a stagnant and declining economy.

Runaway inflation occurred when the government, which issued base metals for coinage, refused to accept anything but gold and silver in the collection of taxes.[19] By A.D. 270 good silver coins all but disappeared from circulation, hence; Gresham's Law.[20, 21] Correspondingly, Romans ceased to trust their common currency and abandoned trust among themselves. The economy reverted to barter-and-trade and the culture of the Western Roman Empire rapidly declined.

The Edict of Maximum Prices

Salvation of sorts came from the backwoods of Dalmatia by a cabbage farmer, who turned shrewd soldier and emperor, named Diocletian. He assumed power the usual way, by assassinating his predecessor and taking command of the army. Realistic about the decline of the empire's fortunes, and pragmatic enough to admit what others only dimly suspected; the vast empire was simply too large to be governed by one man. Diocletian also dealt with the problem faced by every emperor—that of succession. His unorthodox solution: split the empire, and the world as it was then known, in half.

Diocletian handed over the western areas of the empire, where Latin was the dominant language, to his old drinking buddy Maximian. He kept the wealthier and more cultured Greek east for himself, thereby dividing the world into what would later become known as the Roman and Byzantine Empires. He also appointed two junior emperors (Caesars) who were given full authority to command their armies, pass laws, administer, and expand the empire. The new "tetrarchy" was now comprised of four men who claimed imperial rank and vied for the emperor's throne. To Diocletian, competition was a good thing. He further attempted to reorganize the inefficient and corrupt system by dividing the empire into twelve neatly partitioned dioceses, each governed by a vicar who reported directly to the emperor. These reforms were later copied by the Roman Church, with bishops overseeing dioceses and the pope is known as the "Vicar" of Christ.[22] Others would consider the new land system additional bureaucracy.

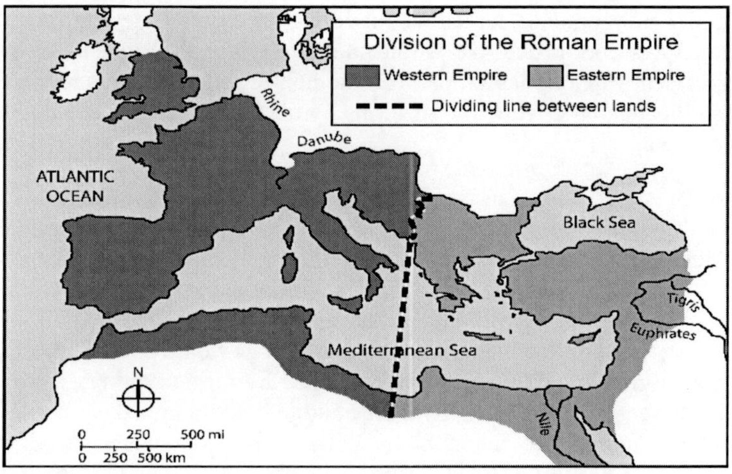

Figure 5-6 *Diocletian's map of the western and eastern empires in A.D 284, delegating in A.D. 294 the new "tetrarchy" or "rule of four." Diocletian would move the eastern empire to Nicomedia (near Byzantium) while co-emperor Maximian would move the western empire to the city of Mediolanum (present-day Milan). Attribution: Map illustrated by Jane Paquette www.janessuncoast works@ comcast.net*

Diocletian further attempted to stabilize the throne through an orderly system of succession and by fostering a public display of awe toward the emperor's authority and his undisputed might. Since Julius Caesar, all emperors went to great lengths to prove they were just like the men they commanded. The common touch was a necessity to procure the public's loyalty, since acting overtly like a tyrant would undermine the principle of an orderly succession, risking the emperor's overthrow and demise.

Diocletian would have none of this and set out to radically revise the position of the emperor's perceived power and authority to reinstate stability within the empire. Religion gave him a perfect tactic to command this new respect. As an emperor, he assumed the role of a god-like figure in the likeness of Jupiter. He was the first Roman ruler who commanded the people to prostrate themselves before him and avert their gaze from the brilliance of his presence. He also dressed the part, as he was the first emperor to adorn his head with a jeweled diadem and drape a golden robe around his shoulders. The Roman Church would soon adopt Diocletian's introduction of royal vestments, customs, and even territorial assignments. The semi-divine emperor established an elaborate court steeped in solemnity and grandeur, which would define the cultural ideology adopted by the Byzantine throne. He would ultimately lose the fight against the advancement of Christianity, as even the non-religious saw his repression as a political gambit, while the suffering by the Christians was equal to that of their own.

In 301 A.D., Diocletian introduced his "Edict Concerning the Sale Price of Goods," otherwise well-known as the "Edict of Maximum Prices." The proclamation was an attempt to further combat the ravages of inflation by establishing maximum prices for goods and official wage rates for workers. The policy attempt turned out to be futile, as many future politicians (including the U.S. Presidents Truman and Nixon) would come to discover. Diocletian greatly expanded the bureaucracy by hiring workers to record and document every plot of land, all buildings, the number of fireplaces, even farm animals, to increase tax collections. Documents show price ceilings for well over a thousand products, freight charges for sea travel, and wage controls for workers and craftsmen. The intricate details of his wage and price controls impacted everyone within his realm.[23, 24] A simple economic alternative would have been to tighten monetary policy, reduce the supply of currency, and increase interest rates in order to bring the economy back into balance.

The Edict doubled the value of copper coins and imposed death penalties for profiteers and speculators who were blamed for the rampant inflation. According to the Edict, all coins were valued against the denarius, which Diocletian hoped to fully replace with a new system of silver coins: the *argenteus* and its fractions. Historians suggest that he may well have succeeded by proclaiming and strictly enforcing the value of the coins even with their low metallic value. However, he made a grave mistake by minting too many coins, thereby stoking hyperinflation and further ravaging the economy.[24, 25]

Figure 5-7 *The argenteus, meaning "of silver" in Latin, was minted during Diocletian's coinage reform of AD 294 to AD 310 and was similar in weight and purity to the denarius of Nero's time. The obverse is the likeness of Diocletian, and the reverse depicts the four Tetrarchs before the city-gate with six turrets. Classical Numismatic Group, Inc. www.cngcoins.com*

Commerce immediately came to a complete halt as those on fixed salaries (especially soldiers) found that their money was increasingly worthless. The artificially set prices did not reflect true costs. Barter and trade became the only way to exchange goods with disastrous results for the economy. Many people fled the cities and took up farming or escaped into the mountains. Diocletian himself retired on May 1, 305 A.D., one of the few emperors to leave office alive, and returned to cabbage farming in Split, Croatia. (His residence still exists and represents the world's most complete remains of a Roman palace). His plans for an orderly succession for the emperors never fully materialized. However, he is well-remembered for dividing the Roman Empire into two halves: a Western and an Eastern Empire. The momentous outcome of his decision would signal the beginning of the Middle Ages and new chapters for the Roman Empire.

The Nugget

Julius Caesar transformed the Roman Republic, one based on "common law" into the autocratic rule of the Roman Empire. The gradual transformation led to corruption, inflation, and the debasement of their currency, as well as, their culture. It was the distrust of their currency, used for everyday trade and commerce, which triggered mistrust among the Romans themselves. Trust help build the Roman Republic, and skepticism gave way to the decline of the Western Roman Empire.

CHAPTER SIX

THE MIDDLE AGES: THE ASCENDANCE & FUSION OF CHURCH AND STATE

Keywords: Constantine's Labarum; Christogram; Chi-Rho; "Manus Dei"; solidus coin

> "Cultures, along with the religions that shape and nurture them, are value systems, sets of traditions and habits clustered around one or several languages, producing meaning: for the self, for the here and now, for the community, for life."
>
> Tariq Ramadan: Swiss academic, philosopher, and writer.

The dawn of the Middle Ages began with Emperor Diocletian's attempt to stabilize the vast Roman Empire and create a planned succession to the throne by splitting the empire into two halves: Western and Eastern. He knew what many others were afraid to say—that the empire was just too big to be managed by one person. To achieve his goal, the emperor drew a simple straight line down the middle of the map of the far-flung Roman Empire. Diocletian retained the more prosperous Greek eastern half for himself while Maximian, his fellow officer, and drinking buddy, was crowned co-emperor of the western Latin provinces. In 293 A.D. he reorganized the empire into a "*tetrarchy*" or *rule of four* as each emperor appointed two junior co-emperors or generals with the title of Caesar. Had the junior Caesars remained focused on expanding and governing the empire, the newly formed tetrarchy might have worked well, but the Caesars began to compete for the sole title of emperor, and soon there were six Caesars engaged in fighting for the title of emperor.

Diocletian should have known better than to pick two men with royal family ties and grown sons. When Diocletian abdicated, Constantius took his place as the senior emperor in the East. Maxentius and Constantine, sons of Maximian (Western Empire) and Constantius (Eastern Empire), each considered the throne his birthright and sought full access to imperial power and the dissolution of the new tetrarchy. They were also brothers-in-law through Constantine's marriage to Maxentius's sister. Once the sons of living gods, both felt bitterly betrayed as they were now nothing more than private citizens of Rome. They were both determined not to let events pass them by. [(1)]

Constantine joined his father's campaign in Britain. He became popular and well-liked by the ranks of his army, largely by ignoring the accepted and commonplace practice of Christian persecutions and oppression. His army was comprised mostly of pagan sun-worshippers. There was little animosity toward the Christians, however, as they equally shared in the misfortune of Diocletian's destructive currency reforms, price controls, and a sizeable debasement of the currency and their salaries. Upon his father's death, Constantine assumed the title of Caesar along with the loyal support of his army. He assembled forty thousand men, crossed the Alps, and descended upon Italy, carrying forward the military standards of his pagan god *Sol Invictus* (invincible sun) before him. He and his army would decide who would become the sole emperor.

The two armies of Constantine and Maxentius faced off near Rome's historic Melvian Bridge over the Tiber River in the fall of A.D. 312. Behind the Roman walls, Maxentius consulted soothsayers and priests representing every god in the pantheon. He stared at the entrails of animals and the flight of birds in hopes of receiving the blessings of divine favor. Outside the walls was the dusty camp of Constantine and his army. He too was looking for favorable omens and blessings from his soothsayers and priests. Both armies prepared for battle.[1]

The Vision of Constantine

Constantine knelt down and said a prayer that would change the course of world history, mark both the beginning and end of the Middle Ages, and generate global repercussions that continue to this day. The battle sowed the seed of Constantine's conversion to Christianity. He retold the story himself some years later. [2] When he looked up to the sky and begged the true God to reveal himself, he and his soldiers were amazed and astonished by a vision that seemed to come from the Christian God, as a great cross of light appeared, bearing the inscription IN HOC SIGNO VINCES ERIS– *"In this sign, you shall be victor."* That night Constantine would interpret his dream as a promising victory if the sign of Chi-Rho, a combination of the first two Greek letters of Christ's name: chi (X) and rho (P), were painted on the soldiers' shields. He led his army with a labarum or military standard consisting of a flag suspended from a crossbar affixed with Chi-Rho, symbolizing the crucifixion of Christ. [2] His soldiers were not only inspired in fighting for him—but for Christ and their religion. The victory gave Constantine undisputed control of the western half of the Roman Empire. He later became the first Christian Roman Emperor to declare Christianity the official religion of the empire, but would remain tolerant of the popular pagan gods.

Figure 6-1 *A coin is depicting Emperor Constantine and the first use of a Christian symbol on Roman currency. The reverse of the coin shows a Christogram (Christian monogram) in the form of a combination of the Greek initials for Jesus Christ. Attribution: FORVM Ancient Coins: www.forumancientcoins.com.* Figure 6-2 Center *The Alpha (**A** or **α**) and Omega (**Ω** or **ω**) are the first and last letters of the Greek alphabet and a Christian reference to Christ Jesus in Revelation 22.13: "I am the Alpha and the Omega, the first and the last, the beginning and the end."* Figure 6-3 Right *The Chi-Rho as displayed above the flag on the military standard of Constantine's Labarum. (CC By-SA-3.0)*

Emperor Constantine now set his sights on the Eastern Empire ruled by his once friend, and fellow Caesar of the tetrarchy, Emperor Licinius. Constantine's son, Caesar Crispus, had earlier defeated Licinius's navy at the Battle of Hellespont while commanding a distinctly smaller fleet. Licinius, fearing Constantine, moved his soldiers out of the small port town of Byzantium to the safer harbor of Chrysopolis on the opposite shore of the Bosphorus Strait. This crucial waterway eventually connects the Black Sea with the Mediterranean Sea, and strategically forms part of the lucrative trade boundary between Europe and Asia.

In A.D. 324 the Battle of Chrysopolis took on a decidedly religious tone, as Licinius had developed a superstitious dread of Constantine's Labarum and forbade his soldiers from attacking or even looking directly at it.[3] He drew up his battle lines with prominently displayed images of the Roman pagan gods. As reported by the historian Zosimus, "*There was a great slaughter at Chrysopolis.*" [4] Constantine won a decisive victory over Licinius, who reportedly lost 25,000 to 30,000 dead, with many others breaking ranks and fleeing. Licinius later threw himself on the mercy of his enemy but to no avail.

Byzantium was chosen by Constantine as the new center for the expansion of the Roman Empire, which he renamed after himself —Constantinople (present-day Istanbul). The Byzantine Empire is a historiographic term, fabricated long after it ceased to exist, making our understanding of the division of the empire an entirely modern convention. The people of the Byzantine Empire considered themselves inhabitants and citizens of the Roman Empire. The Roman Empire would continue for a thousand more years under its new moniker: The Byzantine Empire. [5]

During most of the Middle Ages, its power and status would ebb and flow, but it was widely recognized as the most culturally refined, economically stable, and longest-enduring empire in all European history. Constantinople became the new center of the Roman Empire with the opulence and extravagance surpassing that of Rome. Constantine spared no expense, with new public buildings, temples, and sculptures enhancing his *Nova Roma*. It was dedicated with his name in May of A.D. 330. The city's grand Hippodrome would lavishly host chariot races as the civil form of entertainment. Although the races were still brutal and ruthless, they were less so than the merciless gladiators and animal butchery that commonly took place in the western Latin coliseums.

Byzantium's strategic position overlooking the Bosphorus Strait nourished its economy with trade by both land and sea. It was the center of trade for commodities, and the state held a monopoly over the much sought-after silk. Subsequently, having learned to raise silkworms that were originally smuggled out of China, by A.D. 500 Constantinople had become the first significant silk-weaving center in Europe.

The Byzantine economy was fixed to a gold standard and largely self-sufficient, which allowed it to thrive in both good times and bad. The state provided security and maintained control with a 10 percent tax on all trade and monopolistic control over the issuance of coinage. Tax revenue was used to support the military and thus distributed back into the economy, as well as, being reinvested in building projects throughout the city.[6]

Historians recognize the citizens of the Byzantine Empire in the Middle Ages as the best educated and most prosperous throughout Europe, while the Western portion suffered from the onslaught of barbarian raids and cultural decay. The difference lay in the East's decidedly Greek, rather than Roman, cultural influence and its foundation in Orthodox Christianity. [6] Said to be ruled by God, the Byzantine Empire was a theocracy working through its Emperor. As one historian argues: "*The Byzantine Empire became a theocracy in the sense that Christian values and ideals were the foundation of the empire's political ideals and heavily entwined with its political goals."* [7]

Figure 6-4 Left *A gold solidus coin of Constantine (A.D. circa 307-337) with a depiction of several of his labarum spearing a serpent. The obverse is CONSTANTI-NVS MAX AVG. The reverse is SPES PVBLICA across field, labarum, and medallions on drapery and crowned by two Christograms spearing a serpent. This famous reverse represents the defeat of tyranny with the death of Licinius (depicted as the serpent). Christian imagery portrays the power of Christianity over evil. FORVM Ancient Coins: www.forumancientcoins.com.* Figure 6-5 Right *A 40 nummi bronze coin 8.4 grams 25 mm. circa 491-518 Emperor Anastasius 1. (CC By-SA-3.0)*

Constantine the Great's thirty-year rule not only ushered in the Christian transformation, but also heralded the popularity of the gold *solidus,* which replaced the substantially devalued and scorned silver *denarius* as the official currency of the new Empire. The solidus was a coin of nearly pure gold and remained in continuous circulation from A.D. 300 to 1000. It was likely mined, under the emperor's control, in the Carpathian Mountains that cover Central and Eastern Europe. The solidus was the primary coin and a solid benchmark for the valuation of all things. Decreed by Constantine, the new gold coinage was instrumental in reviving and stabilizing the economy, replacing Diocletian's dreadful currency reforms, and resolving the arbitrary debasement and devaluation of silver coins. Coins were increasingly minted with Christian symbols as Christianity gradually replaced Roman gods as the official state religion. Constantine was the last emperor to bear the pagan title of "*divus*" or the *deified one*, on any coinage.

Solidus is Latin for "*solid.*" However, the Greeks would commonly call it a "nomisma" meaning *coin*. The solidus weighed 4.5 grams of nearly 24-karat gold and functioned as a unit of weight equal to 1/72 of a Roman pound based on twelve troy ounces. It remained stable for over seven centuries. It was highly prized as the main unit of currency, until it eventually deteriorated primarily due to wear and abrasion on the soft gold metal. It was replaced by the hyperpyron (20.5 karats instead of 24) in A.D. 1100. The addition of other metals strengthened the gold coin.[8]

Byzantine currency consisted of two types of coins: the gold solidus, and a variety bronze coins each with a specific value: 40, 20, 10 or 5 nummi—with 576 bronze coins to a Roman pound. These bronze coins were issued with an officially fixed value to the gold solidus, while silver coins were rarely minted nor widely circulated. Western Europe eventually replaced its silver denarius with the *nomisma* but called it the *bezant* named after the Byzantine Empire. The gold solidus remained a standard of international commerce until the early 11th century when it became debased by successive emperors reacting to extreme environmental and cultural circumstances. The solidus was replaced by the Venetian coin the *ducat.*

The "*Manus Dei*" or the Hand of God

The depiction of *Jehovah* or *God the Father* as a full human figure was deemed unacceptable in both Jewish and early Christian art. The Manus Dei motif was used to indicate God's intervention in human affairs on Earth. Paintings and iconography abound, along with numerous metaphorical references to the *right hand of God*, as stated in the New Testament, literature, and early Hebrew Bible. "*Manus Dei*" or the *Hand of God* was the first depiction on a coin of any Judeo-Christian deity!

Divus Constantine I the Great (in a series of coins struck in 337-340 A.D. after his death) is depicted on a quadriga (chariot) with the *Hand of God* reaching down to bring him into heaven. The scene is reminiscent of paintings of the Old Testament prophet Elijah's ascent to heaven on a chariot of horses and fire. This coin exemplifies the ambiguity surrounding the emperor's relationship with early Christianity. Though he was baptized a Christian on his deathbed, he is here named as "*Divine"* on his posthumous coinage—a very pagan concept. [9, 10]

Figure 6-6 *A gold solidus. Obverse: The Consecration of Constantine I, (A.D. 307-337), Nicomedia mint (Izmit, Turkey) A.D. 337-347, veiled head of Constantine, DV (Divus) CONSTANTINVS PT AVGG. Reverse: Constantine veiled and wrapped in a*

robe riding on a quadriga of four horses galloping right, the "Manus Dei" (The Hand of God) extending down from heaven to grasp his extended right hand. Attribution: FORVM Ancient Coins: www.forumancient coins.com

Flavia Julia Helena Augusta a.k.a. Saint Helena

She ranks as an important and influential figure in the history of Christianity. After Constantine's defeat of Licinius, the new Emperor named his mother, Helena Augusta, Imperatrix or Empress, not as a mere symbol—but a way to convey shared power with her. What a son! She soon converted to Christianity and given unlimited access to the imperial treasury to locate the relics of Judeo-Christian tradition. Helena was charged by her son to journey with a royal entourage to the Holy Land in Palestine from A.D. 326 to 328. Her discoveries were indeed miraculous! The newly discovered relics were used with great fanfare to promote the new Christian ideals.

On her well-orchestrated pilgrimage, Empress Helena was informed of the site where Jesus of Nazareth was crucified. In the A.D. 130s, Emperor Hadrian had built a temple to Jupiter over the site of the Temple Mount—the former Jewish Temple of Solomon. Exercising her newly found Christian authority, she ordered the pagan temple torn down. Upon excavation of the site, three crosses were found that were believed to have been used for the crucifixion of Jesus, along with the two thieves, St. Dismas and the unrepentant Gestas.

According to legend, the empress refused to acknowledge the crosses as holy relics unless provided with solid proof. The local bishop arranged to have a deathly ill woman brought to the site and told to touch each of the crosses. Upon touching the last of the three crosses, she suddenly recovered and was thereby thought to have identified the True Cross of Jesus of Nazareth. Constantine then ordered the Church of the Holy Sepulcher to immediately be built over the site. Helena is also said to have discovered the nails of the crucifixion, Christ's tunic, and pieces of the rope with which Jesus was tied to the cross, among many other sacred relics. She also founded and built numerous Christian churches that still exist today, and she is associated with the founding of the historic and expansive Vatican Gardens. [11, 12]

She was proclaimed *Augusta* and many mints started striking coins in her honor, all of which shared similar characteristics. The most common coin of this period showed on the obverse Helena's portrait and read "*Helena Avgvsta*." On its reverse was a personification of *Securitas* (the Roman goddess of security and stability) holding a branch with her left hand

and raising her *pallium* (food bowl) with her right hand with the legend "*Secvritas Repvblicae.*" Its exergue, or inscription, was its mint-mark. For example, a coin minted in Thessalonica noted SMTSA in its exergue. This means: SM Sacra Moneta (sacred money), TS Thessalonica (Mint location), A First officina (Official Roman Imperial Coin).

Figure 6-7 *Helena's Coin, Mother of Constantine, 325 - 328 AD AE Follis, Antioch Mint, 20mm, 2.88 grams Obverse: FL HELENA AVGVSTA, Diademed and mantled bust of Helena right. Reverse: SECVRITAS REIPVBLICAE, Securitas standing left holding a branch and raising her robe with the right hand. FORVM Ancient Coins: www.forumancientcoins.com*

Synopsis

Constantine reigned from A.D. 306 to 337. He founded and built a secure and prosperous empire out of a land hopelessly divided and religiously fractured. A major contribution to the stability of the period was the pure gold solidus, which provided a stable currency for more than seven centuries and served as the basis for international trade and commerce throughout Europe and Asia. He also established the feudal foundations of the early Middle Ages by proclaiming peasant jobs hereditary. This act further stabilized the movement of people by structuring society around collaborative relationships between those holding land and those who labored on it. Feudalism flourished in the collective east, but lacked wide acceptance, and even opposed, by the egocentricity taking place in the western segment of the empire.

Constantine the Great built an empire that served as the foundation for European culture and Christianity for over one thousand years. His empire endeavored to protect the underdeveloped and religiously diverse Western Europe from countless and ruthless Barbarian, Persian, and Asiatic invasions. Despite having murdered his wife and eldest son to retain his throne and authority, he is venerated by the Church as a saint. He became both the last deified pagan god and the first Christian Emperor. He rejected the Roman tradition of cremation and had himself buried in an opulent sarcophagus in the Church of the Holy Apostles that he had built in Constantinople. Around his central coffin were twelve empty caskets—one for each of Christ's disciples. [13, 14]

Upon his death, his four sons battled for the title of emperor and his youngest son Julian, who was well educated in Greek and steeped in pagan literature and philosophy, won out. Emperor Julian would do his best to restore paganism and resurrected the practice of persecuting Christians. Paganism was culturally ingrained and too entwined with classical and intellectual thought to be easily cast off. However, Christianity was the wave of the future. [15] Julian was defeated in a battle with the Persians, while the western branch of the empire was being invaded by the Visigoths (Germany) and the Ostrogoths (Scandinavia). The Byzantine Empire remained in a near constant state of war in an unstable environment typical of that time.

Constantine is recognized as "*the Great*" for his founding of the Byzantine Empire and his extraordinary accomplishments. Fortune would soon bestow upon the empire a succession of other *great* emperors who would reign over long-periods of time. The Eastern Emperors, though often ruthless and brutal, were well educated and versed in both Latin and Greek. Some would be acknowledged as philosophers, and others even authored books. The names of many historical figures are appended by the phrase *the Great*—a colloquial version for *Great King*. The application of this designation varies as there are no set objective criteria for "greatness."

The epithet is believed to have been first used by Cyrus II of Persia and was soon applied to Alexander the Great after he defeated the Persian king. Kings from Alfred to Xerxes have been honored with this title, and they all have one thing in common. They created a stable currency and championed sound fiscal policies—which resulted in a prosperous economy for their people.

Barbarians at the Gate

Emperor Theodosius the Great (A.D. 379 to 395) was the last emperor to rule over both halves of the Roman Empire. He campaigned against the invading Goths (East Germans) and other barbarians but failed to destroy their culture. The Romans initiated contact and achieved domination over other cultures, but the barbarians eventually turned the table and dominated the Romans. The Romans referred to other cultures, which they considered ill-mannered and uncivilized, as *barbarians*, just as today many cultures have equally pejorative words for others unlike themselves. The cultural issue is primarily based on migration. Historians and scientists have agreed on an official "*Migration Period*" during which time the widespread movement of people within Europe began with the Huns in A.D. 375 and ended with the conquest of Italy by the Lombards in 568. Evidence suggests the migrations were a consequence of an extremely cold period in Europe. [16] Buying time, Theodosius allowed the Goths to serve in the Roman legions, but their switching loyalties became a destabilizing factor in the control of the Empire. By the 4th century, the Roman armies experienced an almost complete Germanization of their ranks. [17]

To assimilate the large influx of new immigrants into the empire, Theodosius decreed Orthodox Christianity as the official church of the Roman Empire. He dissolved the order of the Vestal Virgins in Rome and banned many pagan rituals. However, he allowed the continued existence of the Hellenistic temples in consideration of their political influence. [18] Common pagan practices were soon replaced by the new ways of Christian thinking. [19]

The Decay and Decline of the West

While the East rallied behind Christian Orthodoxy and fended off barbarian incursions, Western Europe's allegiance and fealty to the Roman Emperors and their generals declined. The West suffered under continued attacks, invasions, and the sacking of Rome itself. Rome's 50,000 miles of straight stone-paved highways were designed as exits for the military, but were now used by the migrant barbarians as entrances into Rome. Rome was sacked by the Visigoths in A.D. 410, while Attila the Hun latter devastated Italy and the West in A.D. 455. When Attila was unable to take Constantinople, he refocused his assault on Rome by destroying the aqueducts leading into the city. Pope Saint Leo 1, also known as *Saint Leo the Great*, dressed in a plain robe, met Attila the Hun outside the Roman gates and persuaded Attila that invading the city would be sacrilegious and would lead to his demise. Attila left, probably seeing no reason to sack Rome—as there was little left to sack.

Saint Leo declared his primacy as the *Bishop of Rome* based on succession from Saint Peter and Saint Paul. He exercised his authority in the city and well beyond. He claimed title to the universal Roman Catholic Church despite the popularity of the Eastern Greek Orthodox church. His title of *the Great* rests on religious laurels, rather than economic prosperity, as the city of Rome and the rest of Western Europe entered the Dark Ages. The city of Rome, once populated by over 1.5 million people, rapidly declined to just 12,000 and remained nearly abandoned for over a thousand years. [20]

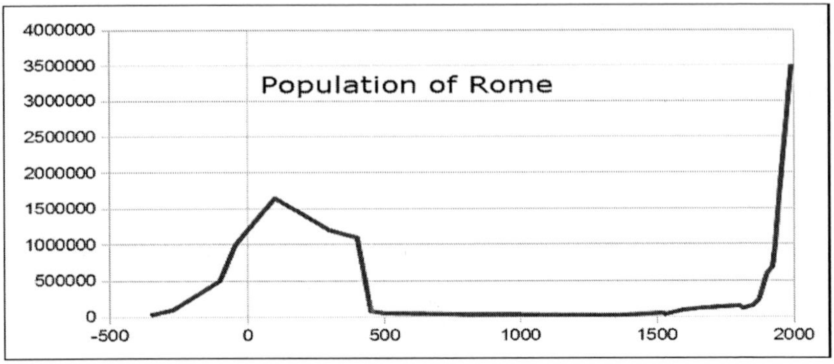

Figure 6-8 *Population of Rome. (GNU Free Documentation License).*

The dying embers of the Western Empire were finally snuffed out by a barbarian general named Odoacer. Half Italian and half German, he had a loyal following among those who were tired of puppet emperors and the ruling elite. He claimed his right to rule as King of Italy. Having conquered the city of Ravenna in Northern Italy, he found the teenager and Western Emperor Romulus Augustus kowtowing, and saved his life by sending him into exile. His given nickname *"Augustulus"* means *little Augustus*. Romulus obediently laid down his crown, left to live with his relatives in Campania, and vanished into history. His abdication on September 4, 476 marks the official end of the Western Roman Empire as established by the British historian, Edward Gibbons.[20] Ironically, the last emperor of Rome had the same first name of the founder of the city of Rome (Romulus), and the same last name as the founder and first emperor of the Roman Empire (Augustus).

Figure 6-9 Left. *An extremely rare small gold coin of the last Western Emperor: Romulus Augustus 475-476, AV 1.52g. The tremisses meaning 'a third of a unit' indicated its value relative to the solidus* [24] *Classical Numismatic Group, Inc. www.cngcoins.com.* Figure 6-10 Right *Odoacer, King of Italy 476-493 AE a rare bronze nummus, mint Ravenna. Obverse: ODO VAC, draped bust. Attribution: British Museum Public domain, via Wikimedia Commons*

Justinian the Great—the "Last Roman"

Peter Sabbatius is one of the most famous of the Byzantine emperors who became known as Saint Justinian the Great. Born of Slavic descent, he was the brilliant nephew of the Byzantine Emperor Justin. Peter adopted his uncle's name in gratitude for providing him with the finest Greek and Latin education. During his reign as Emperor from A.D. 527 to 565, he successfully sought to revive the Empire's greatness and reconquer the lost western half of the historical Roman Empire.

The barbarian kingdoms would nominally recognize the eastern emperors, largely to avoid antagonizing them, while the emperors were too often distracted to respond. That was until Justinian sent his general Belisarius, whose armies were now equipped with lances and heavy cavalry, to subdue the barbarians to the west and suppress the rising Persian Sassanian Empire to the east. Justinian was not frugal and spent lavishly on games to honor his reign. His monumental building programs included ninety new Christian churches and the city's crown jewel—the "*Basilica of the Hagia Sophia*" or the *Church of Holy Wisdom*. [21, 22]

Justinian I, as Emperor of the early Christian Church, organized its governance around five major episcopal sees, named the "*Pentarchy*," of the Roman Empire. The patriarchs (or popes) were given autocratic authority to govern religious matters around the five major cities of the Empire: Rome, Constantinople, Alexandria, Antioch, and Jerusalem. However, the churches that now form the Eastern Orthodox Church had already seceded from the Imperial state church, while in the west Christianity was mostly subject to the laws and customs of nations that owed no allegiance to the Emperor in Constantinople. [23] While the eastern-born patriarchs, who were appointed or confirmed by the Eastern Emperor continued to be loyal to him as their political lord, they refused to accept his authority on religious matters. In A.D. 754, Pope Gregory III became the last Bishop of Rome to ask the Byzantine ruler to ratify his election. [24] A succession of differences and disputes regarding the religious authority between Rome and Constantinople later led to the great East-West Schism of 1054.

Invariably the money for massive building projects and entertainment festivities came from taxes. Justinian appointed a ruthless character named John the Cappadocian who was rumored to be able to squeeze taxes out of stone. He streamlined the tax system, closed loopholes, added new taxes on the rich, and was tenacious in attacking corruption. Justinian's favorite target was the patrician upper class, which had long avoided paying any taxes.

Figure 6-11 *Coin of Justinian the Great A.D. 527-565. Obverse: Justinian was the first of the Roman Emperors depicted wielding the "Globus cruciger" or a cross over an orb (globe) signifying Christ's dominion over the world and a shield with a cross to the right. The Christian symbol remained popular throughout the Middle Ages. Reverse: the small bronze coin is a half-follis or nummus whose value was based on the Greek numbering system (M=40, K=20, I=10, E= 5). 8-10 mm, 0.56 grams. Classical Numismatic Group, Inc. www.cngcoins.com.* Figure. 6-12 *Christian symbol or Christogram of the "Globus cruciger." (GNU Free Documentation License).*

Justinian was also fortunate to meet a gifted lawyer named Tribonian who was a walking encyclopedia of Roman law and taught at the law school in Constantinople. Justinian appointed him commissioner charged with preparing a new imperial legal code, the Codex Justinianus. The *Codex* was organized into book form which compiled the many years of Roman jurisprudence. The Codex eliminated the confusing mess of the conflicts and discrepancies of nearly a thousand years. One member of his jury commission for taxation was John Cappadocian, the much-hated taxman of Constantinople. The *Codex* harmonized much of Roman law and today serves as the basis for most European legal systems. The legal code came to be used throughout the Mediterranean world and was taught in law schools from Alexandria to Rome. The foundation of Roman law for many nations today are based on the Codex. It also serves as a basis for law in the U.S.'s state of Louisiana. Future instructors adopted the syllabus of Professor Tribonian who taught at the University of Constantinople. [25]

The patricians' contempt for Justinian came to a boil in A.D. 532 with the most violent riots in the thousand-year history of Constantinople. The "*Nika*" (meaning *Jesus Christ conquers*!) revolt lasted for more than a week and left tens of thousands of people killed and half the city destroyed. As was customary, the emperor had sponsored chariot races in the expansive Hippodrome next to his Palace. The chariot races allowed the crowd to express its opinion on whether to commute sentences for those who had been convicted. The partisan crowds of the more popular Blues faced off against the Greens by chanting "*Nika!*" for their favorite contestants to be pardoned, much like team competitions that take place today in our sports arenas. Justinian always favored the Blues but often conceded to the Greens based on the outcome of the race. On January 13th the crowds started to hurl insults at Justinian, likely based on the building resentment of the senators and patricians who hoped to overthrow his reign. Justinian sent out his trusted servant Narses with a bag of gold to gain the support of the Blues and ordered them to quickly storm out of the Hippodrome. As the Greens sat stunned, the imperial troops, led by the great general Belisarius, closed the doors of the Hippodrome and slaughtered thirty thousand angry rioters. [26] Soon after, nineteen senators were executed for treason and their palaces were torn down.

Justinian's victory over the nobility, though ruthless, added immeasurably to the prosperity and strength of the Byzantine Empire that would last for centuries. [27] It marked yet another break with the West, as the encroaching aristocracy and landowning nobility continued to erode the authority and power of numerous kings and vandals alike. The West would continue to be plagued by warring factions, petty squabbles, and leave the poor to be crushed by the grip of feudal lords.

The year A.D. 541 was the high point for both the Byzantine Empire and the Middle Ages. General Belisarius conquered the many barbarians, vandals, and Persians along with confiscating their immense wealth and regaining imperial control for Emperor Justinian and the Byzantine Empire. Constantinople became a gleaming architectural marvel with impressive buildings throughout the city along with the rebuilt crown jewel Basilica of Hagia Sophia as its centerpiece. The empire remained stable with a dependable currency based on the gold solidus. However, good fortune and prosperity would soon be ended by a new invading army–rodents.

The Nugget

Charles Dickens's famous opening sentence, *"It was the best of times; it was the worst of times..."* appropriately pertains to the Roman Empire as "A Tale of Two Empires." The Western Empire was largely autocratic, corrupt—and godless. Its currency, the silver denarius, over time became debased and worthless. Its emperors were mostly treacherous and, in the end, left the city of Rome sacked and deserted. However, the Eastern Roman Empire was sophisticated, enlightened, and well educated. Its currency, the gold solidus, remained stable, relevant, and led to long-term economic prosperity. Though brutal but tenacious, they built their cultural foundations and institutions with a standardized Codex of common laws, fair taxation across society, and above all— religious devotion and cohesive values.

CHAPTER SEVEN

THE MIDDLE AGES: THE BEGINNING OF THE END

Keywords: Yersinia pestis; iconoclasm; Islam; Great Schism; Crusades

> "We are certainly influenced by role models, and if we are surrounded by images of beautiful rich people, we will start to think that to be beautiful and rich is very important—just as in the Middle Ages people were surrounded by images of religious piety."
>
> Alain de Botton, British author, and philosopher

Historians would name it the *"Plague of Justinian"* as the first in a chain of virulent pandemics to afflict Constantinople, the Persian Sassanid Empire, and most of the port cities around the Mediterranean Sea, initially killing an estimated one in five inhabitants. Some cities would see two of three dead. The plague closed the overland trade routes, increasing the traffic to port cities which delivered the brunt of the plague. Y*ersinia pestis* is the bacterium responsible for the bubonic plague carried by rodents who were said to have favored ships with cargoes of spices. The infected cargoes were first off-loaded and then the ships burned. Genetic studies indicate China as the primary source of worldwide contagion. The plague would randomly spread across regions and cities throughout Europe for more than 600 years, leading to the peak of the *Black Death* in A.D. 1346 to 1353. The Black Death was the most virulent, having killed an estimated 30% to 60% of Europe's entire population in the 14th century. [1]

The plague reached Constantinople in A.D. 542. Justinian himself fell ill but recovered, but an estimated 300,000 people in the city of half a million were said to have died within the first year. The disease remained virulent for slightly more than two centuries, although it never settled anywhere for long. Instead, it came and went. In addition, a series of earthquakes ravaged the city. The chronicled "A.D. 557 Constantinople earthquake" hit with unparalleled ferocity and almost completely razed the city walls, leaving it open to Hun invaders. There were other troubling signs as the sixth century waned and abated. Many city inhabitants withdrew to their farms or mountain retreats to isolate themselves from the plague. A series of natural disasters and the seizure of foodstuffs by passing soldiers made life difficult for farmers and the growing number of the poor. Powerful landed magnates, enjoying considerable tax breaks, required the Emperor to fill the tax coffers using ever more harsh tactics, which were met with diminishing returns. Persian and Byzantine Empires were both exhausted and the citizens bewildered by the series of dreadful natural events. [2]

In A.D. 622, seemingly out of nowhere, came a new threat from the hot deserts of the Arabian Peninsula. Muhammad, born Muhammad ibn Abdullah, claimed to be a descendant of Ishmael, the first son of Abraham. Abraham, transcending biblical history, is commonly recognized as the patriarch of the three Abrahamic religions: Judaism, Christianity, and Islam—all with a link to a chain of prophets. In the story of Abraham, his second son Isaac (by his second marriage) receives *all of Abraham's goods*, leaving Ishmael and the other family members only token gifts. Scholars have traced the Hebrew biblical narrative to the right of land ownership transferred through the father as head of the family. [3] The feud between religions began over the transfer and ownership of property rights.

The prophet Muhammad revived Ishmael's lineage and rightful place in history. He centered it upon a new religion and renewed religious zeal: Islam. Muhammad united the many tribes of the interior, and his followers' duty was holy jihad—to expand the House of Islam at the point of a sword. The crippled Persian Sassanian Empire quickly fell as they could put up little resistance. Muhammad died of a fever in A.D. 632, but his armies would continue to conquer much of the Mediterranean world making a change of polity from Constantinople to Damascus and Bagdad. By A.D. 656, the Arab assault was only curbed by a civil war among three caliphates.

Though the Islamic empire would expand at an unprecedented rate, not all were committed to Islam but joined to share in the spoils of the change in social order. The plague also facilitated the conquest of stricken cities by the Arabs, who often isolated themselves and waited for the plague to devastate a city before advancing on it, although they would occasionally be stricken too. [4]

Over the years, as if to ward off the many assaults on Constantinople, Emperor Justinian II the Slit-Nosed looked to his coinage to add hope to the empire's turmoil. As the eldest son of Emperor Constantine IV, he inherited the throne from his father in A.D. 685 at the age of sixteen. He made numismatic history when he became the first emperor to place an image of

Christ on a coin. This gold solidus was struck circa A.D. 692-695 and bears a bust of Christ with a full-length figure of Emperor Justinian II the Slit-Nosed on the reverse. Noteworthy of this emperor is that he placed himself on the reverse of the coin, designating himself as subservient to Christ, who occupies the obverse of the coin in the position of honor. [5]

Figure 7-1 Left *A gold solidus coin of the Byzantine Empire struck A.D.705-711. The obverse is the bust of Christ. The reverse is a full-length figure of Emperor Justinian II the Slit-Nosed.* Figure 7-2 Right *Empress Irene of Athens featured on* both sides *of the gold solidus coin holding the Christian symbol of the "Globus cruciger." A.D.797-802 AV (4.36 gm). Constantinople mint. (CC By-SA-3.0) Attribution: Classical Numismatic Group, Inc. http://www.cngcoins.com*

The Byzantines decorated their coinage with the image of Christ both in defiance of the Arabs and to gain God's favor. Almost as quickly as this coin was launched, an inordinate change to Byzantine coinage and culture was introduced with the 8th Century advent of iconoclasm or *image breaking*. Many calamities and military defeats continued to affect the empire, shaking the very foundations of their beliefs. Why had Christ forsaken them? It was plain enough to Emperor Leo III. The culprit was the highly regarded sacred icons designed as worship aids to the faithful. It was one thing to venerate icons to inspire personal faith, yet another thing to cross the line to worship and deify them. The empire was being punished for the sin of idolatry, much like the biblical Israelites who angered God by bowing down to the golden calf. Cultural self-doubt gripped the empire.

Emperor Leo III presented a convincing argument. The Muslims remained victorious by adhering to their strict prohibition of all images, while the Byzantines angered God by praying to paint and wood for their deliverance. Magnificent murals, sculptures, and paintings were deliberately vandalized to the astonishment of its many believers, especially those living in the West. Images of Christ disappeared from the coinage, replaced once again by imperial portraits and figures. The quality of the images on the coinage began to suffer in the crude and rudimentary portraitures of the following line of emperors, especially when compared to the solidus of Justinian II, issued just one hundred and fifty years prior. [5] In A.D. 720,

Emperor Constantine V emerged as the most ferocious of the iconoclasts, as he demanded that the entire clergy take an oath not to venerate religious icons and to destroy those that existed. Perhaps it worked, as Constantine V made a series of unexpected victories, which brought the Empire back to hope but with a much-divided Church.

Upon Constantine V's sudden and unexplained death, his wife Irene demanded that she be the rightful heir to the throne. Irene was devastatingly beautiful, as she had been chosen from an empire-wide beauty pageant to be his wife, as was the custom among many of the Byzantine emperors. She became regent to her son Constantine VI, who was not yet sixteen years old, and lawfully took title to the throne. She dedicated herself to the restoration of icons and summarily executed those who opposed her.

In A.D. 787 Irene convened in Nicaea an Ecumenical Council of the entire church to decide the fate of iconoclasm. When it was condemned by the church elders, not a single voice was raised to defend it. She was expected to celebrate her success by returning to the practice of placing Christ's image on the coinage, but her ambitions far exceeded her piety.[6] Irene mostly put an end to iconoclasm in western culture, but the Islamic religion would fervently adhere to the ban on ideology under Sharia Law. Today, most Islamic societies adhere to a strict policy against visual religious portrayals, statues, or monuments—except for those of their Grand Ayatollah and key clerics.

Western Europe viewed the iconoclastic movement as a 200-year spiritual debacle that contributed to the growing divergence between the Western and Eastern cultural traditions. The opponents of iconoclasm were known as *iconodules* who reasoned that images were inspirational and provided a historical reference to real people and their accomplishments, including that of Christ. They further argued that iconoclasm should not be imposed on the Church by any Emperor.[7] Martin Luther initiated the Protestant Reformation by challenging the Roman church with many of the same arguments. Today statues and monuments of historical figures are found in many western cities from London to Paris, while none are found in strict Islamic dominated societies.

The gold dinar is an Islamic gold coin first issued by Caliph Abd al-Malik ibn Marwan. He was the first to mint gold coins for the Muslim world, and he eliminated images from the coins, replacing them entirely with Arabic words and phrases. Newly discovered gold mines in Arabia coincided with the rise of the Islamic state.[32] The new gold dinar so affronted the Byzantines that they went to war just to protect their Christian coinage. Justinian II conscripted a *special army* of 30,000 Slavs to battle the Arabs. Many of the Slavs were likely paid by the Arabs to defect. In A.D. 692 the Byzantines, struck by a new outbreak of the plague and the desertion of the Slavs, were defeated in battle and forced to pay tribute, yearly taxes, and accept the Arabic currency along with that of their own. [8, 9]

Figure 7-3 Left *Gold Dinar of Umayyad Caliph Abd al-Malik ibn Marwan minted at Damascus, Syria in AH 75 (A.D. 697/698) weighing ~ 4.25 grams (nearly equal to the solidus at 4.5 grams).* Figure 7-4 Right *Fatimid dinar (gold, 4.14 g), minted in al-Mansuriyah in 344 AH (A.D. 955) during the reign of the Fatimid emir al-Moez li-dini Allah (341-365 AH / A.D. 953-975). Public domain*

The Caliph Marwan was a well-educated man who reformed practices in agriculture and commerce and made Arabic the state language. In A.D. 691, he built the Islamic Mosque and shrine *The Dome of the Rock* on the site where it is said that Muhammad ascended on a white horse into the heavens to speak to God. The Dome of the Rock was built over the Temple Mount in Jerusalem as the purported site of Abraham's attempted sacrifice of his son and the founding of Judaism. Later, Emperor Hadrian would build the Temple of Jupiter, followed by Saint Helena with the Church of the Holy Sepulcher. All built over the same grounds. The site would later change hands many times between the Christian Crusaders, Muslim Turkish Ottomans, and the British during the world wars. Today it remains a focal point of the Arab-Israel rivalry and a global hot spot of political and religious contention. The cultural and religious conflict that began in the Middle Ages remains with us to this day.

Irene of Athens Loves Charlemagne?

The Byzantine Empress Irene was a complete autocratic ruler who would not relinquish her position to her son when he became of legal age. Endless purges of her officers and continued defeats by the Arabs, Franks, and Bulgars left the Empire demoralized and nearly bankrupt from the payment tribute. Soon angry mobs called on Irene to step down and be placed under house arrest. Her son Constantine VI, now age twenty-six, proved himself to be totally incompetent and even brutalized his troops by cutting out their tongues for minor offenses. A series of military disasters and overall public dislike convinced him to step down and return his mother to power.

Irene now claimed the title *not* of a regent, *nor* as empress, but as an Emperor of the Roman Empire—the first woman ever to do so. To win the favor of the populace, the *mother* of Constantine VI now did the unthinkable. She had her much-hated son brought to the palace where she viciously gouged out his eyes, leading to his death several days later. The Byzantines were appalled and disconcerted. The next year the Byzantines were at war with the Franks; the Byzantines largely prevailed. However, as if struck by guilt, Irene took to riding around the city on a golden chariot driven by white horses as she tossed gold coins to the crowds. Under tremendous pressure to restore her reputation, and distract her critics, she turned to Charlemagne with a marriage proposal. [10]

Charlemagne, or Charles the Great, was crowned *Emperor of the Romans* by his long-time friend Pope Leo III in Rome's St. Peter's Basilica on Christmas Day A.D. 800. He is widely known as the *Father of Europe*. He united most of Western Europe's autonomous kingdoms nearly four centuries after the fall of the Western Roman Empire. The Carolingian dynasty (German for *descendants of Charles*) began with the Germanic kingdom of the Franks and later evolved into the autonomous Kingdoms of France, Bohemia, Italy, and numerous other territories. The movement gave way to the conception of the nation-states.

Pope Leo III aligned himself with Emperor Irene in her quest to restore the veneration of religious images, but he could not support a woman as a ruler who, by Roman law, was not allowed to head an army or occupy the throne. Irene had declared herself an emperor for just such an occasion but to no avail. The Pope declared the Byzantine throne vacant. He then held a coronation in Rome for Charlemagne, naming him Emperor of the Romans on Christmas Day. The Byzantines were appalled that the Roman Church was not only exerting authority over Constantinople, but it was also supporting the much-detested western barbarians. Irene ostensibly attempted to arrange a marriage between herself and Charlemagne, but the scheme soon failed when she lost power. Irene was exiled to the island of Lesbos in A.D. 802 by officials who were irate that she would even consider marriage to Charlemagne. The Byzantines did not recognize Charlemagne as Emperor until 814, and never recognized him as a Roman Emperor, a title they believed was reserved for their rulers. [11]

To further defy the Byzantines, Charlemagne decreed that the coinage of the newly founded Holy Roman Empire should return to the corrupted monetary system of the old Roman Empire. He proclaimed that it be based on the silver denarius which contained 1.7 grams of silver and weighed 1.9 grams. Western Europe returned to a bimetallic system with 12 denarii equal to one gold solidus.

Rather than weighing the gold coins in the east to verify their precise value as was the typical procedure, the number of denarii was now determined in the west by counting or "*telling.*" The denarii were cut from a one-pound weight of silver providing 240 denarii to one pound (£). Accordingly, a monetary system arose where 240 denarii (d) equaled 20 solidi (s) equaled £1. The uniformity of the coinage soon declined as the local princes exploited the fact that the weight and fineness of the coins were *told* rather than weighed.[12] The same monetary duplicity that had contributed to the decline of the old Western Roman Empire was now reestablished.

Figure 7-5. Left *A very rare and in high demand Charlemagne a.k.a. "The Father of Europe" denarius A.D. 800 or 812.The reverse marks his coronation in St. Peter's Basilica in Rome. Public Domain U.S. Library of Congress*

Under Charlemagne, the Holy Roman Empire was a highly decentralized state divided into many individual entities governed by kings, dukes, counts, bishops, and other rulers, collectively known as princes. There were also some areas ruled directly by the Emperor, but at no time could the Emperor simply issue decrees and govern autonomously over the Empire. His power was severely restricted by the various local leaders. In A.D. 962, King Otto the Great set out to Christianize and unite the German tribes into a single kingdom. He married the Byzantine Emperor's daughter and greatly expanded his recognized authority over the kingdom. Historians later termed this period the "*First Reich*." [13]

The Holy Roman Empire was neither holy, Roman, nor an empire. It saw a series of emperors and kings claiming prestige and heritage to Christ with the tacit approval of the Popes of the Roman Church. In A.D. 1805 the Holy Roman Empire abruptly ended after the most decisive engagement of the Napoleonic Wars. At the Battle of Austerlitz, Napoleon defeated the Russian, Austrian, and German Emperors, including Francis II, the Holy Roman Emperor of the German Nation. Afterward, Napoleon would crown *himself* emperor. Germany dissolved into a confederation of loosely knit German states.

The Great Religious Schism and the Financial Ruin of the Empire

Nothing seemed more galling to the Byzantine mindset than Rome's increasingly insistent papal claim as the only voice that mattered in deciding church policy. The Muslim Arabs had taken over the territories assigned to the patriarchates of Alexandria, Antioch, and Jerusalem, leaving only Constantinople and Rome to quarrel over the papal authority of the Christian church. A series of religious, political, and cultural disputes took place.

In A.D. 1014, Pope Leo IX claimed that only he held authority over the Eastern patriarchs by the full force of excommunication. Pope Leo sent his emissary, the disheveled French Benedictine abbot Humbert of Silva Candida, to make amends. However, Humbert so disliked the Hellenistic culture and its traditions that he laid a papal bull of excommunication for the patriarch of Constantinople on the altar of Hagia Sophia—during a high mass of the Devine Liturgy on July 16, 1054. He did so despite knowing the pope had died a month earlier, which would invalidate the order of excommunication. A few weeks later the patriarch returned the favor and excommunicated the West right back. [14] Christendom would never be united again, as the pope maintained that the Latin Church was the only Catholic, apostolic, and *universal* one, while the patriarch made a similar claim to be the first among equals in the one *true* Orthodox Church. Masked belligerence and distrust remain today with Russia and Eastern Europe predominantly Orthodox and the West tied to the Latin Church.

From the 10th century until the end of the 12th, the Byzantine Empire projected an image of luxury, while visitors were impressed by the wealth accumulated within the capital. However, beneath the image was the reality of an empire in decline still beset by natural disasters, the Black Death, and continued Islamic tributes.

The debasement of their coinage mirrored the empire's gradual dissolution. Emperor Basil II (976–1025) began the process by changing the shape and purity of the gold solidus by introducing a gold "*nomismata*" made wider and thinner, giving it a curious cup shape, hence the name "*nummi scyphati"* or *cup money*. The reason for striking scyphate coins remains obscure. However, in an era obsessed with and determined by the spread of Christian theocracy, the coin shape might resemble that of the Ciborium: the cup which stores the Eucharist as the symbolic body and blood of Christ. A new genre of legends and types of coins were introduced. The figures of the saints appeared on coins in the 12th century. At the same time, the intrinsic quality of the coinage had sunk to a level of frantic confusion, beginning during the time of the first Crusade (1095-1099). It is seen most plainly under Emperor Alexius 1 Comnenus (1081–1118), whose gold appearance as a coin was sometimes no more than billon or even bronze. [15]

Figure 7-6 Left *A Histamenon nomisma (cup-shaped) scyphate gold coin A.D. 1261–1282. Obverse: Bust of Archangel Michael. Reverse: Emperor Michael VIII is kneeling with arms extended to Christ who is placing his right hand on the Emperor's head in blessing. In Christ's left hand he holds the book of Gospels. 23 mm x 26 mm, 3.22 grams Mint Constantinople.*
Figure 7-7 Right *A bronze Tetarteron with the bust of Saint George holding a spear and a shield. Reverse: Bust of Emperor Manuel I Comnenus wearing a crown and loros while holding a labarum and a "Globus cruciger." Saint George was a Roman officer who died a martyr under Diocletian's order to renounce his Christian faith. He is one of the most venerated saints who is immortalized in the legend of Saint George and the Dragon popularized by the Crusaders. The dragon is thought to represent Islam. The coin is 20mm (4.06 grams) struck at the mint of Thessalonica from A.D. 1143-1180. (CC By-SA-3.0) Classical Numismatic Group, Inc. http://www.cngcoins.com*

The debasement of the Byzantine currency coincided with the continuing demise of the empire and fifty years of ineffective and short-lived rulers. The debasement was gradual at first but then accelerated rapidly. The nearly pure gold solidus was debased to 21 carats (87.5% pure) during the reign of Constantine IX (1042–1055), 18 carats (75%) under Constantine X (1059–1067), 16 carats (66.7%) under Romanus IV (1068–1071), 14 carats (58%) under Michael VII (1071–1078), 8 carats (33%) under Nicephorus III (1078–1081), and 0 to 8 carats during the first eleven years of the reign of Alexius I Comnenus (1081–1118).

Emperor Alexius I discontinued the debased solidus and introduced the "*hyperpyron*" as its replacement. The *hyperpyron* was a slightly smaller curved scyphate than the solidus at 4.45 grams of .90 to.95 purity. [16] The last hyperpyra, often named the "*bezant*" or *Byzantine money* by Italian merchants, was last struck under Emperor John VI Kantkouzenos (A.D. 1352). His name (short for karats) is memorialized, as gold remains afterward, as a money account divided into 24 keratia (karats). Karats are measured in parts per 24 so that 18 karats = $^{18}/_{24}$ or 75% and 24 karat gold is considered 100% gold. [16] After 1400, Byzantine coinage became insignificant as the Italian *ducat* became the predominant circulating coinage.

Alexius I Comnenus inherited an empire in its last gasp, but his military ability and diplomatic skills enabled him to briefly revive the economy. He drove back the Normans, headed by Robert Guiscard, who were invading western Greece (1081–82). The victory was achieved with the help of the ruthless "English-Varangian Guard" composed of Anglo-Saxons brutally driven out of England by William of Normandy in A.D. 1066. [17] Emperor Alexius I, knowing the Normans were more than a match for his imperial army, requested help from the Venetian Navy, and in return allowed them to settle a full colony in Constantinople with the freedom to trade in imperial waters essentially free of all tariffs. The Normans were routed, but the merchants of Constantinople were now at the mercy of the Venetians, soon followed by a similar deal made with Genovese businessmen. Whole sections of the city were handed over to the merchants of Venice and Genoa, bankrupting the city tax collections and closing the shops of the local citizens.

Emperor Alexius I appealed to Pope Urban II in an open letter requesting a small army to boost the security of the city. On November 18, 1095, the pope delivered one of the most fateful speeches in history, sealing the decline of the Byzantine Empire. [17]

The Crusades and the Knights Templar

Pope Urban II cited the murder of Christian pilgrims by the Islamic Arabs throughout the Holy Lands, and the sacking of patriarchal Christian cites of Jerusalem, Antioch, and Alexandria. The West could not stand by and watch Muslim oppression. It was the sacred duty of every Christian to march as righteous soldiers and drive them out. All those that marched with "*purity of heart*" would have their sins absolved. Not in the Pope's wildest dreams could he have imagined the groundswell of support.

The concept of holy war was alien to the Byzantines as the Emperor was the only one who could proclaim a war. A ragtag column of forty thousand men and women immediately took up the banner with less than purity of heart. The "People's Crusade" burned and looted its way before carelessly blundering into a Turkish ambush in A.D. 1096. The early crusaders soon were followed by the most disciplined and powerful knights in Western Europe. They successfully stormed both Antioch and the holy city of Jerusalem. However, few inhabitants survived the un-Christian-like bloodbath that spared neither the Muslims, Jews, nor the Orthodox Christians. The Latin crusaders had come to claim the Eastern Empire for themselves and the Roman Church. They would spare no one else. The worst was yet to come as the Fourth Crusade would seal the faith of the Byzantine Empire.[18]

Two French knights Hugues de Payens and Godfrey de Saint-Omer proposed a monastic order to protect the Christian pilgrims as they traveled through Muslim-controlled Holy Lands, where many of them were robbed and killed. The knights were granted permission by the King of Jerusalem and given space for their headquarters on the Temple Mount in the captured Al Aqsa Mosque. The Temple Mount is believed to be the ruins of the Temple of Solomon—that included the room that served as Christ's prison before his crucifixion. The Order of the *Poor Fellow-Soldiers of Christ and the Temple of Solomon* was shortened to the "Knights Templar." The Order started with nine knights, few financial resources, and relied on donations and charity to survive.

Its impoverished status did not last long. The Order of the Knights Templar was officially endorsed by Pope Innocent II in A.D. 1129. By official edict of a Papal Bull, the Order became a favored charity across Europe, receiving money, land, businesses, and the noble-born sons from families who were eager to fight in the Holy Lands. Pope Innocent II reaffirmed his unrelenting support ten years later when he exempted the

Order from any local laws and taxes and allowed its adherents to pass freely across all borders. They were exempt from all authority except that of the Latin Pope, and with the full support of the Venetian merchants.[19] Successful in their ability to break through opposition lines, the knights galloped on their heavily armed warhorses into the enemy at full speed. One famous victory took place during the Battle of Montgisard near Jerusalem, where some 500 Templar knights defeated the Saladin's army of 26,000 soldiers.

In A.D. 1200, Pope Innocent III began by preaching what would emerge as the Fourth Crusade. He appealed to the Venetians of the Italian city-state to conquer Constantinople and claim it for Rome. The Venetian merchants living in the city already had a keen eye for the Byzantine artwork that they could loot, and send back to Venice, before the Crusaders completely ransacked the city. Fortunately, they saved much of the eastern art from destruction and plunder.

The Crusades had their ugly side, however. In 1202, the Pope ordered the Fourth Crusade to attack the Holy Land through Egypt. The Crusaders *never* came within a thousand miles of their objective of re-taking Jerusalem, but instead reverted to pillaging Christian churches, killing many citizens, and carting off the considerable wealth of Constantinople. Some knights refused to participate, but others found the financial incentives too appealing to ignore. Western history turned a blind eye to a series of misunderstandings, carnage, and brutal violence as the Crusaders sacked and burned the Christian city in 1204. Pope Innocent was appalled by the carnage and promptly mass excommunicated them—only to rescind the proclamation upon the return of the knights to Rome. [18]

Constantinople would never fully recover, but it would still retain its prestige as a cultural center for several more hundred years. In the 14th century Emperor Constantine XI, under attack from the Muslim Ottoman Turks, requested help from the Church and the Venetian navy, but again to no avail. Under fire from enormous newly introduced canons and overwhelming enemy forces, Constantine XI waded into the enemy, leading his remaining soldiers into their last charge, where he was gallantly killed in battle. The Roman Empire officially died that day as the city fell on the 29th of May 1453—a date that many historians consider the official end of the Middle Ages. [20]

The Nugget

The posthumous chronology of the Byzantine Empire: Start Date: A.D. 330. End Date: A.D. 1453. *Total Duration*: an astonishing 1,123 years of a prosperous and affluent culture that mostly goes unnoticed in the journals of Western Civilization. The longevity of the Empire's gold solidus reflects the pious and stoic values of the Byzantine culture.

CHAPTER EIGHT

THE DAWN OF BANKING & CAPITALISM

Keywords: letters of credit; ducat coin; florin coin; indulgences for sale; Medici Bank: a holding company

> "You must know your enemy to beat him at his own game, but be ready as well for the ultimate sacrifice, for nobody comes out of hell without a scratch."
>
> Robin Sacredfire, contemporary author.

The Order of the Knights Templar arguably qualifies as the world's first multinational bank.[1] Today's bankers have long known what the Templars first discovered centuries ago, that the profitability of banking is not lending cash in the form of gold and silver coins—but rather lending their notes (bank checks) that promise to be redeemable as lawful money. When people do not readily redeem their checks by cashing them, that cash reserve is held by the bank and loaned out over and over again. This newfound wealth added an enormous infusion of capital into and across the broad European economy. It would be a gift that would keep on giving.

Pope Urban II's edict in A.D. 1095 set in motion the Pope's authority over that of the mere temporal emperors and kings. His decree of a holy war against Islamic oppression unleashed a bottled-up public resentment toward the robbery and murder of the Christians in the Holy Land. The assemblage of righteous soldiers absolved of all their sins needed management, organization, and funding. In A.D. 1129, Pope Innocent II found the management team so desperately needed in the monastic Order of the Knights Templar. The *Poor Fellow-Soldiers of Christ and the Temple of Solomon* quickly became the favorite charity across Europe. Their poverty, however, did not last very long.

A series of papal bulls exempted the Order from any local laws and taxes. They were lawfully allowed to pass freely across all borders and to keep whatever booty, gold or otherwise, that they had acquired during their battles. A knight took a chivalric vow of poverty, chastity, and obedience, and donated all his worldly possessions of land, property, and gold to the

Order. He could later redeem his spoils (with interest) at the end of his service—if he survived. Charitable gifts also added to their vast fortune. At its height, the Order had nearly 1,000 castles, cathedrals, abbeys, monasteries, and nunneries. [2] It didn't take long for the Templars to realize that their castles could easily function as security vaults and full-service banks of that day.

The Templar Order established financial networks and funded numerous building projects around Europe and the Holy Land. In addition to their numerous fortified buildings, they acquired large tracts of land; they bought and managed farms and vineyards; they were involved in manufacturing, import, and export; they owned their fleet of ships, and claimed ownership of the entire island of Cyprus. Tortosa (Tartus, Syria) acted as their main shipping point for incoming goods and outgoing communications. History would depict them as the Arthurian knights governed by the *roundtable* principle of governance.

The Temple Church in London was built in A.D. 1185 to replicate the Church of the Holy Sepulcher in Jerusalem, and it became the Order's English headquarters. It served as their royal treasury, safety-deposit bank, and international banking center. No precise numbers exist, but at the Order's peak, there were between 15,000 and 20,000 Templars, of whom about a tenth were bankers. The Order's financial power became substantial, and the majority of the Order's infrastructure was devoted not to combat, but to economic pursuits. [3]

In A.D. 1150 the Order began generating *letters of credit* for the pilgrims journeying to the Holy Land. It was a common practice for those following their university studies to visit the biblical Land of Israel and historic Palestine. Traveling scholars were guaranteed the right of unhindered passage in the interest of education, based on a charter of "*academic freedom*" first granted by the University of Bologna in A.D. 1158.[4] The pilgrims, many of noble birth simply deposited their valuables with a local Templar *'preceptory'* before embarking. There they would receive an encrypted document indicating the value of their deposit and, upon their arrival, would then use that document to retrieve their funds. The letter of credit is the first recorded instance of the system leading to the use of personal checks drawn on a bank. This innovation enhanced the safety of pilgrims by making them less attractive targets for thieves and further contributed to the Templar coffers. The lending of money in return for interest was officially considered usury and was forbidden by the church. However, the Order sidestepped this with clever loopholes, such as a stipulation that the Templars retained the rights to the production of mortgaged property. Instead of interest, they could now call it—*rent.* [3]

The Order became powerful and highly respected throughout England. King Henry II claimed to be one of the nine founders of the Templars, along with other noble English patrons directly allied with the affluent and dynastic House of Anjou. The Master of the Temple sat in a prominent seat in parliament. When King John imposed excessive taxes and called on the Templar Knights to engage in Pope Innocent III's call for a Fourth Crusade, they revolted. The entrenched Order consequently demonstrated their power over the King.

This revolt would be the first time in history that statutory law was imposed on a monarch by armed force and led to the landmark signing of the Magna Carta on June 15th, 1215. Originally written in Latin, the "*Magna Carta Libertatum,*" or the *Great Charter of Liberties*, is the basis for English Common Law. The charter effectively served as the legal precedent for the U.S. Constitution's Bill of Rights and is the cornerstone of most national legal systems throughout Europe and much of the free world. [5, 6]

The original document is presently exhibited in the Temple Church, located in the financial district of the City of London, and is jointly owned by the Inner Temple and Middle Temple Inns of the Court—the home to the English legal profession. Nearby is the Temple Bar which is the front entrance to the City of London, the Temple Underground station, and other Templar buildings then used to house visiting monarchs, financiers, and knights. Many of their building sites around Europe maintain the *Temple* brand due to the centuries-old association with the Templars. [7]

In addition to the deposit-type of accounts, the Knights Templar also set up international loans to various princes and monarchs. The nobles throughout Europe and the Middle East financed their ventures with funds borrowed from the Templars. The Templar Order was a part of European daily life for more than 200 years, but the situation became more complex as the Templars were occasionally at odds with two other Christian Orders. The Knights Hospitaller and the German Teutonic Knights both were engaged primarily in service to hospitals and housing for the pilgrims. All three Christian Orders were essentially a state-within a state.

The Templar Order soon fell into public disfavor after several ill-fated and unsuccessful military campaigns. The monarch most heavily in debt was the French King Philip IV (1269-1314) who, despite seeing the

Templars as an insurgent threat to the monarchy system, approached the Order with a request for funds to finance the Hundred Years War with the English. When the Templars denied his request, the infuriated king mounted a political campaign to discredit both the Templars and the Jews, and to blackmail Pope Clement V (a relative of the King) into annulling the Crusaders' travel and financial privileges. [9]

When the Templars lost the Holy Land to the Muslims, and amidst rumors that were spread to create public distrust, the Templar Order soon disbanded. On Friday the 13th of October 1307, King Philip ordered the Templars arrested. His decree is considered the origin of the Western superstition: that a Friday falling on the 13th is unlucky.[10] Under pressure from King Philip, Pope Clement excommunicated the Order in A.D. 1312 and initiated a brutal Inquisition, forcing confessions, burning hundreds of knights at the stake, and transferring Templar assets to the Hospitallers. Those Templars who survived simply changed their name to the Hospitallers and gave up the knighthood, while King Edward II of England saw it as his chance to regain control over parliament and confiscate what he can of the Templar assets.

The transfer of power was followed by an economic collapse and widespread famine in Western Europe. Public criticism of the English King mounted as he was forced to resign and later murdered. [11] The vast and uncounted assets of the Order gave rise to many legends involving the Knights Templar. Notably, the 15th century Freemasons revived many of the Templar symbols, rituals, and traditions with a long list of notable politicians, scholars, and scientists claiming title and membership. Freemasons emphasize their fraternal order and allegiance for the good of their members and disassociate themselves from the implied Templar involvement with the disastrous outcome of the Fourth Crusade. President George Washington and many of the signatories of the U.S. Declaration of Independence and Constitution have connections to the Freemasons and their Templar values and ideals. [12] Conspiracy theorists have long associated Freemasonry with distrust and political intrigue. So where did the money go? More than likely much of the wealth found its way to the next big financial center—Venice, Italy.

The Lagoon

The Republic of Venice was founded as a haven for the people escaping from mainland Europe after the decline and fall of the Byzantine Roman Empire. It became home to those fleeing the barbarian invasions, Attila the

Hun, and various enemies that drove the people to hide out on the many islands of the eastern Mediterranean. Venice originally flourished based on the salt trade and grew into a prosperous maritime empire in northeastern Italy. The city-state became a thalassocracy (Greek for *sea power*) as the wealthy merchant class became ever more powerful. The Fourth Crusade and the sacking of Constantinople gave rise to the Venetian Republic. Officially established in A.D. 1205, the Venetian Republic became the dominant global power and center of finance for more than 500 years. It was weakened by the Ottoman navy. Napoleon Bonaparte would see to its official end in 1797.

The lagoon communities were originally under the governance of the Byzantine Empire. The sophisticated culture of the Roman Byzantines substantially influenced the Venetian love of art and architecture. The Venetian Republic would grow as the Byzantine Empire gradually declined. The merchant class took advantage of every opportunity to wrestle control away from the Empire.

The Pope's call for a Fourth Crusade allowed the Venetian navy to be used by the Crusaders for transport and much-needed supplies. The Crusaders, with the approval of the Church, became heavily indebted to the Venetians who were their major financial backers. However, promises of payment were not kept, and the Crusaders were coerced into sacking the Christian cites of Zadar and Constantinople to pay for the transportation costs provided by the Venetian navy. The Fourth Crusade never made it to their original objective of defeating the Muslims in Egypt, and their destruction of fellow Christian cities provoked acrimony and resentment throughout Europe.

Enrico Dandolo assumed one of the more prominent roles as the 41st Doge (or Duke) of the Venetian Republic. Appointed as an ambassador to Constantinople, Dandolo developed a deep hatred for the Byzantines. Already in his mid-70s, he was elected Doge by the wealthy merchants and aristocratic oligarchy. He led the financial negotiations with the indebted Crusaders, and he stood in the front line during the assault on Constantinople. The sacking of Constantinople allowed Dandolo to dictate terms granting the Venetian merchants access to a quarter of the city, exempt from taxes or tariffs. His actions essentially led to the economic decline of the city and the Byzantine Empire itself. Perhaps as a further insult to the Byzantines, Dandolo insisted that he be buried in the Basilica of Hagia Sophia in Constantinople. [13]

Dandolo redefined the office of the Doge. He resolved many of the problems inherent in the doge system of governance by giving Venice an advanced civil code and a constitutional system he named the "*ducal promise*." Venice and other Italian maritime republics played a key role in fostering merchant capitalism along with the issuance of a new dominant currency the "*ducat*" or *the duke's coin.* [14] Dandolo also issued a silver coin called the "grosso" or *large penny* to encourage trade with the East which preferred silver coins. The grosso originally weighed 2.18 grams of pure silver and was valued at 26 denarii.[15]

Figure 8-1 Left *Dandolo stands to the left on the* grosso *coin wearing a cloak and holding the "ducal promise" in his left hand, while St. Mark presents him with the gonfalon (banner) in his right. Reverse: An enthroned Christ 1.90 grams. OTRS Attribution: Numisantica, www.numinantica.com*
Figure 8-2 Right *Venetian Ducat, the very first gold coin made by the City-State of Venice, and a very popular Italian coin minted from about A.D.1284 under the doge (mayor of the city) Giovanni Dandolo. It shows the Doge kneeling before St. Mark, the patron saint of the city, on the obverse, and a figure of Christ standing on the reverse, in an oval frame accompanied by the inscription "Christe datus, quem tu regis, iste ducatus" (Christ to give, that duchy, that you rule). The last word of the legend, ducatus (duchy) is the origin of the coin name "Ducat." The design is perfect political propaganda (who would mess with someone that Christ has blessed?) (CC By-SA-3.0) Classical Numismatic Group, Inc. http://www.cngcoins.com.*

From the 13th century onward, the Republic of Venice minted the nearly pure gold *ducat* coin by recasting the Byzantine coinage and confiscating their gold and silver mines in central Europe. Locally, the Venetians proudly named it the "*zecchino*" after the Zecca building in Venice where it was minted with a weight of 3.5 grams (0.12 oz.). The wide acceptance of the ducat throughout most of Europe reflected the power and influence of Venice. The Venetians patronized the arts and architecture, were influential financiers of Europe, were early contributors to the European Renaissance, home to Marco Polo, and pioneered the opening of new trade routes to the Americas and the East Indies via the Atlantic Ocean.

The design of the Venetian gold ducat remained unchanged for over 500 years, from its introduction in 1284 to the seizure of Venice by Napoleon in 1797. The 500-year run of the *zecchino* is a testament to the economic stability and power of the Venetian Republic. Based on the ducat's consistent purity it remained as one of the dominant currencies among the traders in Western Europe and was widely used as a model for other currencies until it was replaced by the Spanish dollar.[15] In some regions, these coins were stitched to women's clothing such as headdresses and belts. The term *zecchino* was rendered into French as the origin of the more modern word *sequins* to denote small shiny circular decorations sewn onto fashionable garments of that period. Coin collectors often try to accumulate a complete set of *zecchini,* representing all 120 Venetian Doges.

For Sale: Indulgences

To this day, the Roman Catholic Church denies ever accepting the theological premise that indulgences could be sold or purchased. Nevertheless, the sale was HUGE! Indulgences provided Europe with a substantial economic stimulus for over four centuries. Every religion allows monetary donations to construct religious buildings, provide for charities to do good works, and support other righteous causes. Nearly all religions also incorporate rituals for the remission of guilt from sins associated with breaking cultural taboos. The Christian Church's doctrine established that *venial* sins once confessed could be fully forgiven. The Church has traditionally identified three major ways to fully expiate sin: through prayers, fasting, and almsgiving. [16]

In the 8th to 10th centuries, however, the concept of Purgatory as a place seeped into the widely held Christian belief system with a new form of sin. Purgatory was soon envisioned as a waiting station after death but before entry into heaven. [17] *Temporal* punishment remained even after the venal sin was forgiven. An indulgence was considered a remission of temporal punishment, and soon indulgences were attached to a quantification of the number of days and years commuted from time served in Purgatory. Fixed sums of money were attached to various kinds of offenses (tariff penances) and listed in the Church's *"treasury of merit."* The poor could pray, but the rich would pay. The corruption within the Church escalated as bishops marketed indulgences to augment their funds.

After the Knights Templar disbanded in A.D. 1312, a new monetary stimulus was badly needed. In A.D. 1343, Pope Clement VI issued a papal bull "*Unigenitus*" to justify the power of the pope and the use of indulgences to support the Church and various projects like the Crusades. A virulent visitation of Black Death also weighed heavily on the souls of the living, encouraging them to donate generously to the church, both for themselves and their loved ones, and to avoid time in Purgatory. [18]

By the late Middle Ages, indulgences became commercialized, as well as a serious problem, which the Church recognized but was unable to restrain. Under the jurisdiction of a bishop, predatory "*commissaries*" sought to extract the maximum amount of money for each indulgence. Professional "*quaestories*" (pardoners), who practiced the unrestricted sale of indulgences, were sent to collect alms. Their zeal often exceeded the official Church doctrine. There was a tendency to forge documents declaring that indulgences had been granted, and they grew to extraordinary magnitude, regarding longevity and breadth of forgiveness.[18] The indulgences became ingrained in the European economy to fund expensive projects, cathedrals, and the continuation of the Crusades simply by distributing mere sheets of paper. They were used by the Church the way some governments use bonds today.

Many of the cathedrals built during the construction boom years of A.D. 1100 to 1500 were financed by a city's "cathedral chapter" of leading citizens and the locally seated bishop. Like our city sports arenas of today, cathedrals were the landmarks that would put cities on the map and bring tourism, employment, and prosperity. The city would first need a patron saint—preferably the saint's dramatic and captivating physical remains. The cathedral chapters financed construction by taking the holy relics, and saintly remains, on a promotional tour. They also cashed in on the fruitful sale of indulgences. Many afflicted with the Black Death would leave their family largess to the Church in exchange for a written and sealed indulgence contract. Numerous trades, from architects and artists to stone masons and sculptors, were needed to construct the costly spiraling Gothic churches—with their devilish gargoyles facing outwards over the entrance to the Church's inner celestial sanctuary.

Historical examples of the building boom abound. The Milan Cathedral, or *Duomo di Milano*, whose construction began in A.D. 1386, remains the largest in Italy and the 3rd largest in the world. It is the most famous landmark in the city and features the golden "*Madonnina*" statue atop the main spire that is 108 meters (354 ft.) in height—or 35 stories. The Cologne Cathedral is today among the tallest cathedrals in Europe with a height of 157.4 m (516 ft.). The "*Butter Tower*" of the Rouen Cathedral in Normandy, France, earned its moniker because the money was largely raised from the sale of indulgences that allowed for the use of butter on Fridays and during Lent.[19] Italy has 365 official cathedrals with seated bishops, France has 110, and Spain 87. [20] The list doesn't include basilicas, monasteries, parish churches, abbeys, and nunneries. The impact of the building boom was substantial with the money widely dispersed throughout the European economy.

The Dominican friar Johann Tetzel (A.D. 1465 to 1519) was the marketing genius and Grand Commissar behind the sale of indulgences in exchange for money in Germany. He became widely known for a brilliant couplet attributed to him:

As soon as the gold in the casket rings
The rescued soul to heaven springs [21]

With the introduction of the Gutenberg press in A.D. 1439, there was born a demand for stories, news, gossip, and other printed content. The conflict between the Dominican friar, Johann Tetzel, and his nemesis Martin Luther, the St. Augustine monk, brought wide attention to what without the printing press would have been a discreet and guarded church problem. Martin Luther would question the very men and institutions that allowed for the pay-for-play action behind the sale of indulgences.

According to Martin Luther, after Tetzel had received a substantial amount of money in his hometown of Leipzig, Germany, a nobleman asked him if it were possible to receive a letter of indulgence for a future sin, one about to take place. Tetzel quickly confirmed the request and insisted that the payment be made at once. The nobleman did so and received a letter of indulgence with a seal from Tetzel. When Tetzel left Leipzig, the nobleman attacked him, gave him a thorough beating, and sent him back empty-handed with the comment—that was the future sin which he had in mind! Duke George at first was quite furious about the incident, but when he heard the whole story, he let it go without punishing the nobleman. [21]

The conflict would further escalate upon Luther's writing of his famous "Ninety-Five Theses," along with his effective use of the Gutenberg printing press to spread his views on Lutheranism. The resulting Reformation brought severe limitations to the Church's sale of indulgences. King Henry VIII of England might simply have purchased an annulment from the Pope to marry Ann Boleyn had the Church not been politically constrained in its sale of indulgences. Frustrated, King Henry would break from the Roman Church, confiscate the Church's vast properties, and initiate the English Reformation. The transfer of the Church's assets eventually bolstered the English Parliament's control over their monarch and ushered in a new attitude toward private ownership and early capitalism.

Max Weber's book, "The Protestant Ethic and the Spirit of Capitalism," first identified the Protestant *work ethic* as the foundation of capitalism. However, he further noted that the spirit of capitalism could be divorced from religion within a larger cultural context and seen more broadly as a *Spirit of Rationalization.* Protestantism would mark a cultural change in attitude. The new work ethic would challenge the Catholic Church's widely condoned and accepted desire for profit with minimum effort, seeing work as a burden to be avoided, and doing no more than what was enough for a pious and modest life. [22]

The Roman Church would eventually question and come to suppress its dependence on the sale of indulgences. As a result, the Church's pricing power would diminish, leaving many Christians without a way to set a price for their sinful transgressions. The Church would thereby need another form of economic stimulus.

The Money behind the Renaissance

The word "*Renaissance*" literally means *rebirth*, as it identifies the era following both the fall of Constantinople and the end of the European Hundred Years War in A.D. 1453. It is considered the cultural bridge between the Middle Ages and modern history. A gradual transition of economic wealth and power favored the rich agricultural Tuscan countryside, particularly the city of Florence, over that of the maritime merchants of Venice. Much of Florence's early wealth came from the husbandry of sheep, and the export of wool, glass, and ceramics. The Florentines played a prominent role in the Italian Renaissance as the leading patrons, and political dynastic families, behind the fine arts and architecture of that era. [23] The innovation of movable metal type also sped the dissemination of humanistic study and a search for realism and human emotion in the arts.

Greek scholars, texts, and art from the Byzantine Empire found a home and patronage in the wealthy families of the northern Italian city-states of Venice, Genoa, Bologna, and particularly Florence. [24] The Italian city-states were a political phenomenon of small independent states from the 9th to the 15th centuries, as opposed to the continued existence of the feudal territories of northern and central Europe. France and Spain remained absolute monarchies under pressure to resist further Islamic invasions and encroachments, while other regions remained under direct Church control. Scholars consider the Italian city-states as a marriage of responsive government, Christian values, and the birthplace of capitalism.

Leading Church theologians like Augustine and Thomas Aquinas gave their approval of private property, profit, and interest. The 13th-century German philosopher and Christian theologian, Albertus Magnus, wrote that a just price was simply what "*goods are worth according to the estimation of the market at the time of sale.*"[25] This was a significant turning point in the Church's attitude toward the consumption of goods and the treatment of accrued interest, as it had previously condemned all interest that earned money without labor. Based on Aristotle's writings in his book Politics, the Church had historically adopted this restricted view of capital and accrued interest. Strict usury laws were now relaxed as capital wealth was now allowed to make a profit from lending money, only as long as the lender also assumed some of the risks with the loan. In Muslim countries, by contrast, the charging of any interest at all is illegal to this day.

The Papal States, a series of territories in the Italian Peninsula under the direct sovereign rule of the Pope, embraced the principles of capitalism originally invented on the Church's self-reliant monastic estates. The Benedictine Order had become the standard form of autonomy and monastic life throughout the whole of Western Europe. The Augustinian friar and abbot Gregor Mendel is recognized as the founder of the modern science of genetics based on his pea plant experiments and rules of heredity. The essential features of capitalism—individual enterprise, innovation, advances in credit, commercial profits, speculation, etc.—are found in the 12th-century Papal States. [25]

The French historian Fernand Braudel notes that the term "*capital*" first came into use in the 14th century to identify funds having the capacity to return income, or the use of wealth (money) to return wealth (money). [26] The Papal States energized an unprecedented commercial revolution that preceded and financed the Renaissance with the full support of the Church Papacy.

By far the best customer of the Italian banking and mercantile companies was the Church. The Church was still the largest landowner with holdings spread throughout Europe and loosely managed by monasteries and various religious orders. They often specialized and introduced innovative methods and science to commodities like wine, beer, cheese, animal husbandry, and later focused primarily on education. [24, 25, 26] Profits from these holdings found their way into the coffers of the Church in Rome.

The Papal States were a manifestation of the temporal power of the pope, as opposed to his direct ecclesiastical primacy. The popes of this period reflected the thinking of the College of Cardinals that elected them and played an integral part in various reforms within the Church. From the 13th to 15th centuries the size of the College of Cardinals never exceeded thirty members, which allowed for a more active voice in church matters, versus the more unmanageable 216 Cardinals in the College today. (Most large corporations currently have less than a dozen board of directors.) It was dominated by cardinal-nephews (relatives of the popes that elevated them), crown-cardinals (representatives of the Catholic monarchies of Europe), and members of the powerful Italian families that convened to discuss and settle matters of the Church.

During this period, there were two popes each selected from the House of Borgia, House of della Rovere, and the House of Medici, along with monarchs and numerous princes. The wealthy popes, cardinals, and bishops increasingly patronized Renaissance art and architecture. They commissioned the corporate families in rebuilding the landmarks of Rome. The Papal States began to resemble a modern nation-state, and the papacy took an increasingly active role in mediating European wars, diplomacy, and the settlement of family disputes. [27]

Figure 8-3 *Gold Florin coin the "Fiorno d'ore" of nearly pure gold, circa A.D. 1252–1422 (20 mm, 3.50 g.) The obverse is the hallmark Florentine fleur-de-lis. The reverse is John the Baptist standing holding a cross-tipped scepter with his right hand raised in benediction. (CC By-SA-3.0) Classical Numismatic Group, Inc. http://www.cngcoins.com*

In A.D. 1252 the Republic of Florence minted the gold florin coin which, along with the Venetian ducat, soon became a preferred currency in Europe. Significantly, the Florentine bankers kept their accounts in gold florins, thereby establishing an unofficial gold standard. Silver-based florin coinage "*piccioli*" (or *loose change*) was used by the general public for common everyday transactions. While there was no official fixed ratio between gold and silver, the value of the silver *picciolo* was allowed to inflate next to the gold florin, providing the bankers with a common and stable standard of gold currency for tracking commercial transactions.

The florin was made of nearly pure gold, had a stable weight, and was designed, minted, and stamped as a high-quality coin of beauty. It was the first European gold coin struck in sufficiently large quantities to play an important commercial and international role. The weight of the gold florin was equal in value to one lira (£), 20 solidi, or 240 deniers, and used primarily in commercial and wholesale business transactions, while the silver *lira di piccioli* was originally equal to 20 solidi di piccioli, or 240 deniers di piccioli. [28]

The Florentine direct tax, the "*catasto*," also provided monetary stability and support for the currency. The income tax was based on individual returns filed with tax officials much like the income tax in the United States and other countries. The existence of tax records details the financial and social status of the Florentine society and have many traits in common with modern income taxes. [29] Wars with other Italian states, supported by the money raised by the *catasto*, proved a drain on the national debt and contributed to the decline of the Florentine banking system.

Soon other Italian cities and foreign countries adopted the use of the florin to express their independence and copy its commercial success. Imitations of the gold florin were widely minted in Turin, Rome, Milan, and Bologna, as well as in Germany, Austria, Poland, Czechoslovakia, Greece, Turkey, Hungary, and Holland. Each portrayed different imprimatur images of the local saints, landmarks, or rulers. The gold content of the florin did not change while the money of account (silver coinage) continued to inflate. By A.D. 1500, the gold florin was worth seven silver Florentine lire. The value of other countries' money continually varied against each other, reinforcing the solid gold florin's utility as a common measure of value by bankers in foreign exchange transactions.

The distinctive feature of the Florentine business organization was the existence of large interlocking family mercantile and banking companies which controlled a network of branches abroad. The companies were family-based partnerships, rather than corporations, and trust among the oligarch families was the basis of the economy.

The most powerful Florentine companies were those of the Bardi, the Peruzzi, and the Acciaiuoli, known as the "*pillars of Christian trade*." At one point, the Peruzzi had fifteen branches scattered all over Europe and employed a staff of about 90 clerks or "*factors*." In A.D. 1348, all three companies collapsed due to the Black Death, overextension of credit, and excessive loans to bankrupted foreign governments defeated by wars. It was the cost of doing business as it allowed the merchants to sell and trade their luxury goods. After the collapse of the big three companies, the Pope was unable to find a banking firm that offered him the same services for the transfer of paper revenues within the Church. The Alberti family took advantage of the situation but due to family quarrels fell into disgrace among the ruling Florentine oligarchs. [30]

In A.D. 1397, the Medici family interceded with the founding of the Medici Bank. The Medici were the richest family in the entire city of Florence and occupied the uppermost rung of the social ladder. The Medici Bank became the most powerful banking house of the 14th century. Headquartered in Florence, it established branches in Rome, Venice, Geneva, Lyons, Bruges, London, and many other cities. The bank served as the sole financial agent of the Church, extended credit to monarchs, and facilitated international trade in Western Europe. The family's extensive connections reformed the Church's ban on usury and made the bankers respected citizens who now prided themselves on being called the Pope's *money-changers*. [31]

By their social influence and the private use of their profits, the owners and administrators of the bank contributed significantly to the development of Florence as the greatest financial center of the time. The hegemony of the Medici Bank rested largely with its superior management organization and the evolving innovative structure of a bank holding company. *"It is, for example, decidedly a legend that the Medici ever invented the bill of exchange, but were creative in devising the 'holding company' form of organization and in forming the alum cartel."* [32] Credits and debits were made within the same Medici Bank organization, but were *not* made across independent banks—as would occur with the later innovation of the bill of exchange.

A holding company is a business that owns the outstanding stock of other companies and thereby controls the *held* company through a single board of directors. The holding company usually does not produce goods or services; rather, its' purpose is to own shares of other companies to form a corporate network. Holding companies reduce their risk by not being liable for the debts of the companies they control. The Italian family oligarchs could pool and track their wealth based on stock ownership. Holding companies can also limit their tax liability by placing subsidiaries in locations with lower tax rates. The Medici Bank could now devise clever ways to avoid payment of the *catasto*.

Challenges faced by a holding company include management's limited knowledge of the day-to-day operations of the controlled companies, a lack of understanding of the controlled companies, and all compounded by the then slow and mistaken communications over long distances. Holding companies frequently end up owning unprofitable assets or lines of business contained in their subsidiary corporations. In A.D. 1464, the Medici Bank was suffering from a lack of coordination with branch managers who failed to understand each other's problems. Mounting bank losses sharpened the conflicts as the plague and wars added to the economic stagnation that lasted for over three decades. [32]

To track their account balances, the Medici Bank adopted the innovation of the new double-entry accounting system which developed in the Republic of Genoa in A.D. 1340. [33] The new accounting system allowed a holding company to focus on the ownership of stock and pay less attention to company assets. The depreciation of assets was a new accounting principle known to the bookkeepers using the rules of double-entry accounting. Since these banks operated on a fractional reserve principle, they created transferable deposits that were not entirely covered by what was in the bank till or vault.

The Medici Bank emphasized banking—not trade nor production. It added little to capital investments in machinery and production but was encouraged by the Church in the commissioning of the arts and real estate. Perhaps much of the money that paid for the artworks and buildings of the Renaissance period came from contrived bankruptcies, manipulation of stock prices, questionable depreciations, and the inflation of everyday silver coinage coordinated by the bank holding company. All are examples of financial operations that might take place among central banks with little effective oversight. Industrial capitalism did not appear until the Industrial Revolution that would later take place in northern Europe. [34]

The sudden bankruptcy of the Bank of Medici occurred in A.D. 1470. It resulted from a convergence of poor management, ill-advised policies, and inherent weakness in the structure of its business model, and other adverse business conditions that worsened with the contraction of international trade. Conventional ledgers indicate a breakdown of the central control of investments and unauthorized withdrawals by the branches that led to the downfall of the Florentine Medici Bank network. [32]

The rebirth of the global financial order would follow two widely separate economic roads. The "*Reconquista*" (or *reconquest*), by the Christian Spanish and Portuguese kingdoms, led to the fall of the Nasrid Moors of Grenada, Spain, ending a protracted war with the Muslims in A.D. 1492. This event turned the Spanish and Portuguese attention to the discovery and mercantile conquest of the riches of the "*New World*." The other economic road was followed by the Protestant-dominated countries of northern Europe, which set the stage for the "*Dutch Golden Age,*" and a new form of—industrial capitalism.

The Nugget

The English proverb "*necessity is the mother of invention*" infers that the primary force behind invention is a need. When it comes to investing money, two questions involving need arise: The first is: *Where do I place my money to preserve my wealth*? The second is: *How best to invest my money to make even more money*? The Latin Church was challenged by the fall of the Byzantine theocracy, the Protestant Reformation, public scrutiny over the sale of indulgences, and its old ways of thinking about usury and interest. The bulk of the Church's profits, however, continued to flow from its vast land holdings and operations on its thriving monastic estates. The Church needed to redefine how it made and spent its wealth. Along the way, the newly reformed Church, by both necessity and invention, would invent and nurture early capitalism.

CHAPTER NINE

THE ORIGINS OF MODERN CURRENCY & THE DUTCH GOLDEN AGE

Keywords: stadholder; bill of exchange; agio; guilder; Tulipomania, Central Banks

"Money goes to where it is most wanted."

Anon

Most school children are taught about the Norman conquest of England by William I the Duke of Normandy, France. William the Conqueror became renowned for his decisive victory at the Battle of Hastings in A.D. 1066. He forcefully conquered the indigenous Celtic Britons and Germanic tribes of the Anglo-Saxon world, made French the official language, redistributed land to his elitist Normans followers, and built castles (new to England) commanding military strongholds throughout England. It was 350 years later that King Henry V, born into Norman society—but raised as an Englishman, reintroduced English and reestablished Anglo-Saxon culture. The King of England later came close to turning the tables by conquering all of France as he became regent and heir-apparent to the French throne and heir to the Holy Roman Empire. The historical adventures of the House of Plantagenet were made popular through the writings of William Shakespeare.

Figure 9-1 Left *Penny of William I the Conqueror 1066-1087 Sandwich mint.*
Figure 9-2 Right *William III on a gold guinea coin in 1695. Public domain*

Not as well commemorated, but equally important is the *other* King William. The Dutch-born William arrived 600 years after the Norman William. He was crowned as the English King William III of Orange (more commonly referred to as in the married couple of William and Mary). Much like a hostile corporate takeover of today—the Protestant English Parliament, in opposition to the standing Catholic English King James II, requested the assistance of William from the Netherlands to take over as King to the English throne along with the official bloodline of a fixed marriage to Mary the Queen of Scots. William was *not* a king or monarch, having turned the offer down from his father, but adopted the title of "*stadtholder*" or chief magistrate of the Dutch provinces. He assumed command over the Dutch military, soundly defeated the Spanish, and held the formidable French King Louis XIV at bay. Otherwise, he acted more as a financial corporate executive officer overseeing the Dutch government—and was soon *hired* by parliament as the King of England.

The English had suffered a series of calamities and disasters including: a plague that decimated much of England in 1665; the London fire of 1666; the defeat of their Navy by the Dutch in 1667; and 150 years of simmering religious turmoil dating back to Henry VIII's break with the Catholic Church and Holy Roman Empire. The English Parliament acted in the best interest of their stakeholders (and themselves) and crowned William King of England in 1685. However, his position came with one notable and outlandish exception. The King worked for the Parliament and the people—*not* for the King himself.

Parliament's somewhat peaceful takeover was named "*The Glorious Revolution*" of 1688 which secured the English Bill of Rights, parliamentary democracy, and largely influenced the United States Constitution. The Dutch-born William of Orange was a Protestant, and the vested English interests of the day had converted to some form of Protestantism initiated 150 years earlier by King Henry VIII. Henry, through the legalities of the published "*Dissolution of the Monasteries,*" had confiscated all properties and wealth from the Roman Church which he then shared among his loyal aristocracy. His dispute with the church over his marriage to Ann Boleyn conveniently provided a cover for his feigned motives. The expropriation provided a vital source of newfound wealth as the abbeys, priories, convents, and monasteries were the greatest landowners in England—an estimated one-third of all the land belonged to the Church.

The Protestant parliament wanted the status quo to stay that way as large financial interests were at stake. They *fired* King James II and replaced him with William and Mary. This was the beginnings of the world's first modern nation-state with power vested by the people through parliament. Another great advantage, King William brought with him the financial building blocks founded in Holland, along with the wealthy Dutch elite, and most of the capital wealth of the Dutch Golden Age. [1]

The Dutch Miracle

The Dutch Golden Age bridged the years A.D. 1550 to 1815 and globally dominated the 16th and 17th centuries. It began in a time of peace after the cessation of the Thirty Years' War. The war dragged Central Europe through the fragmentation of the Holy Roman Empire and religious conflicts between the Protestants and Catholics (colloquially the *Prods* versus the *Popists*). The Netherland's transformation from a mere possession of the Holy Roman Empire in the 1590s to a preeminent maritime and economic power in the world was acclaimed as the "Dutch Miracle" by historian K.W. Swart.[2] A number of factors converged bringing about economic innovations and changes to the status quo. The financial lessons learned by the Dutch *stadholder* were quickly incorporated by the new English King William and his astute entourage of entrepreneurs and savvy corporate financiers from Holland.

One vital condition for the Dutch transformation to occur was cheap energy converted from harnessing the winds of the North Sea with the newly invented Dutch windmills. Before the windmill, peat was the primary source of energy which was laboriously farmed from bogs and transported via the canals into the cities. New more powerful wind-driven innovations amplified the economy.

One such innovation was the circular sawmill which powered the construction of a massive fleet of ships for trading and military defense. The Dutch-designed and originated a new ship called the "*fluyt*." It was a sailing vessel dedicated to transporting cargo. Most ships of the day were built primarily as warships and converted to cargo ships when needed. The *fluyt* was cheaper to build and carried twice the cargo along with a smaller crew than building a warship-sometimes-cargo ship. The new style ship provided a major competitive advantage for Dutch merchants as it led to sharply lower costs of transportation and far larger distances. Add to this the fortunate geographical advantage of Dutch ports located on the confluence of the Rhine River as it empties into the North Sea—and the sea-born empire of the Dutch Golden Age arrived.[3]

The Dutch were the quintessential middlemen of Europe as they occupied a strategic geographic spot midway between France, Germany, and England. The Netherlands, no more than the third the size of the state of Indiana, had little landmass which incentivized many to become merchants, traders, and financiers. With just two million people, they had a penchant for religious tolerance and a work ethic leading to the highest productivity in Europe. They introduced such services as marine insurance and other risk management innovations. For example, ship voyages were financed by shares of stock with as many as 16 merchants, each holding perhaps 1/16 share, to both minimalize risk and provide an opportunity for profitable gains.

The Netherlands, considered the first "modern economy" by the scholar of that period Jan De Vries, spanned from the early 1500s to a far-flung maritime empire in the 17th century.[3] Also, the Dutch textile businessman Pieter de La Court published the bestseller *Interest van Holland* in 1662. His book focused on the reasons for the economic success of the Dutch Republic. Central to their argument was the need for nurtured competition and a republican form of responsive government. They were particularly critical of monopolies, and of unionized trade and craft guilds, becoming established institutions. Both correctly forewarned of the economic demise these events would later bring.[4]

Their insights were an inspiration to the first noted economist, Adam Smith, who published his famous and popular book: *An Inquiry into the Nature and Causes of the Wealth of Nations* in London in 1776. Today it is casually referred to as "*The Wealth of Nations*" ignoring the scientific *inquiry* into why some nations become wealthier than others. The founder of classical economics investigated a country's advancements based on a productive balance of land, labor, and *capital*—which are the foundations for international trade and prosperity in an open free market economy.

In the early 15th to 16th centuries, merchants and traders found it easy to export textiles from Leiden, porcelain form Delft, cheese from Gouda, sugar first imported and later refined in Antwerp, herring, and other Dutch agricultural commodities for foreign trade. "Trading Clubs" of investors would financially back nearly anyone with inventory to sell. Dutch and Portuguese voyagers were the first Europeans to make contact with Japan and Asia, and by the 1600s dozens of Dutch merchant ships regularly made the trip. The Japanese were at first astonished by the Dutch desire for their plentiful silver, which was considered as of little value by the Japanese. Silks, porcelains, and spices were in great demand throughout Europe, and the Dutch merchants were the first main suppliers. Soon countless ships were making the trip and intense competition destabilized prices. The Dutch merchants called upon the government to avoid commercial ruin. [5] Their requests eventually led to the incorporation of the lucrative Dutch East India Company.

The Two East Indies Companies

Queen Elizabeth I defeated the Spanish Armada in 1588 allowing her to grant a Royal Charter to the British Honorable East India Company (HEIC) in December 1600. The act laid claim to being the oldest of the East India Companies which provided wealthy aristocrats and merchants private ownership of issued shares of stock. Originally formed to trade with the East Indies, the British (HEIC) focused mainly on the subcontinent of India and the far east of China. The Dutch East India Company (VOC), established in 1602, concentrated on Indonesia and Japan.

The Dutch VOC forcibly seized two essential trading routes around the Straits of Malacca from the Portuguese. It was then granted a 21-year Dutch charter and monopolist oversight in 1602. The Straits were the primary routes to the Spice Islands which connect the Indian Ocean in the east to the Pacific Ocean to the west. The VOC collected a 10 percent corporate *royalty fee* on goods shipped in both directions through the Straits. The charter legally prevented the British easy access to the West Indies and Japan which readily led to extensive naval battles that sided with the Dutch. The second charter gave the VOC exclusive access to the West Indies without a liquidation clause. The VOC became substantially wealthy and a company of firsts.

The VOC became the *first*-ever multinational corporation financed by corporate stock sold publicly on the first modern (Amsterdam) stock exchange. They were granted the *first* monopoly on Asian trade and would maintain their control for nearly two centuries. It became the world's largest commercial enterprise of the 17th century, and a state unto itself with the ability to wage war, imprison and execute convicts, negotiate treaties, strike its own coins, and establish colonies.[6]

Based on its peak net worth the company is still considered the most valuable in history estimated at $7 Trillion in U.S. 2014 dollars.[7] (Today in comparison, Apple Inc., and Alphabet Inc. each have a net worth around a mere $850 billion). The British Honourable East India Company (HEIC) was a far second competitor, but still commanded military and administrative control over all of India, along with jurisdiction over its private army. The intense competition between the two East India Companies resulted in four major Anglo-Dutch wars over the control of disputed trade routes, colonies, and globally dispersed company factories.

Figure 9-3 Left *The flag of the Dutch Vereenigde Oost-Indische Compagnie;* **VOC**: Figure 9-4 Right: *The flag of the British Honourable East India Company* **HEIC** *commonly referred to as the John Company. Note the uncanny resemblance to the flag of the U.S.A. (Public domain)*

The First Central Bank

The Bank of Amsterdam (*Wisselbank* or the *Amsterdam Exchange Bank*) was established in 1609 primarily as an exchange bank to finance the growing international trade and to resolve the practical problems faced by merchants with the circulation of multiple currencies. This was the early precursor to, if not the first true central bank and vouched for by the city of Amsterdam. It was nearly half a century before its time. Endorsed by the city of Amsterdam, it was not technically a *national* central bank—but was followed by the oldest *national* central banks in operation today: the Riksbanken of Sweden (1668) and the Bank of England (1694).

The Bank of Amsterdam was originally chartered by the city government to facilitate trade, suppress usury (not to eliminate it), and granted a monopoly on all currency trading. The bank's chief function was to withdraw from circulation all gold and silver coinage from any currency that was damaged, debased, or counterfeit and reissue them as Dutch guilders with standardized value.

The new coins could be deposited and exchanged with credits known simply as *bank money*, based *not* on the face value of the coins—but on the purity of the metal's weight or standardized metallic value of the Dutch guilders. Thus, a perfectly uniform coinage was created from a variety of other national coin issues. The new paper *bank money* was backed by a standardized coinage, and along with its convenience, security, and a guarantee by the city government of Amsterdam. It caused the bank coins to trade at a premium or "*agio*" over all other coins. The premium varied 4 to 6 ½ percent which represented the depreciation and normal wear rate of the deposited coin below its nominal or face value.[8] Essentially, the convenience of a secure paper currency likewise held a premium of 4 to 6 percent over other precious metal coins—a historical first for the preference of paper money over precious metal coins.

The Bank of Amsterdam was the first public bank to offer ledger accounts not directly convertible to coin. One merchant could credit or debit their account with another merchant if both were customers of the bank. This action alone attracted many merchants to become bank customers. The Bank of Amsterdam was limited to exchange and deposits of capital, but by 1614, it was legally allowed to become a lending bank. It could now offer full commercial capital and financial services throughout the Netherlands, and the first to issue private bonds to purchase other foreign government debts.[10]

Eventually, the bank established its paper bank notes allowing merchants to set up accounts (for a fee) in a bank currency note backed by standardized Dutch guilders. The inconvenience of exchanging large sums of precious metal coins was solved, and the bank became a huge success among merchants and traders. A merchant could make a payment to another simply by arranging for his account at the bank to be debited and the counterparty's account to be credited. The bank pioneered the system of transfers between account holders (for a fee) that we commonly take for granted in currency transactions today.[9]

The Bank of Amsterdam perfected the main negotiable instrument of trade the "*bill of exchange*" commonly used to expedite foreign money payments in any international transaction among various banks. A bill of exchange is a written order by one person to his bank to pay the bearer of another bank a specific sum on a specific date or commercial delivery. A buyer could deposit money into his bank account to be paid to the seller upon the merchant's receipt of the delivered goods. Typically, a "*bill of lading*" acted as the signed receipt that the goods were accepted by the buyer and the seller could then redeem or cash-in his receipt. The seller's bill of exchange verified that money was held by the bank for payment. However, the bank or creditor rarely held on to the maturity of the bill of exchange preferring to sell it, or otherwise use it to pay off other debts, mainly due to the time vagaries of unreliable transportation.

The Bank of Amsterdam became the only bank to buy, discount, and sell bills of exchange thus freeing up capital and enhancing further expansion of commercial activity among merchants and traders. The country and economy flourished with a new source of capital! By the latter half of the 17th century, many wealthy merchant families moved away from trade and commodities into speculative financial ventures such as the trade in commodity values (futures), the offer of shares in joint stock companies, privately held currency exchanges, and various types of insurance. Once the providence of Jewish financiers, the Protestant break from the Roman Church's restrictions on usury allowed the Bank of Amsterdam to operate in the open public market—yet another historical first.[11]

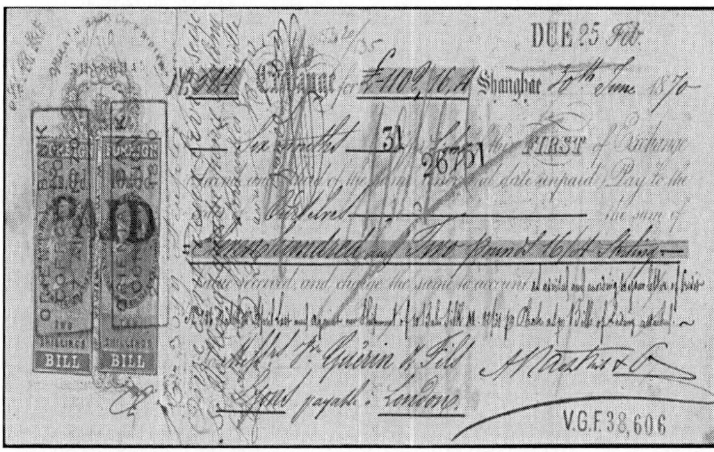

Figure 9-5 *A "Bill of Exchange" of 1870 with a London Revenue Stamp marked "Paid." Public domain*

The Bank of Amsterdam adopted the *guilder* as its standard coinage in a transition from the *florin* coins of Florence, and the *ducat* coins of Venice, Italy. The guilder became internationally accepted in A.D. 1517. *Gulden* was a generic European term used in reference to all gold coins. In Renaissance Europe, many states shared their florin or ducat coins with other neighboring states based on the metal content and purity which often varied significantly. Over time much of the coinage became debased, chipped, worn, broken to make change, illicitly scrapped or filed down. A new stock of freshly minted coins became more valuable than the older worn coins. The difference in value, both perceived and real, is the "*agio*." An *agio* (from the Italian *aggio*) is a term for the discount or premium for the exchange rate of currencies. Most European countries used a gold standard and tried, often unsuccessfully, to keep a uniform point of fineness. For example, a newly minted English sovereign coin was in a fixed relation (thereabouts) with a French ducat or a German florin.[12] The *agio* also occurred between the value of gold and silver coins within the same country if both metals were of legal tender.

Figure 9-6 *Netherlands Silver 3 Guilder, 1794. A guilder coin in good condition was perceived of higher value or "agio." The obverse illustrates the goddess Athena with her left arm resting on a large book on top of a pedestal. In her left hand, she holds a spear peacefully pointed downwards. The legend translates to "We defend the one and are protected by the other." The "one" is the helmet and spear of Athena, and the other is the book on the pedestal, which likely is the Christian Bible of that era. The reverse depicts a shield with a crown, in the middle of the shield is a lion holding seven arrows which represented the seven provinces of the Netherlands. The legend is translated as "Silver Coin of the United Netherlands of Holland." OTRS Attribution: Numisantica, www.numinantica.com*

The Bank of Amsterdam began with offices in city hall and soon became the central hub for commercial credit and insurance. Amsterdam was a major port city in Northern Europe, and the Dutch merchants generated bills of exchange in various foreign currencies. Merchants from all over Europe preferred bills of exchange quoted and bought on the secure Amsterdam exchange. The Dutch bankers revolutionized foreign exchange trading particularly if the transactions were backed by official licenses, various marine insurance contracts, and other security-oriented transportation and administrative documents.

The city of Amsterdam became a commercial information hub or a de facto "*entrepôt*" which is a port city were goods are brought for import and export and further processed for collection and distribution. Transportation, at the time, was slow, expensive, irregular and the supply and demand of goods erratic and unpredictable. These circumstantial risks put a premium on defining the fair market price of each commodity along with clarifying the costs of storage, transport, and insurance, among other transactional costs. One derivative of the primary function of physical distribution was the ability to assess supply and demand and therefore post a fair price.[13] Modern-day global financial institutions and technology companies now provide the role of an *entrepôt* in world trade, along with just a few modern port cities of Rotterdam, New York, Los Angeles, Singapore and Hong Kong. Internet websites like Amazon and E-Bay, or dominant retailers like Walmart, now provide their clients with valuable pricing data like the historical role that Amsterdam provided as an early entrepôt port city.

Futures Contracts on Tulips

Throughout the 17th century, precious metals from Japan and the *New World* were channeled into Europe creating inflation and price increases. Japanese silver mining production expanded from trade with the Dutch East Indies Company, which had a virtual monopoly on trade with Japan from 1624 to 1853. Large quantities of bullion also arrived in Europe from the Spanish and Portuguese conquests in the Americas.

The European monarchies tempered rampant inflation by debasing the purity of their coinage while expanding the quantity of their coins. However, the Bank of Amsterdam offered a sound haven with a money policy backed by 100 percent gold or silver backed coinage and paper currency. Immense quantities of precious metals found their way to Holland with a corresponding rapid rise in prices. The increased supply of precious metals and coins fostered an atmosphere of speculation and malinvestments which led to the first recorded European financial panic and a speculative bubble. The monetary bubble formed around the Dutch fondness for—tulips.[14]

A curious mania of buying tulips at ever higher prices consumed much of Holland during the 1630s. Tulip trading clubs were organized not only for the beauty of the flower—but more so as an effective way to keep up with the monetary inflation of European currencies and to smooth financial transactions in their trade. Dutch interest rates had sharply declined, allowing the futures market to be traded with little or no required margin. In 1636, an official futures market developed for the tulip market with trade taking place in taverns by groups known as "*colleges*" with rules governing the bidding and fees of futures contracts. Speculators piled in as they could borrow to trade with no required margin. Neither the buyer nor seller of a futures contract intends to take physical delivery, but only to speculate on the difference between the contract and expected settlement price at some future date. The boom came to bust in 1637 as the market collapsed and growers could not find buyers or recover money owed them by those under contract. The Court of Holland judged the tulip contract to be speculative bets under Roman law and canceled all the contracts leaving many of the growers and traders to bankruptcy.[15]

The Exposed Secrets of Finance

Financial innovations both in services and products (e.g., insurance, stocks, derivatives, etc.) were the covert practice of Jewish traders and financiers throughout 16th century Europe. The origins are due to usury laws first introduced to the West by the ancient Greek philosopher Aristotle. These activities were first fully explained by a Sephardic Jew, Joseph de la Vega in his 1688 book *Confusion of Confusions,* originally published in Amsterdam. The religious expulsion of Jews from Spain, along with the Protestant reforms in Holland, led him to take a job at the Bank of Amsterdam. Notably, he dedicated his book to the *stadtholder* William of Orange of Holland—soon to become King William of England. His stated purpose was to "*describe business which was, on the whole, most honest and useful—and to describe the tricks that rascals knew how to employ in business.*" [16]

Although speculation in goods has always existed, the trade and speculation in stocks and equities were indeed new to the average person of the 16th century Protestant Europe. Joseph de la Vega provided the first insiders' ethical and moral look into how these new financial products: stocks, options, futures, and all sorts of hedges and the laying odds, were transacted. He viewed them from an economic, monetary, and personal perspective. The first and oldest book ever written on the stock exchange business, it takes the form of an insightful dialogue between a philosopher, a merchant, and a shareholder.

The decline of the Dutch Golden Age was primarily attributed to the issuance of private bonds to foreign governments. Bonds are a surety for the guaranteed reimbursement if the principal holder fails to make payment. The Venetians, in the 1100s, were first noted for their issuance of bonds (*presiti*) by their government to its citizens primarily to fund local wars. Bonds issued to other foreign governments were introduced by the Bank of Amsterdam in 1517 with a guarantee underwritten by the city of Amsterdam. King William brought to England many of the Dutch financial innovations and, in short order, made the questionable indebtedness of England equal to the creditworthiness of the Netherlands. Enormous amounts of foreign direct investment, backed by the Bank of Amsterdam's bond and stock markets, flooded into England from the overstuffed capital markets of Holland. It also provided an escape route by the Dutch elite from their ever more dangerous French neighbors. This auspicious and well-timed event brought enormous investment and necessary capital to England which largely financed and expedited the Industrial Revolution of the mid-17th century.

The Bank of Amsterdam was committed, from the time of its creation, to continually maintain a 100 percent reserve ratio on *demand* deposits. As evident from its account history of over one hundred fifty years, the Bank scrupulously fulfilled the commitment upon which it was founded. Noted for its ability to handle any demand from its depositors for the return of their money, it became a refuge for capital fleeing inflationist speculation in other countries. The prestige of the Bank grew throughout Europe and beyond. David Hume, the Scottish philosopher and historian, noted the success of the Bank of Amsterdam in his book *Political Discourses* published in Edinburgh in 1752. His opposition to fiat paper money was resolved based on a 100 percent cash reserve bank policy.

In the 1780s, the bank systematically violated this legal principle to provide large loans to the British government, the Dutch East India Company, and to its municipality of Amsterdam, among other violations. A small committee of Amsterdam city officials was placed in charge of the bank from its founding. They kept the affairs of the bank secret from its depositors, who eventually learned they could not redeem their deposits. In 1819, several years after the Napoleonic Wars—the Bank of Amsterdam failed when it couldn't make good on withdrawals. The Fourth Anglo-Dutch War (1780 to 1784) ended the Golden Age of Holland as the Dutch saw their foreign investments lose value and the savings by the Dutch investors dry up.[17]

The end of the Dutch Golden Age was foretold by Pieter de La Court in the bestselling book of its day *Interest van Holland* published in 1662. He was critical of monopolies like that of the East India Companies and the consolidation of worker guilds. He watched as craftsmen, artisans, and merchants began as something akin to professional associations and trade unions—only to later evolve into monopolistic and restrictive trade cartels. The guilds often depended upon "patent letters" provided by the monarch or other authority to enforce the flow of trade. Eventually, the apprentice structure and craft "certification" led to self-serving restrictions on who and how many apprenticeships were allowed.

The City of London in 1516 granted the status of guilds based on the Lord Mayor of the time. Soon, the ranks had grown to well over a hundred different specialized guilds. They were given public charters to incorporate and soon consolidated into the "Great 12 Livery Companies" of the City which controlled every aspect of daily life and trade. Each of the 12 Great Companies had their buildings. The Mercers' Company (merchants), the Draper's Company (cloth), the Fishmonger's, and The Goldsmiths Companies, etc. still today maintain their economic clout within the City of London.[18] The lack of competition was obvious to La Court and inspirational fodder to the free market ideals of Adam Smith and the Austrian School of Economics.

Since the Glorious Revolution of 1688, the Dutch Republic and Great Britain had shared a co-monarchy. However, the Dutch soon became junior partners to the dominance of the British finally ending with the pro-British stance of King William V in 1806. The British had expanded their naval warships, excelled at trade based on their rapidly growing industrialization, adopted financial and improved monetary expansion originally learned from the Dutch, and won many economic concessions from their wars with other countries. Standing by were the Dutch people who silently watched as the British expanded both their empire and economy by winning the War of Austrian Succession and the Seven Years' War. The Dutch also remained neutral and sidelined by the British colonization of North America.

Emperor Napoleon Bonaparte hammered the nail in the coffin of the Dutch Republic as it was annexed to France in 1813. Most of the Dutch coinage was melted for its intrinsic metallic value and re-stamped into French francs. Later, the defeat of Napoleon by the Duke of Wellington's Anglo-allied army brought what was left of the French francs back to the British Empire.

The Nugget

Astonishing that a small country of only two million people, a third the size of Indiana, and comprised of seven united provinces each with their own distinctive language, would eventually command global wealth for nearly two centuries! A fortunate confluence of cultural factors, from a new work ethic to a cooperative and responsive government, formed the foundation of a successful monetary system and the envy of world commerce. That envy was smartly seized upon by the British Empire—as money goes to where it is most wanted.

CHAPTER TEN

THE UNITED KINGDOM & THE WIZARD OF THE GOLD STANDARD

Keywords: pound sterling; mercantilism; the gold standard; classical economics; Royal African Company (RAC): "letters patent"

> "I can calculate the motion of the heavenly bodies, but not the madness of people."
>
> Sir Isaac Newton, Master of the Royal Mint.

Sir Isaac Newton is today recognized and remembered for his laws of motion, optics, and universal gravitation. Little known by many, however, is his pivotal role in significantly accelerating the Industrial Revolution. As a physicist and mathematician, the 17th century scholar also served in the Parliament of England representing Cambridge University. He later moved to London as the Warden of the Royal Mint (A.D. 1692) and assigned to protect the currency from counterfeiting at the request of King William. Working under the Chancellor of the Exchequer, he soon earned the title of "Master of the Royal Mint," a position he held for thirty years. He took his job seriously and vowed to reform the currency and discipline counterfeiters and clippers who scraped (clipped) the edges of gold and silver coins to filch the metal. He successfully prosecuted, and severely punished, 28 "*coiners*" for various forms of currency debasement and outright counterfeiting. [1]

Isaac Newton, as Master of the Royal Mint, was responsible for the establishment of a standardized monetary system that many countries would adopt for over 200 years and set the stage for classical economic theory. He pegged a fixed amount of British currency to one ounce of gold. Prior to this time, any gold or silver coin was accepted as payment, based on its apparent purity and visible condition. The bi-metallic system created a series of complications and disputes in establishing a fixed exchange rate. The new monetary policy established a gold exchange standard based on a government guarantee of a fixed exchange rate, regardless of what type of officially backed notes or coins were used as a means of exchange. A gradual move to a classical gold standard began as other nations adjusted their currencies to a national standard exchange rate—or just fixed their currency to the established British exchange rate. Newton created a de facto currency standard where the value of the means of exchange has a fixed external value explicitly benchmarked to gold, independent of the inherent value of the means of exchange itself. He presented his clearly reasoned approach to Parliament on September 21, 1717.[2, 3]

The new monetary system provided a stable and secure method for merchants to convert currencies between nations, giving Britain a jumpstart in international trade and setting the stage for its leadership in the Industrial Revolution of the 1700s. Newton saw, what others would come to see: pegging currencies to an official gold standard expands and facilitates trade, investment, and trust between merchants and furthers cooperation among the nations involved. The fixed exchange rate allows for more transparency over the effects of inflation as it constrains a government from using domestic monetary policy to achieve macroeconomic stability.

The sovereign manipulation of the value of a nation's currency was now open for all to see. The gold exchange standard encouraged nations to avoid monetary manipulation by way of inflation and to apply sound fiscal management for the improvement of the economy and the wealth of its people. The Bank of England wittingly sanctioned and enforced a global gold standard which helped establish long-term price stability over several centuries of its existence. Although wartime situations and other fiscal emergencies briefly halted the practice, a return to the gold exchange standard soon reoccurred based on its merits in facilitating global trade.

Since medieval times, English currency had always found its way to some form of physical debasement. The origin of the British term "sterling silver" began with the reign of King Offa of Mercia (A.D. 757 to 796). A powerful Anglo-Saxon king, he smartly adopted the French King Charlemagne's system of 240 pennies to a pound of silver—which became the standard unit of coinage in England. [4] Sterling silver is said to be derived from the iridescent glitter of starlings as they take flight in the morning sky. Fine and softer pure silver was traditionally used until 1158 when King Henry II based the new coinage on 92.5 percent silver. The addition of tin or lead made for a harder and more durable coin. By the reign of Henry III, the new *silver long-cross penny* was introduced with clearer markings to prevent clipping. The new penny made it easy to cut the coin into halves and quarters to make change.

Figure 10-1 Left *King Offa of Mercia penny (circa A.D. 757-796) Public domain.*
Figure 10-2 Right *Long-cross penny of Henry III (A.D. 1216-1272) OTRS Attribution: Numisantica, www.numinantica.com*

The English silver penny was constantly recast, stamped, and revalued during the reigns of numerous monarchs. The penny was often found to be underweight because of clipping, dividing the coin to make change, and the addition of other base metals to expand the supply of coinage (providing the monarch more revenue). New terms and designs for the coins were based on the demand for a currency to fit the current supply and demand for the traded goods and services of the time. The English gave affectionate names to a variety of new coin denominations. The pound itself was fondly called a "*quid*" which is Latin for "*something.*" Hence the saying "*quid pro quo*" which is Latin for "*something for something*" or "*this for that*" as in a money exchange transaction. Despite the debasements, many European countries admired the English currency and copied it extensively, often with lesser amounts of gold or silver. The stronger the currency, based on the given perceptions of the strength of the government and culture, along with the reality and trustworthiness of the metal content, provided a trading advantage to the English merchants with other nations.

The Dutch William of Orange, upon his ascent to the British throne from the Netherlands, found the English economy and currency to be in serious disarray. King William granted a Royal Charter to create and establish the Bank of England to serve the government along with other commercial banks. The Bank was privately owned by stockholders from its foundation in 1694 until it was nationalized in 1946. (In 1998, it became an independent public organization owned by the Treasury Solicitor on behalf of the government with a monopoly to issue banknotes in England and Wales and to regulate commercial banks in Scotland and Ireland). King William found the country was on a bi-metallic currency standard with silver used by its citizens, and gold for sovereign foreign exchange between governments and for large commercial purposes. Silver traded at a ratio of 15:1 to gold and the ratio fluctuated among countries depending on supply and demand. The fluctuating disparity between two metal markets created an opportunity to profit from the difference in prices, otherwise termed—arbitrage. The new world was a budding source of precious metals constantly flowing into sovereign European coffers. Today, the silver to gold ratio is around an 81:1.

In 1662, the Royal Mint had largely stopped the clipping of coins by introducing engraved, decorated, and milled edges. They also tried to prohibit the shipping of raw bullion outside of the country. Early on, the Bank of Amsterdam had become a legal repository for coins of other countries. The Bank would issue a banknote, take the old clipped, debased, and worn coins, and recast them into more refined forms of metal coinage, thus increasing their value. The value of silver became greater in Paris and Amsterdam than the face value in London. The Royal Mint had inadvertently triggered the counterfeiting of its currency, as forging coins and moving them outside the country was the easiest way for criminals to avoid prosecution. Vast quantities of silver coins were melted, recast in counterfeit die stamps and molds, and illegally shipped abroad. The Great Re-Coinage Act of 1696, supported by Newton, made counterfeiting an act of high treason, resulting in the convicted felon being hanged, drawn and quartered. A condemned traitor was hanged (almost to the point of death), emasculated, disemboweled, beheaded, quartered, and prominently displayed as a warning to others.[5] Despite all of that, counterfeiting remained a popular trade.

Figure 10-3 Left *Isaac Newton on a Halfpenny 1793 Public domain.*
Figure 10-4 Right *Milled and stamped edges on British currency Public domain*

It proved impossible to maintain a system based on both gold and silver due to the variation of bullion prices between the two metals. Silver is much easier to access, mine and mint. In practice, silver was usually worth more melted down into silver ingots and cast into jewelry, sterling silver tableware, or used by industry. England committed itself to the gold standard and found that the only way to maintain silver as a coin was to reduce the silver content so that the nominal value was more than the bullion of the same weight. By the late 17th century, 50 percent of silver was missing from British coins. Historically, this was comparable to the Roman Empire's debasement of its silver coins. Over time, people began to distrust the value of the coin. The debate over how to avert a monetary crisis arose after the passage of the Re-Coinage Act of 1696. Prior to that time, the British treasury secretary planned to melt down and remint all its coins in order to devalue the currency to help pay for the government's financial mess. John Locke, the political statesman and philosopher, and Isaac Newton teamed up to oppose the planned devaluation. They argued that this was a violation of *natural law* equivalent to the arbitrary seizure of property. They won this argument.

The Re-Coinage Act of 1696 proclaimed that a counterfeit or clipped coin would no longer be legal tender and no longer accepted for tax payments. Isaac Newton had discovered that 20 percent of the coins sampled were counterfeit. Draconian enforcement called for a £500 fine for anyone caught with a clipped or counterfeit coin. The offender would also be branded on the right cheek with a capital "R" as if stamped by the Royal Mint. Furthermore, only professional goldsmiths, under the strict supervision of the Royal Mint, could buy and sell bullion.

The Royal Mint was unprepared for the depositors who flocked to the Bank of England for the coins to conduct everyday transactions. The lack of coins led to a monetary contraction and subsequent massive unemployment, poverty, and civil unrest. The alternative use of the gold guinea, the smallest gold coin, and various forms of credit provided the only remaining liquidity in the market. At the height of the crisis, news that the Duke of Beaufort was forced to pay for dinner by entering his name in a book was the late 17th century equivalent of a social media tweet going viral.[6]

The Dawn of a Gold Exchange Standard

Parliament's decision not to devalue the currency was a victory for advocates of a stable and sound money system. In 1717, Isaac Newton, then Master of the Royal Mint, by royal proclamation and with the full support of Parliament, fixed the British pound to one ounce of gold. One ounce of gold was pegged by Newton as equal to £3.17s.10$^{1}/_{2}$ d. (three pounds, seventeen shillings and ten and one-half pence) or nearly four pounds to an ounce. Just shy of £4 (by less than three shillings) the difference provided a distribution and transaction fee to the bank for the conversion of gold backed by the bank's gold reserves. Psychologically it would provide an incentive to buy into the convenience of a banknote and a three-shilling disincentive to cash it back in for gold bullion.

The idea of pegging a currency to a set weight of gold was born in the early 17th century when a new gold coin was introduced to Great Britain—the 22-karat fine gold "*guinea.*" It was eventually fixed in weight at $44^{1/}{}_2$ guineas to the troy pound (1 troy pound = 12 troy ounces ~ 373.24 grams – or about a ¼ ounce of gold per guinea). The coin's value varied considerably until 1717 when, by royal decree at the behest of Isaac Newton, it was fixed at 21 shillings (equal to 1.05 pounds). The customer would now pay the up-front transaction fee for conversion to paper currency. Guineas offered a psychological edge over the common pound, based on the slightly added value and latest image of the monarch. Merchants sent silver abroad in payments for imports, while goods for export abroad were paid for in gold by the foreign customer. Therefore, silver flowed out of the country and gold flowed in, leading to a situation where Great Britain was effectively on a solid gold standard. [7]

The beggar-thy-neighbor era of mercantilism was gradually replaced by Isaac Newton's new gold standard, which would give rise to the theory of classical economics soon forwarded by Adam Smith. Mercantilism was the widely accepted and standard practice of governments from 1500 to 1750. It advocated government regulation of the nation's economy to bolster the power of the state. The theory posited that the purpose of international trade was to acquire bullion by running a trade surplus (a positive balance of payments) with other nations. Mercantilism promoted creative fiscal protectionist practices that stymied free trade and complicated industrial growth. The more gold and silver in the government treasury the better off the nation. This is otherwise known as the Golden Rule: "*He who owns the gold—rules*."

Mercantilism set the groundwork for many of the European wars and foreign conquests aimed at acquiring gold and silver. The results of mercantilism are personified by King Louis XIV of France with his opulent Palace of Versailles, the excesses of King Henry the VIII at Hampton Court Palace, and by other monarchs with their castles built on hoarded and confiscated precious metals. Whether the citizens prospered is of course highly debatable, if not deplorable, but then there was no other alternative economic system at hand. Mercantilism was repudiated by economists like Adam Smith and David Ricardo.

The theory of classical economics was first advanced by Adam Smith. His theory argues that each nation has a comparative advantage based on its unique specialization of labor and resources. The emphasis on price stability among currencies based on a gold standard complemented the theory of comparative advantage. It is still common today, however, for one country to adopt fiscally deceptive practices that can manipulate a nation's trade surplus over that of the fair value of its currency—even based on a gold standard. Countries in economic crisis often revert to mercantilist trade policies that manipulate currencies to their advantage. Eventually, mismanagement of currency often results in a deferred calamity or a serious financial bubble obvious to all.

King Charles and the Goldsmith's Tally Sticks

In the 1620s, during the reign of Charles I, the London Goldsmiths Company (a chartered guild of goldsmiths) had pioneered the concept of "fractional reserve banking." The gold and silver stored in their vaults was collateral to issue individual "bearer receipts" that the depositor could use as a convenient and secure payment method without lugging heavy coins. The bearer receipts would soon become "banknotes" as one gold coin was as good as any other based on its metal content and fineness. The goldsmiths of London soon found that they could lend more out in banknotes than they had gold reserves needed for daily withdrawal by depositors. The fractional reserve made them very wealthy—if only they could avoid a bank run. One of the safest bets was lending money to the king; the landed gentry and affluent merchant traders. The Bank of England would initially set the fractional reserve ratio of 2:1, with the intent to keep half of the value it lent out in their faults as a reserve. [9, 10]

The "Divine Right of Kings" was restored to Charles II after the beheading of his father Charles I during the English Civil War. King Charles II, however, had to beg Parliament for money, as Parliament had expressly banned usury or the charging of interest on borrowed money. The Great Plague (1663) and the Great Fire of London (1666) had emptied the King's purse just as the Dutch fleet was spotted massing off the Thames Estuary in preparation for an invasion. To avoid strict usury laws, Charles sold his nation's future tax receipts at a discount to the goldsmiths, thus avoiding the payment of interest. He revived the use of "Tally Sticks," first introduced to England by King Henry II in the 1100s, to keep track of recording tax payments. Charles II successfully circumvented Parliament by selling government debt based on future tax receipts, a questionable practice widely used to this day, and accumulated numerous tally sticks based on public debt.[11]

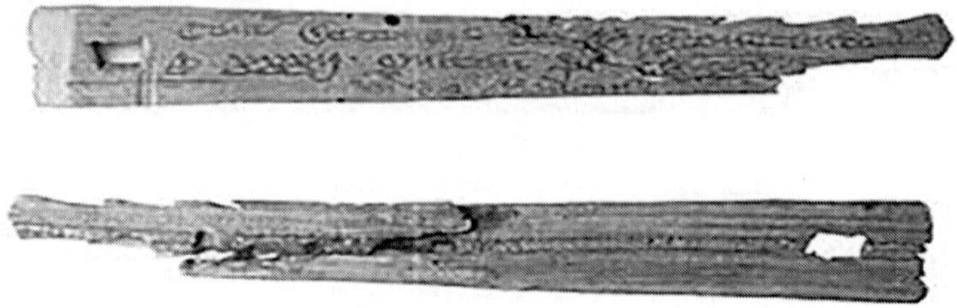

Figure 10-5 *Medieval English split tally stick. The handle was called the "stock" for those advancing the funds and the other half the "foil" for what is owed. The term "stock" evolved into stock offered by public traded corporations as in the word "stock market." (CC By-SA-2.0)*

The Advent of the "Letters Patent"

To obtain legal protection against potential infringers of new and inventive devices, the Venetian Republic is regarded as the first to introduce a simple statutory patent system with the passage of the Venetian Patent Statute of 1450. The patents were mostly in the field of glass making and were protected for ten years. The Venetians sought similar patent protections as they pioneered the idea of a patent system to other countries.[12] In contrast, royal charters were granted by monarchs for perpetual use for cities, universities, and learned societies. The granting of a letters patents and royal charters often gave way to the emergence of craft and trade associations, or *guilds,* to retain member ownership of the tools of their trade. The first of the medieval guilds can be traced to the University of Bologna founded in A.D. 1088, and Oxford in 1096.

The English patent system evolved into the first modern patent system to recognize *intellectual property,* or intangible creations of the human intellect, to stimulate invention. Historians recognize this as the crucial legal component upon which the Industrial Revolution would emerge and flourish. [13] Queen Elizabeth I (from 1561 to 1590) granted about 50 patents whereby the recipients were provided monopolies in the manufacture and sale of such items as soap, leather, salt, glass, knives, sailcloth, iron, and paper. [14]

In 1623, Parliament usurped the discretion of the monarchy and passed the Statute of Monopolies Act that restricted the King's exclusive power to issue a letters patent to inventors or founders of original inventions. The issuance of a letters patent was slowly incorporated into the statutes and by the court of law.

James Puckle's autocannon (1718) was one of the first inventions that required a specification for a patent. This legalized approach was followed by many other inventors including James Watt (steam engines), Richard Trevithick (locomotives), and Edmund Cartwright (the power loom). Through a slow process of the judicial interpretation of the law, and influenced by the philosopher John Locke, the granting of patents as a form of intellectual property became a human right, rather than a simple economic privilege. The English legal system became the foundation for patent law in countries with a heritage in common law. Many founders and inventors were granted a letters patent as private investors happily provided the less risky capital to kick-start the Industrial Revolution. The comparably tiny nation of Britain, with just eight million people in 1750, embarked upon a remarkable economic expansion that would propel it to global domination in little more than a century.

The Royal African Company (RAC)

Between 1663 and 1813, the Bank of England minted a new gold coin—the guinea. It was named after the Guinea Coast in West Africa where the British first procured most of their foreign gold. Silver and lead were the primary metals mined in England and the discovery of gold provided for highly welcomed revenue. King Charles II and his brother James, the Duke of York, granted a royal charter to the *Company of Royal Adventurers Trading to Africa* otherwise known as the Royal African Company (RAC). It was established to exploit the West African gold fields on the Gambia River but soon engaged in other commodities including the lucrative slave trade. England was nearly bankrupt, and any source of revenue was considered acceptable. [15]

The slave trade was well established in Africa many years prior to the British arrival. Slavery was a commonplace result of early Muslim conquests, the enslavement by local tribes of their enemies, and of dealing with common debtors and criminals. African tribes conveniently sold off their captured enemies and criminals simply to get rid of them. While the Spanish and Portuguese purchased and then resold slaves as hard labor to South America, the RAC traded slaves as "indentured servants" along with other commodities using the Virginia Company of London. Under the protection of the British Navy, the RAC transported across the Atlantic some 5,000 slaves annually between 1672 and 1689, which later increased to an estimated 90,000 to 100,000 slaves annually. The slaves were branded on their backs with "*DY*" for the Duke of York (King Charles II's brother) until 1685. Later, when King James II ascended the throne, the slaves were branded on their chests with "*RAC*." The Virginia Company of London was established under British royal charter to settle and manage Jamestown, Virginia. The profits from the slave trade made an enormous contribution to the financial power of those who controlled the City of London, a designated one-square-mile financial district within the city of London. The City elects its mayor and serves as the financial headquarters for many merchant banks to this day.[16]

The RAC provided gold from Africa to the Royal Mint from 1668 to 1772. By 1731, RAC had completely abandoned the slave trade and returned to the trading of gold and commodities, as it had lost its chartered monopoly on slave trading. The slave trade was now open to any English merchant who paid a 10 percent levy to the Virginia Company on goods or slaves exported from Africa. The number of slaves transported by English ships, however, increased dramatically even after RAC's exit from the slave trade.

Figure 10-6 *Depicted on this guinea gold coin is King James II: Iacobvs II Dei Gratia (James II by the Grace of God) The obverse is the logo for the Royal African Company known as "The Elephant and Castle," which is a major road junction in Central London derived from a local coaching inn or transportation hub. It resides within the City of London. Public domain*

William Wilberforce, an independent Member of Parliament from Yorkshire, lead the movement by English abolitionists to stop slavery—the first national attempt in recorded history. The Slave Trade Act of 1807 charged the Royal Navy to stop anyone from trafficking slaves by sea. The Act was immediately signed by the heads of many nations, including President Thomas Jefferson who insisted that he be second in line to sign it. However, slavery was not abolished in Britain until the passage of the Slavery Abolition Act of 1833—again led by William Wilberforce and the English abolitionists. [16]

The Corn Laws

Despite economic expansion and trade, the English national debt had increased, and the gold standard was briefly discontinued. A series of bad harvests suddenly inflated food prices, resulting in civil riots in 1801–2, as well as a war with France. When trade resumed with Europe after the Napoleonic Wars, corn prices halved. Parliament passed the Corn Laws of 1815 to protect farmers and keep the price of domestic grain from falling. The unintended consequence was to depress the domestic market for manufactured goods as people had to use all their ready money just to buy food. Likewise, European countries, which relied on exporting corn to Britain to buy British manufactured goods, were no longer able to afford to do so.

The Corn Laws and the suppressed use of silver led to a shortage of coins throughout the country. The alternative use of paper money gradually moved to fixed denomination banknotes. Previous handwritten bearer notes or receipts were provided to those who deposited gold. The £ sign and the first digit were printed, with other numerals added by hand, as were the name of the payee, the cashier's signature, the date and the number. Notes allowed for uneven amounts, but the majority were for round sums.

By 1745, printed notes were found in denominations ranging from £20 to £1,000. Most people, however, went through life without ever seeing one, as the average annual income during this time was less than £20. By 1797 the Bank was running short of gold and issued £1 and £2 notes instead. The Bank Charter Act of 1844 provided the Bank of England, a monopoly as the sole provider of banknotes. [17]

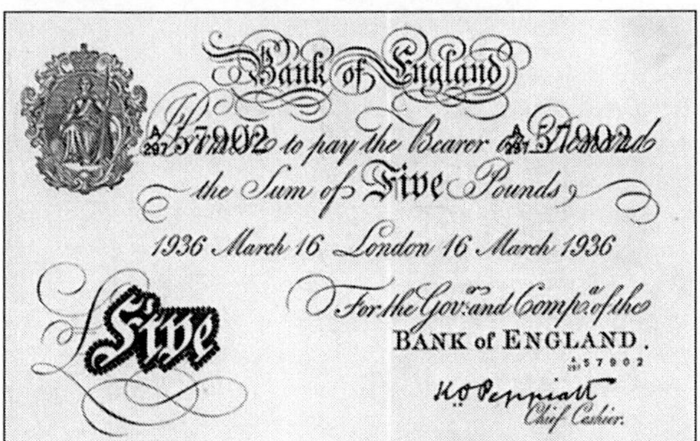

Figure 10-7. *Banknote. Public domain*

The Great Re-Coinage Act of 1816

Military campaigns, as well as economic trade issues, in the 18th century, contributed to British financial instability. Britain financed a series of coalitions opposed to the regimes of the French Revolutionary Wars (1792 to 1802) and the Napoleonic Wars (1803 to1815). King William, along with his Dutch entourage and investors, had long been enemies of the French. In 1810, Napoleon annexed Holland to the French Empire, further enraging the British aristocracy. Large cash subsidies were given to Austria, Prussia, and Russia for their armies to use to defeat Napoleon. The British government needed to find a way to further stabilize its currency.

King George III had lost the American colonies and now saw the possibility of a French conquest at his doorstep. Through the Re-Coinage Act of 1816, the Royal Mint reintroduced silver coinage only for sums of legal tender up to £2. It also changed the worth of a guinea from 21 shillings to a slightly lighter-weight coin worth 20 shillings. This propelled a flood of new coins into the economy. Crowns and half-crowns were now stamped with the famous image of St. George & the Dragon that was designed by the Italian engraver Benedetto Pistrucci.[18] Also crafted was a portrait of King George III that came to be known by collectors as "bull-head George." The design met so much public hostility, as the King was widely known to be mentally insane, that the coin was soon withdrawn.

Figure 10-8 Left: *Benedetto Pistrucci designed coins for Napoleon and the Pope. His designs won many awards and he soon became the Chief-engraver and Chief-medalist for the London Royal Mint. The depiction of St. George & the Dragon on the new English Crown refers to the Golden Legend. A fanciful legend in which the Christian St. George slays the evil dragon during the First Crusade. Public domain*
Figure 10-9 Right *King George III on a half-crown known as "bull-head George." The face value of a 1£ sovereign in 1816 with a total weight of 22 carats (91 $^{2}/_{3}$%) of 0.25682 ounces has the same purchasing power as £68.36 in 2016. One £ maintained a value of $5 USA dollars from 1817-1925 Public domain.* [18]

The Rothschild's family interests were called upon to lend money to fund the English who were fighting against Napoleon. Their family patriarch was Mayer Amschel Bauer Rothschild who founded the Rothschild (Red Shield) banking dynasty and is believed to be the ancestor of the wealthiest family in human history. A German Jewish banker, he is referred to as the founding father of international finance. [20] The banking firm of Jacob Oppenheimer taught the young Amschel foreign trade and currency exchange and he became known as a dealer in rare coins.

He won the patronage of German Prince Wilhelm of Hesse and in 1769 he became the "Court Factor." He handled the British funds in payment for 30,000 Hessian mercenaries to fight for the British in the American Revolutionary War. It was less expensive to hire German soldiers than to send more British troops. Business opportunities expanded rapidly following the French Revolution. His four sons would soon branch out across Europe, enabling them to profit from numerous opportunities, including that of financing Wellington's armies in Portugal which required the sourcing of large quantities of gold on behalf of the British government.

The timely payment in gold to the British troops incentivize them to defeat the unpaid and bedraggled French legion. Nathan Rothschild made his initial fortune by creating and selling British government bonds across Europe. The Rothschild family fortune was the largest in the world as they controlled key financial institutions. It was the London financier Nathan Rothschild who in 1810 voiced the oft-repeated saying: "*buy on the cannons, sell on the trumpets*." The maxim is commonly retold today on Wall Street as "*buy on the story—sell on the news.*"

The Rothschild family successfully built an intelligence network of agents and shippers across all of Europe. Their network of messengers and carrier pigeons kept them informed of military information even ahead of the military itself. The family kept close tabs on the British gold guineas they had lent to the king and secretly sent to the Duke of Wellington's army deployed in Portugal and Spain. The commissions earned on these financial transactions grew the Rothschild family fortune even more.

According to popular legend, when the Battle of Waterloo was being fought in 1815, other speculators watched the Rothschild's bond holdings to guess who would win. When Nathan began to sell some of his bonds before the war's end, it led everyone to believe that Napoleon had won the war and the speculators began to sell their bonds and stocks. Panic selling ensued, and after the prices crashed, Nathan Rothschild bought everything in sight—and made an immense profit.[20]

In 1821, the British Parliament formalized the gold standard by law, replacing the de facto standard earlier set by Isaac Newton. The United States and Germany officially enacted their gold standards in 1834. The U.S. adopted the eagle on its gold currency and Germany the Gold mark (*ℳ*). The German Hapsburg Empire used the Gold mark as legal tender from 1873 to 1914. It was distinguished from the fiat *Papiermark* (paper mark) which suffered a serious loss of value through hyperinflation following World War 1. The Gold mark was placed on a gold standard with 2,790 *ℳ* equal to 1 kilogram of pure gold, or approximately one Gold mark to one U.S. $0.25 quarter.[21]

The United States slightly devalued the price of gold to $20.67 per ounce from 1834 to where it remained until 1933. (Alexander Hamilton originally fixed one ounce of gold to $19.39). Other major counties officially adopted the new gold standard in the 1870s. The period from 1880 to 1914, known in its ideal form as the *classical gold standard*, was the time during which most countries adhered to varying ratios of gold to each currency. It was also a period of unprecedented economic growth and relatively free trade in goods, labor, and capital.[22]

The United States fixed the price of one ounce of gold at $20.67, while the United Kingdom set it at £3, 17s, 10 -1/2d. Thus, the dollar/pound exchange rate was perfectly computed. The fixed exchange rate of about $5 U.S. dollars per one English pound was referred to as the par exchange rate.[22] The convenience of an easy to determine exchange rate was advantageous to trade and business between the two countries. Under the classical gold exchange standard, constant trade deficits or surpluses were offset by the physical movement of gold from one nation's treasury to another to rebalance the fixed exchange rate. In practice, however, the ratio was rarely followed as national economies were expected to rebalance their currency in an open economy based on their balance of trade and fiscal prudence.

The gold standard provided a benchmark for long-term price stability between currencies. The Bank of England was adamant in reporting government manipulation of currencies and infractions by other nations. While nations pledged support to a pegged gold standard, they were often found to manipulate the exchange ratio to their advantage. Trade surpluses or deficits indicated which currencies were suspect or suspiciously inflated.

Currency manipulation by other countries only made the British currency more stable and preferred for use in trade. A regulated gold standard simply balanced the supply and demand of the currency without being fully dependent on holding metals. National inflation and interest rates were adjusted to the pegged price of gold.

Inspired by the success of Great Britain and the U.S., other nations began to follow their example, and by the 19th century, Germany, Italy, Spain, France, Russia, and Greece had adopted the international gold standard set by the United States and the United Kingdom. The shared currency standard helped facilitate world trade and broke down the barriers between nations that had heretofore been adversaries. Before World War I, the British shilling, French franc, German mark and Italian lira were all valued roughly equally–about four each to one U.S. dollar. However, while some central banks played by the rules of the gold standard, other nations reverted to quietly manipulating their fiscal policies to gain a trade and monetary advantage. Colonialization and monetary distrust between nations helped fuel the conflict leading up to WWI.

Colonial jealousies contributed to the unexpected outbreak of World War I which led to the brief cessation of the classical gold standard among nations. Countries reverted to their old mercantile practices. In response to the war, Germany floated massive bond issues, appealing to patriotism to pay for the war rather than hard cash. Kaiser Wilhelm II borrowed heavily from other nations to pay for the war effort. The Reichsbank suspended the redemption of banknotes for gold and gave out unbridled credit for more war-bond subscriptions. The U.S. reacted to the withdrawal by stockpiling European gold safely in its central bank. From August 1913 to August 1919 the U.S. stock of monetary gold increased 65 percent. Great Britain, in contrast, was more prudent in financing the war with Germany. London met the cost by raising taxes, primarily on those industries and groups that stood best to profit from the war.

British Currency

The "pound sterling" is unique to the U.K. currency as other nations use just the general term of "pound." Although there are many plausible explanations for the origin of the term, the Encyclopedia Britannica refers to silver coins known as "*sterlings*" that were issued by Saxon kingdoms. Some consider the origin of the term to come from starling birds as they flock and glitter into the morning sky. The pound sterling coins were minted 240 pence to one pound of silver dating back to King Charlemagne in A.D.

800. Large payments were weighed in pounds of sterling; a phase later shortened to pound sterling. Before the advent of decimalization in 1971, the pound was divided into 20 shillings, with each shilling worth 12 pence, hence 240 pence to a pound.

Figure 10-10 *The guinea coin depicts the co-monarchs King William and Queen Mary after the removal of King James II in the Glorious Revolution of 1688. From 1717 to 1816 the value was officially fixed at twenty-one shillings. The diameter of the coin was 1 inch (just over 25 mm) and was 22 karats or 0.9100 pure gold. The legend on the obverse reads MAG BR FR ET HIB REX ET REGINA (Of "Magna Britannia" Great Britain, "Francia" France and "Hibernia" Ireland King and Queen) The designers were James and Norbert Roettier. (CC By-SA-3.0) Classical Numismatic Group, Inc. http://www.cngcoins.com*

The pound sterling and the guinea both shared the same £ symbol. The guinea was worth £1.1s or one pound and one shilling (252 pence) or £1.05p. It was based on a 22-karat gold standard with 44-½ guineas to a troy pound. Twenty shillings equaled one pound, and each shilling was subdivided into twelve pennies, or pence, with one pound equal to 240 pence. The guinea was close to a pound by just 5 pence. The posting of prices in guineas made the price seem equal, however, the merchant received more money. The guinea became a popular coin as it was perceived to be a quarter of an ounce of gold (almost). One troy pound (comprised of 12 troy ounces versus today's 16 ounces) converted to 44-½ guineas. The troy ounce was later abolished by the British in the 19th century in favor of the 16-ounce pound.

The U.K. as a Global Financial Center

"*Time is money.*" The famous quotation is attributed to the American statesman and polymath Benjamin Franklin. During Franklin's day, however, there was *no* set standard benchmark time—not even by local time standards. Isaac Newton had set the classical gold standard to a finite measurement, whereas, time was still relative. Farmers set their own time according to the seasons, while shopkeepers, postal clerks, and railroad timekeepers often assumed various local times in use around the country and globally. While the compass and sextant were used by mariners to calculate solar time on the open seas, the advent of railroads proved a dilemma when traveling even short distances without an acceptable time standard.

Local “railway time” was first synchronized by large station time clocks in the early 1840s. The Shepherd Gate Clock, developed and patented by Charles Shepherd in 1852, was mounted on a wall at the Royal Greenwich Observatory in London for public view and displayed Greenwich Mean Time or GMT. It was an electric master clock that controlled a network of slave clocks throughout England. By 1866, the transatlantic cable sent clock signals to the United States.

The railway's use of timetabling gradually gave way to a series of statutes to establish Greenwich Mean Time, based on longitude and latitude. In 1687, Isaac Newton (again!) confirmed that the earth is an “oblate ellipsoid” giving a known meridian arc. In 1884, at the International Meridian Conference held in Washington, D.C., 22 countries voted to adopt the Greenwich prime meridian as a basis for the world’s time standard. London became the timekeeper of the U.K. financial markets and with it the capability of spanning both eastern and western financial hemispheres. London markets can process trades and currency transfers within a window of time between Berlin and New York while both markets are open.

Figure 10-11 *The Shepard Gate Clock “Where east meets west.” The Royal Observatory, London England. Public domain*

The political convention of a standard of time thus became an intangible geographical and ecological natural resource, allowing institutions to exploit it to their financial advantage. A long history of cultural evolution, trade, and currency transactions have placed the United Kingdom in the top tier of global financial centers.

British Currency and Nomenclature

The British conferred mostly affectionate names to their currencies. British novels like those of Arthur Conan Doyle, creator of Sherlock Holmes, made many references to the currency of that period. Below is a quick guide to British currency along with some slang terms. The terms were often used before decimalization took place on February 15, 1971, which is officially known as "*Decimal Day*" in the United Kingdom and Ireland.

Pound (£): Often called a "*sovereign*," as it is imprinted with the current Monarch's name or face. It takes the form of either a gold coin or a paper-note convertible to gold or silver. The slang term for a pound is a *quid*; £500 is a *monkey*, and £25 a *pony*, still terms to be heard in the English horserace business.

Shilling: The word derives from *skilling* an Anglo-Saxon accounting term meaning "*division*." This was the currency's workhorse, with 20 shillings equaling a pound. Often called the *bob*, it was used to buy food and household necessities. The shilling was typically silver or a composite of silver.

Penny: The plural is pence. There are twelve pence to a shilling and 240 pence in a pound. The penny was made of copper or other nonprecious metals.

Prior to decimalization: 4 farthings = 1 pence, 12 pence = 1 shilling, 2 schillings = 1 florin, 5 shillings = 1 crown, 20 shillings = 1 pound (sovereign) and 21 shillings = 1 guinea. Multiples and fractions of the pound, shilling and pence evolved as needed for transactions.

A *guinea* was often referred to as a "*yellow-boy*" for its gold content and was used for commercial transactions.

Half-crown: A coin worth 2.5 shillings
Tuppence: A coin worth 2 pence
Thrupence: A coin worth 3 pence

Groat: A coin worth 4 pence
Tanner: A coin worth 6 pence
Ha'penny: A coin worth 1/2 of a penny
Farthing: A coin worth 1/4 of a penny
Mite: A coin worth 1/8 of a penny

The Nugget

Sir Isaac Newton not only calculated the motion of heavenly bodies but attempted to solve what he termed as "*the madness of people*" with the repression of the sin of counterfeiting and the launch of a new gold exchange standard. His shrewd and logical monetary actions stabilized global currency transactions—which helped launch the Industrial Revolution.

The purchasing power of gold has been preserved over a remarkably long period. The same quantity of gold that a Roman centurion earned annually under Emperor Augustus (27 B.C. to A.D. 14) would cover one year's pay ($46,500 to $65,000) for a U.S. Army captain today.[22] Gold has retained its value and can be purchased and sold instantly on the open and transparent financial markets.

CHAPTER ELEVEN

THE AMERICAN EXPERIENCE: A CURRENCY & CULTURE IN TRANSITION, PART I

Keywords: wampum; Spanish pillar dollar; "$" symbol; U.S. banking system; era of free banking; "cross of gold."

"An investment in knowledge pays the best interest."
Benjamin Franklin, American statesman.

Before the American Revolution, the Pilgrims, Puritans, Virginians, and other mainly English colonial settlers in North America all faced a chronic shortage of currency due to the British mercantilist policies toward the colonies. The restricted access to British currency meant that the bulk of economic transactions had to be carried out with tedious barter and commodity trade. The scarcity of hard currency was partially alleviated with a variety of coins the immigrants brought with them from Europe. The most popular currency in circulation, however, was the Spanish silver dollar obtained largely by illicit trade with the Spanish West Indies.

The Spanish and Portuguese were quick to conquer the heavily populated lands close to the warm weather climes of Central America, while the British colonial pioneers found the cold and inclement North America largely uninhabited with less than one person per square mile. The largest indigenous enclave was located at Cahokia Mounds in Southern, Illinois, which had peaked in the 13th century, with an estimated population of only 40,000 inhabitants.[1] These native North American "*Mississippians*" consisted of many different nomadic tribes who had little or no interest in gold and silver, unlike that of the insatiable colonial pioneers. In 1620, the chartered Virginia Company at Jamestown insisted that their parent Virginia Company of London stop sending them goldsmiths—and to send more laborers! [2]

The early settlers adopted the Native American Indians use of "*wampum*" as money to trade with the native tribes. Simple wampum is a white string of ornate shell beads and was declared legal tender by the colonists in New England from 1637 to 1661, along with standardized exchange rates set by the colonists in New York, New Jersey, and Delaware until 1673. North Carolina briefly accepted wampum as a currency of legal tender as late as 1710. Wampum served as a native person's identity and credentials and was often made into elaborate garments or jewelry. Dutch colonists began to manufacture wampum with modern machine tools and glutted the market. By the early 18th century wampum was no longer used as a currency or as a means of exchange in the colonies.[3]

Figure 11-1 *Native American tribes used wampum shells to create promise belts. The promises given were often treaties that the tribe made with another group of people. Wampum promise belts were also given to individuals as a way of creating a "written" promise.*[3] *Attribution: https://simanaitissays.com/2016/03/02/*

The Origins of the U.S. Dollar

In the early 1500s, the Spanish conquistadors shrewdly focused on Central and South America where the large population centers of Mesoamerica (Central America) and Norte Chico (Peru) civilizations were to be found. The Aztecs, Mayans, and Incas, fractured by years of internal dissent, quickly succumbed to the Spanish onslaught which led to the conquest of their vast holdings of gold and silver. A Spanish colonial mint was established at Potosi, Bolivia, where more than 40,000 tons of silver were mined, coined, and shipped by the end of the 18th century. The Spanish expanded production by transporting some 40,000 natives to work as slaves in their silver mines in western Hispaniola (the Greater Antilles). [4]

A vast shipping convoy dubbed the "Spanish treasure fleet" became the first permanent transatlantic trade route in history. Shipments from all of their colonies were required by law to dock at Seville, Spain, designated the only legal port of entry. The Crown of Spain taxed the precious metals and other cargo at a rate of 20 percent for the use of the port and in support of the government. The tax or tariff became known as the "*Quito real*" or the "*Royal one-fifth*" which reflected the standard levy charged by the monarch of the day. Much of this new wealth was inflationary, monetarily mismanaged, and used by the Spanish Hapsburgs to finance armies against the Ottoman Empire and other European and Muslim powers. Some of the silver was illicitly diverted to Japan and China to avoid the Spanish taxes altogether. [5, 6]

The "*real de a ocho*" (Spanish for "the royal eight"), also became known as the Spanish pillar dollar or peso. Widely accepted as an international currency for its uniformity in standard and milling characteristics from the 1500s to 1850s, it was a one-ounce (28 g) silver coin and was based on a denomination of eight reals to one silver peso, or colloquially as "a piece of eight." Other coins were issued as four-reals, two-reals, one-real and ½ real (little more than 12 mm in diameter). The Spanish pillar dollar was the coin upon which the United States dollar was based. It remained legal tender in the United States untill the Coinage Act of 1857. The origin of the $ sign is derived from the draping of the two pillars on each side of the globe on the reverse of the coin. [7]

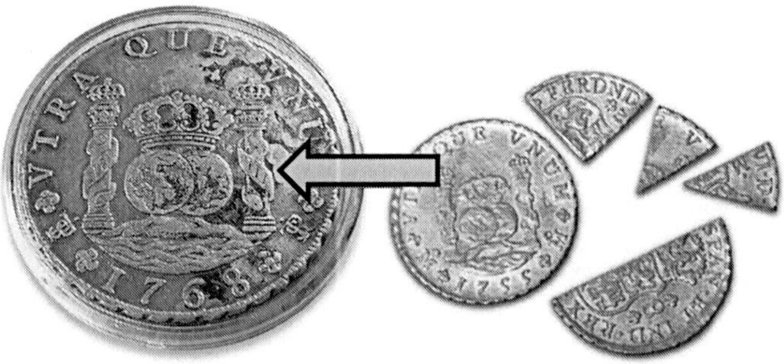

Figure 11-2 *One-ounce Spanish pillar dollar 1768* or *"Pieces of eight." Public domain*

The term "dollar," however, was derived from the "*thaler*" a silver coin used throughout Europe for over four hundred years. It served as the precursor to the silver coins of Spanish Mexico and Peru. Mined and minted in the Kingdom of Bohemia (now the Czech Republic), it was originally named the "*Joachimstal.*" Joachim is the Bohemian city named after Joseph the father of the Virgin Mary, while "*stal*" meant valley. It became the favorite, and predominant local coin as the silver mines at Joachim financed the expansion of the Hapsburg Empire and helped to subsidize the Roman Catholic Church. The Dutch and German immigrants to North America later called it a "*tolar*" which evolved into the English term "dollar." These coins are popular among professional coin collectors for their cruelly realistic depiction of monarchs and rulers of their time. [8]

Figure 11-3 *A silver Count Schlick of Joachimsthaler, 1525. Obverse: The Kingdom of Bohemia with Saint Joachim and the Bohemian Lion on the reverse.* [9] *Public domain*

Few precious metal coins were minted in the thirteen colonies, as the Spanish pillar dollar served as the main currency in circulation while gold and silver were yet to be locally discovered. The Spanish dollar was an illicit currency as the British imposed trade restrictions between the colonies and Spain. Paper money was issued by the colonial governments to facilitate needed economic activity and became known as "bills of credit." Based on fiat paper money, these bills could not be exchanged for fixed amounts of gold or silver. The Parliament of Great Britain, with the full endorsement of the Bank of England, decreed in a series of Currency Acts the regulation of any paper money from the American colonies. These currency regulations sought to protect British merchants and creditors from depreciated colonial currency. The early colonists cited this yet another grievance which would lead to the American Revolution.

The issued bills could, however, be accepted and retired by the local colonial government in payment for taxes. Inflation resulted when, in defiance of British law, the colonial governments would not take them out of circulation. To fund the Revolution, the Continental Congress also issued paper money, known as *Continental currency.* Rampant inflation ensued, and the near worthless currency was dubbed "not worth a continental." [10]

The American colonies were founded on fiat paper currency subject to a printing press and given to hyperinflation. Alexander Hamilton saw to it that the U.S. currency would be stabilized under a gold and silver standard. [11]

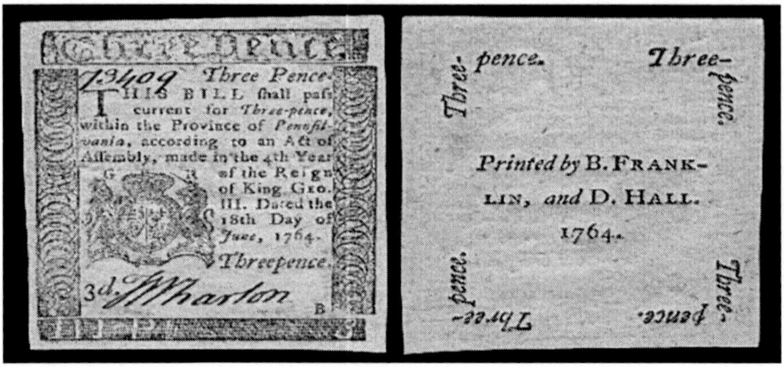

Figure 11-4 *A three pence note of paper currency issued by the Province of Pennsylvania and printed by Benjamin Franklin in 1764. Public domain*

Alexander Hamilton was a founding father of the American Revolution and one of the 55 "Framers" who crafted and signed the U.S. Constitution. Acclaimed as the founder of the nation's financial system, he was orphaned as a child and raised in the British West Indies. Good at numbers, he processed bills of exchange and other financial transactions at the Caribbean shipping ports. Recognized for his abilities, he was sent to King's College (now Columbia University if New York) to complete his education. Hamilton closely studied and was highly influenced by the works of the economist Adam Smith and his newly published book: *An Inquiry into the Nature and Causes of the Wealth of Nations (1776).* The book dispelled the common mercantilist practices of the era and supported the new premise of classical economics with its focus on the specialization of labor, productivity, private property, capital, and free market economies.

Hamilton became the financial chief of staff to General George Washington. Elected to the Congress of the Confederation from New York, he helped write the U.S. Constitution before resigning to practice law and later founded the Bank of New York. Disgusted with the weak financial foundation of the national government, he led a movement to establish the first central bank of the United States.

Two Strikeouts for a Central Bank

Hamilton was constrained by the U.S. Constitution as to how the currency should be managed. George Washington and the other Founders wanted nothing to do with paper money or central banks as is evident from the chronicles of debate.[12] The Constitution mentions money only four times. 1: The first and most significant is in Article 1, section 8, clause 5, whereby Congress is granted the power "To coin Money, regulate Value thereof, and of foreign Coin, and fix the Standard of Weights and Measures." 2: Clause 6 allows Congress: "To provide for the Punishment of counterfeiting the securities and the Coin of the United States." 3: Article 1 section 10 *prohibits* the states from "…coin Money: emit Bills of Credit; make any Thing but gold and silver Coin a Tender in the Payment of Debts." (States cannot create their own money.) 4: Lastly, the Seventh Amendment provides common law rights, "where the value in controversy shall exceed twenty dollars, the right of trial by jury shall be preserved…."

The Constitution does not control the government's issuance of currency—only that of its regulation, which includes coining to ensure standard weights and measures. In other words, parties can transact with any market medium of exchange so long as it meets lawful standards. The government does not have statutory supremacy over alternate currencies that private parties might use for settlement, such as, the cryptocurrencies of today. It is fine for the government to issue currency or security for settlement of its debts—just as long as others decide to accept it. Although Congress was given enumerated powers to coin money (from any metal), those powers didn't necessarily have to be enacted. Encouraged by Hamilton, Congress passed the Coinage Act of 1792 which established the U.S. Mint. The United States now had a hard currency, with regulatory control over the minting of gold and silver, brought to it mostly by wealthy interests.

The creation of money has many origins. Like King Midas, numerous monarchs and dictators hoarded precious metals to demonstrate their power and status. The government of ancient Athens nationalized their silver mines, minted, and coined their currency, and used it as payment to build their city-state. Alexander the Great confiscated gold and silver from those he conquered and created coins to pay his soldiers, who would then use it to expand trade and commerce. The Spanish conquistadors enslaved the Incas and Aztecs and shipped their plunder back to Spain. Hamilton would simply, and brilliantly, create the U.S. Mint. It was freely open for holders of gold and silver to convert their metals into a marketable and standardized currency—and invest in the new nation.

The Bank of North America was a private bank first chartered, after much political debate in 1781, by the Congress of the Confederation at the urging of Alexander Hamilton. It opened in Philadelphia across the street from the Continental Congress in 1782. Although there were regional private banks in existence, this institution, headed by the Founding father and financier Robert Morris, became the Nation's first de facto central bank, along with serving as the origin of the stock market. Morris had arranged financial backing in gold, silver, and bills of credit from the French and Dutch governments. He was able to issue 1,000 bank shares at $400 each. [13] As a sign of good faith in the new bank, Benjamin Franklin was first to purchase one share ownership. Today, we find his portrait on the popular $100 bill. Morris then issued new paper money that was backed by the reserve of hard currency. In 1783, Congress allowed Americans to pay their taxes with Bank of North America certificates.

Figure 11-5 *Today there are 11.1 billion $100 bills in global circulation or $1.1 trillion in cash. More than 75 percent of all $100 notes are held outside of the United States as the dollar is the dominant international reserve currency. It is conveniently used globally, in both legal and illegal transactions. A million dollars in $100 bills would weigh 22 pounds and fit into one standard briefcase. One-hundred-dollar bills make up 12 percent of all U.S. currency in production.[14] Public domain*

The Bank offered America's first IPO—the country's first initial public offering—with shares sold to the public. The formal establishment of a central bank as the "First Bank of the United States" began in 1791 by way of a Congressional charter not to exceed twenty years. A year later, 24 stockbrokers signed the Buttonwood Agreement of 1792 which founded the first national stock exchange—the New York Stock Exchange. Shares of the Bank itself were publicly traded along with tobacco and cotton stocks. The

Museum of American Finance is located at 48 Wall Street in New York and offers exhibits and seminars on the history of U.S. currency.

Bens, *Benjamins*, or *Franklins* are terms commonly used to refer to the $100 U.S. bill with his portrait on the current denomination. They are also known as "*C-Notes*" based on the Roman numeral for 100. On the reverse is Independence Hall, home of the Declaration of Independence and Second Continental Congress—the only building pictured on U.S. currency not located in Washington, D.C. The first $100 bills were issued in 1862 as gold or silver backed notes with various portraits. The use of Benjamin Franklin's portrait on the $100 Federal Reserve Notes was first issued in 1914 under the Federal Reserve Act.

Curiously, the Independence Hall's bell tower clock reads 4:10 on the back of $100 bills printed before 2013, but those printed after read 10:30. Mystery, and much debate, surrounds why either of these times was chosen, but both images—the north and south views—were engraved by J.C. Benzing in the 1910s. It is assumed that he took pictures of the building at different times of day, which would explain the time and shadow discrepancies. [15]

Following a coinage study by Alexander Hamilton in 1791, Congress passed a resolution calling for the establishment of a national mint which was officially authorized by the Coinage Act of 1792. Hamilton set the value of an ounce of gold at $19.39, which allowed the bank 61¢ to cover the bullion transaction cost (and profit) in return for providing the convenience of a $20.00 paper banknote. The $20 note was subsequently made convertible to the British for 4£s or $5 per one £. The currency was placed on a decimal system with silver to gold ratio of 15:1. Silver coins were issued in denominations of $0.05, $0.10, $0.25, $0.50 and $1.00. The first silver and gold coins were struck in 1794. [15, 16] Robert Scot, the Chief Engraver of the United States Mint, designed the then-popular and now-rare *Flowing Hair dollar* along with the *Liberty Cap half-cent* and the *Draped Bust of Liberty*.

The *Flowing Hair* dollar was the first dollar coin issued in 1794-5 by the United States federal government. Its size and weight were based on the Spanish dollar and featured the likeness of Alexander Hamilton with a purity of 90 percent silver. It was replaced in 1795 with the Draped Bust of Liberty with a reduced purity of 89.2 percent to make for a harder coin, but also to save on the silver.[15] On January 24, 2013, a specimen from the 1794 production sold for $10,016,875—the highest price than ever paid for a coin. [17]

Figure 11-6 Left *The first coin ever struck by the U.S. Mint in 1794. Known as the "Flowing Hair" dollar with the image of Alexander Hamilton. Sold to a collector in 2013 for more than $10 million.* Figure 11-7 Right *Draped Bust dollar depicting Lady Liberty replaced the Flowing Hair dollar with an 89.2 percent silver content, making for a more durable coin. The reverse is the Heraldic Eagle which introduced the first national motto: E Pluribus Unum (Out of Many–One). The motto "In God We Trust" was added at the height of the Civil War. Public domain*

Between 1793 and 1857, the United States minted copper half cents. A seemingly unusual denomination, it became an important part of the monetary exchange when wages were $1 for a 10-hour workday.

Figure 11-8 *The Liberty Cap half-cent was a widely distributed copper coin with five major design revisions until the Coinage Act of 1857 replaced it with the one cent. The Coinage Act also forbad the use of foreign coins for transactions in the United States. Public domain*

In 1811, the twenty-year charter granted by Congress for the First Bank of the United States expired and the bank closed, with the U.S. Treasury assuming the role of a central bank. The nation's finances, however, had suffered greatly due to the conflict with the British during the War of 1812—essentially a continuation of the Revolutionary War. Since there was no national income tax, U.S. revenue came mainly from tariffs and partly from excise taxes. The British navy, however, with their blockade of New Orleans and the Eastern ports, stopped the collection of all tariffs. The British armies occupied the strategic water trade routes of Baltimore and the Erie Canal, further choking off revenue. After General Andrew Jackson decisively defeated the British in the Battle of New Orleans, and then routed the Spanish from Florida, both the British and Spanish reassessed their financial positions and withdrew from North America to focus their attention on the Napoleonic Wars raging in Europe. [18]

To pay for the war, Congress granted another twenty-year charter for the Second Bank of the United States beginning in 1816. This private bank was chartered and authorized to provide loans, pay bills, collect taxes, move money around the country—and to print paper money. The Bank started with $35 million in capital ($492 million in 2016 dollars), some coming from the Treasury but most from individual investors. The exclusive privilege of a chartered central bank allowed the initial investors to provide loans and print money—making its public stockholders very wealthy. When Nicholas Biddle, the bank president, wanted to renew the Bank charter in 1836, he was confronted by the former general and now President Andrew Jackson.

The chief opponent to renewing the bank charter was Senator Thomas Hart Benton of Missouri. He saw the bank as too great and powerful, as "it made the rich richer and the poor poorer." While the West was being developed, money flowed to the Eastern bankers and the establishment. President Jackson, a favored populist among the people and the first Democratic president, vetoed the renewal of the bank charter that was passed by Congress. Biddle, in retribution, demanded that borrowers immediately repay their loans. Businesses struggled, and the economy tanked.

At first, the Panic of 1837 was blamed on President Jackson, but when the governor of Pennsylvania was denied a loan by Biddle, the tables turned. The Speaker of the House of Representatives, James Polk (later to become President), proposed four resolutions. One denied the bank a charter. The second was that no government money be deposited in his private bank. The third stated that the government should continue to put money only in state banks. Lastly, the government should investigate Biddle, his bank, and the reasons for the economic panics of 1819 and 1837. Biddle was arrested and charged with fraud but died before civil suits were adjudicated. [19]

The Era of Free Banking

Over the next 75 years, from 1836 to 1913, the United States had neither a formal central bank nor an income tax, resulting in interesting and creative approaches to constructing a financial system. The U.S. Treasury was charged with collecting taxes, mainly from tariffs, and to a lesser extent from excise taxes and duties placed on the consumption of specific classes of goods, like alcohol, and of required governmental services. The U.S. Treasury would provide the needed currency to its ever-expanding territories through privately owned banks which were chartered and overseen by the Treasury and regulated by each state.

President Andrew Jackson signed into law the Coinage Act of 1834 which attempted to torpedo the upcoming 1837 renewal of the central bank's charter. A contentious political debate ensued over who would control the United States currency. The value of the dollar was devalued by 6 percent, from \$19.39 to \$20.67 per ounce of gold, by raising the official silver to gold ratio from 15:1 to 16:1. Silver coinage became undervalued and flowed out of the country into the international market where it was worth more. Gold soon supplanted silver coins as the standard bearer of U.S. currency with the circulation and convenience of paper money. The Act further required the Treasury Department to pay, within five days after deposit at the mint, the full amount of the paper money in gold. [20] A hard currency, backed by gold, became stable and free from speculation and manipulation.

Figure 11-9 *President Andrew Jackson is handsomely portrayed on a twenty-dollar gold certificate. Arrow points to a gold-colored stamp. Public domain*

Private banks were viewed as part of a healthy banking system when left alone, whereas poorly run financial institutions were regularly put out of business or absorbed by those better managed. The profitability and management of a well-run bank was the responsibility of both the investors and savers. Consequently, competition for deposits and loans based on prudence and judgment served to strengthen the banking system. This was the opposite of Gresham's Law which promotes the theory that "bad money drives out good money." Gresham's Law is the cited justification for ever more government regulation of banks and currencies. However, the U.S. banking system in the era of free banking reflected the country's founding principles of minimal government involvement and its inherent distrust of government rule.

The lack of a central bank led to an era of free banking in the United States. Free banking systems have historically existed in many other countries, but by the mid-20th century, they were replaced by central banks, partly due to the overall success, trust, and popularity of the Bank of England. The "free banking era" is a partial misnomer, as regulations from the U.S. Treasury and each state stipulated and enforced the protection of the currency. The wide disparity of economic development within the U.S. and its territories allowed a free banking system more financial flexibility without central planning. Citizens would deal directly with the U.S. Treasury which supported the ideals behind the foundations of the U.S. Constitution.

Privately held banks were granted charters by each state, and the Treasury stipulated the money reserves required for each bank. A fractional-reserve banking system arose as private banks collected deposits, made loans or investments, and kept a fraction of their money in reserve to cover short-term withdrawals—as still exists to this day. The system allows the money market to expand to meet liquidity needs, but only if the bank retains sufficient reserves to cover any losses.

Banks do not create money (but do create credit) as that function is reserved for the Treasury with the issuance of notes to the banks. The expansion of credit is based on those willing to offer credit with a suitable interest rate as determined in the open money marketplace and based on the reserve requirements. However, the base currency remains stable, pegged by the Treasury to gold and silver. Each state had its bank regulators who oversaw the bank's reserves, and the Treasury also kept the money supply in check. Nonetheless, there was no central bank of last resort, and some mismanaged banks failed. [21]

Tariff Disputes Leading to a Civil War

The United States was a vast and expanding agricultural economy. As a result, there were occasional bank runs and foreclosures as farmers needed loans to plant their crops. The incredible demand for bank loans occurred before each harvest, which resulted in money flowing back into the banks after the harvest. The U.S. government, faced with the vagaries of an agricultural economy, derived most of its income from the inconsistent collection of tariffs and various excise taxes. The U.S. looked to Great Britain which had imposed both tariffs and a national income tax (in 1601) to provide both fiscal balance and monetary stability.

Without a secure national tax to rely on, the United States suffered many tariff blunders. President Thomas Jefferson enacted the Embargo Act of 1808 which was intended to keep merchant ships safe from the conflict between the British and French navies—only to see trade evaporate, federal revenues decline, and a severe economic contraction. [22] Another staggering blunder in the management of tariffs came with the passage of the "Tariff of Abominations" of 1828 which set in motion the beginnings of the U.S. Civil War. [22] The northern states authorized high tariffs on goods from the southern states. The southern states had supported low tariffs, as their competitive advantage was the export of commodities such as cotton and tobacco. The northeastern industrialists favored high tariffs to protect themselves from international competition and to grow their factories and businesses at home. [23] The economy slid into recession in 1828 on expectations of higher trade barriers *and* lower tariff revenues.

The southern states sold their agricultural goods both to the northern states and abroad but had to purchase expensive northern manufactured goods to protect the northeastern business and banking interests. The Coinage Act of 1857 later outlawed the use of foreign coinage within the United States—which further inflamed the southern states. The new law affected some 80 percent of the currency in circulation within the southern states as they were paid mostly in foreign currency for goods they had traded abroad. [24] They now had to deal with a domestic currency increasingly controlled by northeastern industrialists and bankers.

The new Confederate States of America had an agrarian-based economy, primarily cotton and tobacco, for export to the northern states and Europe. Had it been an independent nation in 1860, it would have ranked as the fourth richest country in the world. [25] It relied heavily on slave-worked plantations, and with the earlier invention of Whitney's highly efficient cotton gin, expanded the growing territory into ever more unproductive land in the Deep South. The practice of importing slaves, however, was stopped by Great Britain with the passage of the Slave Trade Act of 1807. The Act required the British navy to stop any transport of slaves across the high seas. The growing demand for both domestic slaves and the new and more desirable short-staple cotton drove prices higher. [26]

As the domestic slave market became the only source of hard labor, plantation owners began to breed slaves and practice chattel slavery. Britain officially abolished slavery within most of the British Empire in 1833 with the passage of the Slavery Abolition Act. By 1860, 11 percent of blacks in the U.S. were freed slaves, either through manumission or simply the retirement of spent labor. In fact, numerous freed blacks owned black slaves in a number disproportionate to their population based on census figures .[27] Colonel Robert E. Lee, in a letter to his wife in 1856, called slavery "a moral and political evil." He concluded that black slaves were immeasurably better off in the U.S. than in Africa, morally, socially, and physically. [28]

Today, economic historians disagree on whether the U.S. Civil War was ever necessary. Phillips argues that large-scale U.S. plantations had reached their economic limits and that cotton production would decline and eventually move to Brazil or a country with lower labor costs. [29] (Brazil didn't ban its dependency on slavery until 1888—more than twenty years after the U.S. Civil War). Economists Conrad and Meyer countered that the economics of the south would not have ended in the absence of the U.S. Civil War as the slave labor market would continue to grow and thrive. [30] Today, U.S. cotton farming is highly mechanized, indirectly subsidized, and continues to be a major world exporter of cotton next only to China and Brazil. The mechanization of agriculture contributed to the migration of many blacks to the industrial north for jobs in private industry.

Without any substantial source of revenue besides tariffs, the Confederate States relied on war bonds to self-finance the war with the northern states. European investors remained on the sidelines unsure of the results. The Union immediately set out to blockade the port cities of the South and to stop their trade with Britain and France. The early success of the blockade signaled the likely outcome as to which side would win. By July 1861, only three months from the start of the war, the Union Navy had established blockades of all the major southern ports. Economically the war was in effect over.

The southern states had hoped that Britain and France would intervene on their behalf to avoid losing the supply of low-cost cotton critical to their textile mills. One of the first acts by the Confederate Congress was to lower import tariffs on British and French goods from 20 percent to 10 percent and to raise tariffs on all imports from the northern states. In practice, almost no tariffs were collected. With a weak and nascent banking system, the Confederacy turned to smaller banks and speculators who bought \$15 million in war bonds with gold to finance the civil war. The gold was used to back their new currency to buy warships and supplies. However, the newly issued Confederate currency was soon inflated and irredeemable as the European powers refused to take sides. That left each state to issue its own bonds. The South's finances were so in disarray that corporations and individuals wrote their own promissory notes and passed them on hand-to-hand.

Flush with Cash

The northern states relied on private banks with more affluent depositors to support their currency. Still, there was a need to fund the war effort. The Treasury, in clear violation of the U.S. Constitution, issued its own U.S. bank notes known as "greenbacks" to pay the Union soldiers and for other expenses of the war. The value of the notes decreased rapidly as they were unredeemable for gold. Congress soon passed a series of Legal Tender Acts that required creditors to accept the notes despite their lack of backing by gold or silver, bank deposits, or government reserves. The green color was selected as it was believed to convey dependability and assurance, but the paper dollar soon destabilized. By war's end in 1865, the dollar's value had sunk to $57 to an ounce of gold or a nearly 3:1 devaluation, while the Confederate notes were devalued by an astonishing 28:1. [31] Commodity prices soared across the nation.

The California Gold Rush began in 1849, just before the start of the U.S. Civil War. The miners, called "49ers," used much of their gold to purchase food and supplies—and entertainment of all sorts. Those who got rich were the merchants, vendors, and businessmen, many of whom went on to achieve great financial success. As time passed, local banks and gold dealers issued their own convenient banknotes and "drafts" of locally accepted paper currency in exchange for the gold.

Private mints created their own gold coins—a practice observed with great concern and dismay by the U.S. Treasury. The Treasury quickly established a U.S. Mint in San Francisco and by 1854 turned the gold bullion into U.S. gold coins for circulation. California banks later sent the gold to the eastern national banks in exchange for paper currency to be used in the booming California economy. [32] Gold holdings in the U.S. Treasury began to swell towards war's end. Based on the newfound wealth, the Union held the financial advantage as the northern states would rapidly recover from the devastation of the Civil War. The U.S. gradually returned the dollar to the prewar parity of $20.67 per troy ounce of gold, fully redeemable into either gold or silver.

Ten years after the beginning of the Gold Rush, silver was discovered in large quantities. This was both a blessing for funding the Union during the war and a curse to the nation after the war. The Comstock Lode of 1859 generated immense personal fortunes and growth in the territories of Nevada and San Francisco. The mines yielded vast amounts of silver and some gold as a byproduct. Both the U.S. Treasury Secretary and Congress became concerned as they feared that the large quantities of silver were likely to devalue the gold-and silver-backed paper currency—and endanger the status quo of a global gold standard.

The Coinage Act of 1873 abolished the right of holders of silver bullion to have their metal struck into legally backed dollar coins.[33] The U.S. Mint continued to stamp silver coins but only based on the face value of the coin. Once silver became more valuable than the face value of the coin, collectors would take the coins out of circulation, and the U.S. Mint would begin using other metals like copper, zinc, and nickel. Proof sets with precious metals remain for sale today—but not for circulation—as the metal became more valuable than the face value. The end of bimetallism in the United States placed the nation firmly on a gold standard, much to the dismay of those who held significant amounts of silver.

Figure 11-10 Left *The Coinage Act of 1873 abolished the Seated Liberty silver dollar issued from 1840 to 1873. Public domain.* Figure 11-11 Right *The Silver Trade dollar was authorized by Congress to improve trade exclusively with China and the Orient and minted from 1873 to 1885. Public domain*

The U.S. Adoption of a Classical Gold Standard

The Coinage Act became known as the "Crime of '73." The Act itself was cited as the cause of the "Panic of 1873," and its effect persisted throughout most of the 1870s and beyond. A large sector of the public favored inflation generated by the increased quantities of mined silver and the resulting devaluation of gold and paper dollars. Inflation makes loans cheaper and easier to pay off in the long run but eats into the creditor's real profits.

Legislation was again passed in favor of bimetallism, which required the U.S. Treasury to purchase silver and pay in banknotes that could be redeemed in gold. Gold flowed out of the Treasury, leading to yet another depression in the 1890s. William Jennings Bryan, the Democratic presidential candidate in 1896, is famously known for his "Cross of Gold" speech in which he decried the gold standard, concluding *"you shall not crucify mankind upon a cross of gold!"* [34] He lost overwhelmingly to Republican William McKinley. The United States officially returned to the gold standard in 1900 upon passage of the Gold Standard Act—and the economy boomed.

Only India, Japan, Korea, and China continued to prefer silver. The silver United States "Trade Dollar" was coined for the exclusive use in Asian trade. In 1792 the official ratio of silver to gold was 15:1. By 1900 it had fallen to 33:1, and by 2018 the ratio was 81:1. Silver-only based economies suffered from growing inflation and trade distortions.

The Morgan silver dollar replaced the Seated Liberty dollar which was no longer produced following the passage of the Coinage Act of 1873. The Morgan dollar was named after its designer, George T. Morgan, and was minted from 1878 to 1904. A common misperception is that it was named after the financier J.P. Morgan who gladly assumed the notoriety.

Mining interests lobbied to restore free silver under the Bland-Allison Act and later the Sherman Silver Purchase Act. These laws required that the Treasury purchase set amounts of silver for coinage and distribution through the banking system, rather than accepting all requests for silver to be coined and returned to the owner. The Morgan dollar ceased to be struck in 1904 when the Treasury depleted the purchased silver reserves, but production resumed on an occasional basis and large quantities of Morgan silver dollars accumulated in bank vaults around the nation.

Figure 11-12 Left *Morgan Silver Dollar 1878 to1921 Public domain*
Figure 11-13 Right *Peace Silver Dollar 1921 to 1928, 1934-1935 Public domain*

Minting of silver dollars began anew in the aftermath of World War I. During the war, in hopes of destabilizing British rule in India, the Germans had spread rumors that the British didn't have enough silver to redeem their money. The rumors led to the hoarding of silver, drastically reducing the currency supply. The British war effort was threatened by driving up the price of silver and the goods and services on which it was based.

The British government asked the United States to begin purchasing silver from its domestic suppliers so it can increase the supply and lower the price of silver in India.[35] The U.S. responded with passage of the Pittman Act of 1918, which authorized the United States to melt down 350 million old Morgan dollars held on reserve in bank vaults and sell the silver to the British for $1 per ounce. The British paid with gold from the Bank of England. The Pittman Act directed the U.S. Treasury to *again* replace the melted coins with the purchase of new silver from American mining interests and mint new silver dollars. The resulting "Peace dollar" was minted from 1921 to 1928 and again in 1934 and 1935, with a new design commemorating America's victory in WWI. Numismatists lobbied Congress: "*we gave our silver dollars to help win the war, we restore them in commemoration of our victory and peace.*" [36]

In 1964, based primarily on demand by Las Vegas casinos and other Western interests, Congress again passed legislation that resulted in the production of 45 million new silver dollars. The casinos were well-aware that slot-machine customers preferred the sound of silver coins as they fell from the slots. The distinctive and pleasant sound of a silver coin struck by another metal is commonly used as a test of silver content. Many in Congress opposed this legislation as the new coins would not benefit the entire country. A public uproar occurred when the new coins were announced in May 1965. Coin dealers immediately offered to buy them for their silver content at $7.50 each. Placing such a high price on the newly minted coins meant that they would never be used as currency, as they would yield more than seven times as much from a coin dealer in exchange for the metal content. As a result, Congress halted the production of silver coins for circulation. The last silver coin put into circulation was the 1964 quarter. Based on the silver content, a $10 roll of silver quarters can currently be purchased online for more than $150.

The Nugget

As Benjamin Franklin stated, "*An investment in knowledge pays the best interest.*" After more than a thousand years of cultures experimenting with the vagaries of bi-metallic currencies, the United States and most of the Western industrial world were finally on a solid gold-only footing.

Many economists and politicians have simply forgotten how the classical gold exchange standard operates and how it led to over two hundred years of stabilized currencies with a public spotlight on government excesses. However, wars, fiscal imprudence, economic shocks, and natural disasters caused governments to suspend the classical gold exchange standard and embark on an entirely new fiat financial system—at least for the time being.

CHAPTER TWELVE

THE AMERICAN EXPERIENCE: A CURRENCY & CULTURE IN TRANSITION, PART II

Keywords: a moral hazard; fractional reserve banking; FDIC; bonds; Internal Revenue Service; Nixon shock; Special Drawing Rights (SDR)

> "It's very difficult to explain to a normal working citizen the implications of what $18 trillion in debt means and what it means when the Federal Reserve buys the U.S. Treasury bonds to finance our loss every month."
>
> Steve Wynn, casino and hotel mogul

The Bankers' Panic of 1907 served as the prelude to the creation of the Federal Reserve System in 1913. The Panic took place over a three-week period in October when the value of securities on the New York Stock Exchange fell almost 50 percent from the previous year's peak. It was sparked by a failed attempt to corner the stock market of the United Copper Company. The event led to a run on numerous banks across the nation which, lacking access to market liquidity and adequate management supervision, went bankrupt.

The financial contagion continued into November when financier J.P. Morgan personally intervened to prevent further economic collapse. Republican Nelson Aldrich also interceded and was instrumental in founding the Federal Reserve System—the newest attempt at a central bank. Chairman of the powerful Senate Finance Committee and the newly created National Monetary Commission, Aldrich dominated all tariff and monetary policies and was fondly known to the public as the "General Manager of the Nation." Although some were critical of his daughter's marriage into the powerful Rockefeller family, his efforts were presented as a way to stabilize the currency markets from speculators.

After having abandoned the idea twice before, the United States became the last major country to adopt a central bank. The distrust of central banks stemmed from the colonialists' experience with the Bank of England. The newly created Federal Reserve Bank (FRB) was given oversight of twelve Regional Banks which, at that time, were officially allowed to set their own discount rates and reserve requirements.[1] Prior to the passage of the Federal Reserve Act in 1913, the U.S. currency was an obligation of the private banks and their bondholders. However, the new Federal Reserve note (dollar) was now an obligation of the U.S. Treasury—and its taxpayers.

The Federal Reserve Act was originally granted a twenty-year bank charter, to be renewed in 1933. The original mission of the FRB was for two simple monetary purposes: act as a bank of last resort and stabilize the liquidity of the currency by supervising other banks' reserve requirements. It now assumed complete control of the nation's currency, as it was hoped the new central bank would prevent a liquidity crisis like that of the Panic of 1907. As a bank of last resort, the FRB, along with state regulators, required that private banks have ample reserve capital to fund any withdrawals. Today this system is known as fractional reserve banking. How much a bank must keep in reserve varies considerably depending on economic conditions and political interests.

Fractional reserve banking is a monetary system that allows a private bank to keep only a fraction of the bank deposits, held in actual cash and liquid securities, to be available for withdrawal. The Bank of England set a reserve requirement of 2:1 when it was first chartered. The amount in reserve frees up underutilized capital that can be lent out to other parties—and must obviously be carefully managed to prevent a bank run.

Bank reserve requirements vary considerably based on how much the Federal Reserve wants to stimulate or depress the economy. If the reserve requirement is 20 percent, for example, a bank that receives a $1,000 deposit may lend out (with interest) $800 of that deposit. If the borrower then writes a check to someone who deposits the $800, the bank receiving that deposit can lend out $640 etc. This may occur many times over. For example, at the start of the 2007 financial crisis, many financial institutions held a historically low 2.5 percent reserve (or just one-dollar reserve to every 40 dollars loaned out) due to the repeated practice of re-lending. Reducing the reserve requirement adds money and generally stimulates the economy while increasing the reserve withdraws money from circulation and depresses an overstimulated economy.

The FRB also has the exclusive authority to sell and redeem U.S. government securities, such as saving bonds (non-marketable securities) and marketable Treasury bills (that mature in one year or less), notes (mature in 2 to 10 years) and long-bonds (20 to 30+ years). Privately owned banks are required to hold part of their reserves in U.S. Treasury notes and bonds.[2] Transparent economic statistics like interest rates, inflation rates, international balance of payments, etc. are expected to provide for economic information to help investors interpret how the FRB would (or should) react monetarily given the current health of the economy.

The Federal Open Market Committee (FOMC) of the FRB simply adjusts the demand for currency through the discount rate that it charges private banks to borrow money or set bank reserve requirements. Like a home thermostat, the central bank releases more currency to stimulate or heat up the economy and to offset deflation—and reduces the amount of currency to cool and slow an overheated economy and avoid inflation.

The FRB was created (in 1913) to prevent private banks from failing. However, the Wall Street Crash of 1929 and the Great Depression that soon followed dashed those expectations. At the height of the banking crisis, and on the eve of Franklin D. Roosevelt's presidential inauguration, there were no long lines at the teller windows of the big New York banks. They had prudently kept 20 percent of their deposits as bank reserves and remained highly solvent. It was the small rural farm banks and unsupervised state regulators that did not see the events that led to the Great Depression.

The 1933 Banking Act was passed to shore up and restore badly needed trust in the American banking system—only twenty years after the Federal Reserve System was established to prevent just that.[3] The Banking Act notably created the Federal Deposit Insurance Corporation (FDIC) which proved extremely controversial as it provided taxpayer-subsidized insurance coverage for depositors at U.S. banks.

Before 1933, state governments strived to limit private banks' propensity for excesses. Injured depositors were legally allowed to bring lawsuits against equity stockholders for *double* their original investment—a process that brought prudence and vigilance to both bank managers and shareholders. District Judges up for reelection often sided with the injured depositors against the bank owners who were ordered to pay large penalties.

The FDIC switched the liability and responsibility from the bank owners onto the U.S. taxpayer. Under the present-day banking structure, shareholders and boards of directors face no personal liability for mismanagement or imprudent risk-taking. Proven embezzlement and larceny, however, is another matter. Initially, in 1933, insurance on bank deposits was limited to $2,500 per depositor ($47,000 in 2016 dollars). However, in response to the financial crisis of 2007-2008, the passage of the Dodd-Frank Wall Street Reform and Consumer Protection Act of 2010 significantly increased the amount to $250,000. The Dodd-Frank Act also set new compliance requirements that eventually led to 1.1 regulatory bank examiners for every one private bank manager. [4] The criticism that bank examiners have grown too close to the bankers they oversee is a phenomenon known as "regulatory capture." [5] Large banks have prospered—as the high cost of government regulation closed many smaller banks.

Depositors who once were responsible for the financial success of a privately-owned bank would now rely on the U.S. taxpayer-funded by the FDIC under the Federal Reserve System. Gresham's law of bad money driving out good money became the fully adopted financial norm. Gresham's law was popularly presented by the news media as the new "moral hazard" where one person or organization assumes the risk—while another person or organization bears the cost. Essentially, a company or bank that can profit from protective policies will attempt to do so.

Figure 12-1 *FDIC Public domain*

Glass-Steagall legislation

The Banking Act of 1933 also included Glass-Steagall legislation resulting from the Senate Banking Committee's investigation into the causes of the 1929 crash. The insightful inquiry conducted by Chief Counsel Ferdinand Pecora led to simple legislation (~ 15 pages) that required banks to register as either an investment bank or a commercial bank. Essentially, investment banks are legally allowed to speculate in the market with their own or other investors' money, while the function of commercial banks was to protect depositors' savings and service merchant accounts. Savings accounts at commercial banks would be insured through the FDIC.

Glass-Steagall provisions were gradually watered down with loopholes, technicalities, and escape clauses arising from the changing definition of the banking business and the evolution of banks into large and complex bank holding companies and corporate trusts. By 1999, the Glass-Steagall Act was entirely repealed by the bipartisan passage of the Gramm-Leach-Bliley Act, also known as the Financial Services Modernization Act. Among other effects, this Act resulted in a megamerger between two financial giants, Citigroup (as the owner of Citibank) and Salomon Smith Barney, one of the world's largest securities firms. The repeal allowed the financial industry to create new corporate financial institutions that became popularized as "too big to fail—and too big to jail."

After the global financial crisis of 2007-2008, noted economist Joseph Stiglitz argued that "*when the repeal of Glass-Steagall brought investment and commercial banks together, the investment-bank culture came out on top*." [6] Banks that had previously been managed conservatively turned to riskier investments to increase their returns and thus destabilized the entire banking system leading to a financial crisis and the Great Recession of the 2010s. Throughout history, economic booms and busts follow a repetitive and cyclical routine: their overly permissive expansion creates economic bubbles, followed by the over-regulation of banks *after* economic downturns.

Despite depressions, wars, and other calamities, the FRB and the Bank of England coordinated, championed, and supported the classical gold exchange standard for nearly 200 years. Their efforts were largely successful as both the U.S. and U.K. maintained the gold standard throughout the economic tumult of WWI with no major liquidity shortages from 1914 to 1971. During the first war, however, U.S. gold sovereigns were withdrawn from circulation, and the gold was converted to 400-ounce bars, thus limiting and discouraging physical gold ownership while still maintaining access by U.S. citizens mainly through the Bank of England. British Parliament, to help stabilize its currency, imposed tax increases on those companies most likely to profit from the war.

The House of Morgan in 1914 (now JPMorgan Chase & Co.) organized massive credits for the U.K. which maintained its gold standard and fiscal responsibilities—while none for Hapsburg Germany which had not. The financial credits alone likely swung the military outcome of the war to Great Britain and its allies. [7] After the war, the allied nations slowly returned to the gold exchange standard, although with revised exchange rates. The vanquished Central Powers would not, which led to more disastrous conflicts yet to come.

New Sources of Money

Normally the U.S. would borrow money from other countries to pay for a war effort, as did Germany—but there were no other countries from which to borrow, as none had any funds available to lend. Printing more money only results in inflation which discourages the population from joining in the war effort. The U.S. Treasury reacted by issuing Liberty Bonds as the first financial security marketed to the general American public. Buying Liberty Bonds was promoted as a patriotic duty and encouraged by a variety of public relations events and spokesmen. Four issues were made of Liberty Bonds during the war years with interest rates of between 3.5 and 4.25 percent. Both the principal and interest were exempt from all taxation except for estate and inheritance taxes. Ultimately the government raised $21.5 billion for the war effort, while the full cost of the war exceeded $30 billion made payable to the U.S. government and its taxpayers. [8] The majority of bonds were sold to banks and financial institutions. Ordinary citizens were apprehensive about the new non-marketable financial instrument as there was no established market where they could be exchanged or traded. Indeed, many small savers of Liberty Bonds experienced significant losses when they were forced by personal circumstances to sell their bonds before maturity.[9]

Figure 12-2 *A sample of a Liberty Bond.* [10] *Public domain*

The passage in 1913 of the 16th Amendment to the U.S. Constitution established a national income tax, which currently generates more than half of all government revenue. After Arizona became the last of the contiguous states to be admitted into the Union in 1912, there was nowhere left in the country to hide from the national tax and the U.S. Treasury's Internal Revenue Service. Indeed, U.S. currency often flowed out of state-regulated banking and into the unchartered U.S. territories where investors had more leverage over their money. Congress floated the narrative of a "community of interest" that required taxpayers to serve as a backstop to prevent future financial calamities. Democratic President Woodrow Wilson and Republican Nelson Aldrich were in full bipartisan support. The big financiers were euphoric. J.P Morgan, Carnegie, Rockefeller, and other moguls of that day had already established private foundations to avoid the proposed federal income tax.

Private foundations fall outside the reach of the Internal Revenue Code, as they are considered 501(c) (3) nonprofit organizations and are subject to a 1 to 2 percent excise tax on net investment income. So long as new money is not defined as *income*, no income tax is due.[11] Foundations are often funded with stocks that have reached their peak value and the donations deducted from personal income taxes over a period of several years. Family foundations include many tax benefits as control of the foundation's assets can be passed onto their heirs who often become the well compensated and paid managers of the foundation. Foundations grew in number from 18 in early 1910 to 267 by 1930. The Foundation Center states that in 2014 the U.S. was home to well over 87,000 private foundations, which include some 40,000 family-managed foundations. [11]

The federal income tax began with a minor 1 percent tax on personal and corporate income over $3,000 (about $73,000 in inflation-adjusted 2016 dollars) with a surtax of up to 6 percent on incomes over $500,000 (about $12 million in 2016 dollars). By 1918, after the U.S. had become fully involved in the war and global trade stopped, the top tax rate that was 6 percent in 1913 jumped to 77 percent (on income over 1 million dollars) and continued to climb well after the war. [12] Exacerbated by high wartime tax rates and little revenue from tariffs, global trade came to an end and a recession ensued. The Democratic Party campaigned in the following 1920 election to keep the tax rate high to pay off the war debts. Voters thought differently, and the Republican Warren G. Harding won the presidency in a landslide.

After the war, tax rates were steadily reduced to 58 percent in 1922 and continued the slide to 24 percent by 1926. The stimulus of more currency into the market led to an economic boom that became known as the Roaring Twenties. Roaring indeed, the 1920s saw the electrification of the nation, the large-scale adoption of automobiles, telephones, motion pictures, and unprecedented industrial growth—not only in the United States but Western Europe as well.

Republican President Harding had aptly chosen as his Treasury Secretary Andrew Mellon. Mellon was a wealthy industrialist who established many successful business ventures including the Aluminum Company of America (Alcoa, Inc., since changed to Arconic), Union Steel, Pittsburgh Coal, and Gulf Oil. Republican President Coolidge reappointed Mellon and continued with a pro-growth agenda. The tax rate fell further to just 1.125 percent on the lowest wage earners and 24 percent on the highest. The Dow Jones Industrial Average peaked in 1929 at 381 points from 120 points in 1924—over a 300% increase in just five years. The whole economy grew alongside the stock market, and Andrew Mellon was heralded as the best Treasury secretary since Alexander Hamilton.

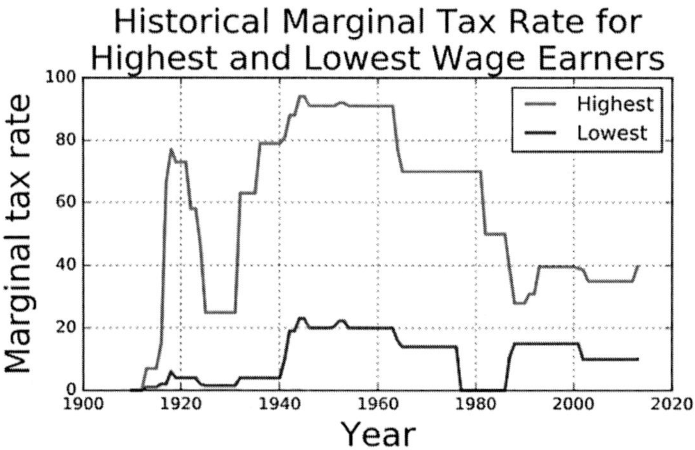

Figure 12-3 *Tax Chart Attribution & Source: Battiston, S.P. (2017, May 12)*[12]

Left behind was the German Weimar Republic whose severe economic downturn resulted from demands to pay oppressive reparations for WWI. The London Ultimatum of May 1921, largely pressured by France, demanded annual reparations be repaid in gold-backed hard currency. The first of many annual balloon payments were paid in June 1921 with two billion Goldmarks *plus* 26 percent of the value of Germany's exports! Germany suspended the circulation of Goldmarks at the beginning of the war and replaced the notes with printed fiat papiermarks (paper marks).[13] Papiermarks were simply printed in mass to buy hard foreign currencies to pay for ever-increasing annual reparations. Initially, the papiermarks had a stimulus effect on the domestic German economy as their imports were being paid with fiat money.

The Los Angeles Times in 1924 estimated that there were more worthless German papiermarks spread among the farming communities of the western United States than existed in all of Germany. [14] The Germans were buying American farm commodities with worthless paper. The exchange of hard U.S. dollars for rapidly worthless German notes contributed to a deflationary currency spiral starting with U.S. agricultural commodities, rural banks, and western farmers. Bankers from the northeast took advantage to purchase farmland on the cheap from unsuspecting local banks holding worthless paper. The bankers demanded their tenant farmers to plant every square foot of land they could cultivate contributing to an environmental calamity.[15]

First to feel the Great Depression, as early as 1920, were the 50 percent of Americans who lived on farms and didn't own stocks.[16] The hyperinflation of the German currency was ultimately exported worldwide, creating unexpected havoc in global currency markets and world trade. Also, Germany's major trade partner went bankrupt due to the Russian revolution in 1917. Poland, Hungary, and Eastern Europe would feel the effects of currency inflation as well. In the early 1930s, the United States faced a severe drought resulting in a calamitous dust bowl from over farming. The turn of events would have a devastating impact at home and on the entire global financial system.

Figure 12-4 Left *A Reichsbanknote (5 Trillion Marks 1923)* [17] *OTRS. Attribution: National Numismatic Collection, National Museum of American History.*
Figure 12-5 Right *A 5 million Mark coin worth $714.29 in January of 1923—about 1 thousandth of one cent by October 1923.* [18]*(CC By-SA-3.0)*

The Dirty Thirties—a Major Change of Events

The "Dust Bowl" in the United States also became known as the "Dirty Thirties." Decreasing global commodity prices due to inflationary currencies, cheaper imports, and a persistent drought forced tens of thousands to leave their farms and request financial assistance from the government. The problem in great part was with the divergent economic goals of the two political parties. The Republican Party, in support of northeastern industrial businesses, advocated lower income taxes and higher tariffs to protect industries from foreign competition. The Democratic Party favored higher taxes as the main source of revenue and supported lower tariffs on foreign goods to keep their mostly agrarian and commodity exports competitive in foreign markets. Eventually, the two parties reached a compromise and agreed that *both* higher taxes *and* higher tariffs should be enacted!

The Smoot-Hawley Tariff Act of 1930 set retaliatory tariffs that already were enacted by other countries in a "beggar-thy-neighbor" return to an earlier mercantilist era. It raised U.S. tariffs on over 20,000 imported goods and imposed an additional tax rate of up to 60 percent on more than 3,200 goods. [19] Congress didn't pass the Smoot-Hawley Act until early 1930. However, investors and industrialists saw the writing on the wall in 1929. On October 24 (Black Thursday), October 28 (Black Monday) and October 29 (Black Tuesday) the market saw a cumulative 40 percent downturn and the start of a worldwide Great Depression. The Dow Jones Industrial Average would lose 89 percent of its value before finally bottoming out in July 1932. The economic downturn would continue, fueled by increased government spending and taxation—and continued debasement of the hard dollar in exchange for increasingly worthless foreign currencies.

President Hoover's response was to push through an enormous 42 percent expansion of government spending and massive public works projects, including the building of the Hoover Dam, the San Francisco Bay Bridge, and the Los Angeles Aqueduct. In 1932 the top marginal tax rate was increased to 63 percent and by 1945 reached 94 percent on all income over $200,000 ($2.7 million in 2016 dollars). Tax increases and wage-price controls further depressed the market, causing the economy to plunge even further.

Democrat Franklin Roosevelt campaigned on sound money and lowered tariffs, but by 1933 as the newly elected President, issued an executive order that made physical ownership of gold a crime under the Trading with the Enemy Act of 1917. The enemy was presumably the American people since the U.S. was not at war in 1933. Citizens were required by law to redeem their gold coins for banknotes. More importantly, he ignored any effort to modify the effects of the Smoot-Hawley Tariff Act and reduce the impact of increasingly worthless foreign currencies entering the U.S. and global markets. Roosevelt further shocked the world markets by devaluing the dollar nearly 70% from $20.67 to $35 per ounce of gold and making it a federal offense to *hoard* gold by Executive Order 6102. [20, 21]

The abrupt change in the value of gold was considered an unpardonable act of economic nationalism by foreign nations, especially by the Japanese who depended heavily on foreign trade for necessary commodities like oil, and the Germans who were dealing with the aftermath of hyperinflation. Both Japan and Germany were seemingly goaded into taking extreme actions. Austria, in concert with Germany as its major trade partner, was the first to break from the gold exchange standard totally and were soon followed by twenty other nations most of whom raised tariffs, increased taxes, suspended their gold exchanges—and went to war.

To help pay the huge government debt leading up to the war, President Roosevelt issued saving bonds, popularly called "baby bonds." These were sounder investments than the previous Liberty Bonds, as they were sold at 75 percent of face value and paid 2.9 percent annual interest when held to their full 10-year maturity. They were issued from 1935 to 1941 in denominations of $25 to $1,000. The savings bonds were registered and could be replaced in the event of loss or destruction. The last of the "baby bonds" matured and ceased earning interest in April 1951.

Beginning in 1941 with the start of WWII, the U.S. Treasury and the President began marketing the previously successful *baby bonds* as "*war bonds*" with an appeal to patriotism. Those issued from 1941 to November 1965 accrued interest for 40 years; those issued from December 1965 to June 1980 accrued interest for 30 years. Like the baby bonds, they were sold for as little as $18.75 and matured in ten years, at which time the United States government paid the bondholder. They were issued at 75 cents per dollar face value, maturing at par in a specified number of years that fluctuated with the rate of interest. Denominations available were $25, $50, $75, $100, $200, $500, $1,000, $5,000 and $10,000. Series E bonds were issued only in registered, physical form and were not transferable. The guaranteed minimum investment yield for the bonds was 4 percent, compounded semiannually. Bond Series EE, F, and G would later be introduced. Over the course of the war, 85 million Americans purchased bonds totaling approximately $185 billion (over $2.1 trillion in 2016). The budgetary expenses for the years 1941–1945 amounted to an estimated $323 billion, of which $211 billion was directly borrowed by the government. [22]

Figure 12-6 *Series E Savings Bonds series issued 1941 to 1980 Public domain*

The Revival of the Gold Standard

With the end of WWII near, representatives from 44 countries convened at the Mount Washington Hotel in Bretton Woods, New Hampshire to reestablish the classical gold standard and revive world trade. They agreed that the United States would anchor gold at $35 an ounce and act as the world's only reserve currency. Countries that opted-in benchmarked their currencies to the U.S. dollar—many had no other choice. The U.S. government sponsored the creation of several global economic agencies. The International Monetary Fund (IMF) would help countries maintain their currencies pegged to gold and the dollar. The World Bank would help maintain financial stability, and the General Agreement on Tariffs and Trade (now the World Trade Organization or WTO) would seek to reduce tariffs. Key world commodities like oil and precious metals would be priced in dollars, and the world's oceans protected by the vast presence of the U.S. Navy.[23] Countries would be encouraged to produce and trade—not go to war. Devastated by WWII, both Germany and Japan, who had previously attempted to seize resources through conquest, became industrial giants through global commerce and trade.

In 1940, due to the high cost of the war, the U.K. and U.S. agreed to set the pound to the dollar exchange rate at £1 to $4.03. The result was a 20 percent devaluation of the pound since the U.S. first set the exchange rate in 1792. The exchange value remained until 1949 when the British government further devalued the pound by 30.5 percent to the dollar (£1 to $2.80) due to the lingering financial pressure of WWII and its gilt (bond) remittances.[24] Other countries reassessed their economies and adjusted their currency exchanges to the U.S. dollar based on a benchmark $35 per ounce of gold. Many foreign countries had already safely stored their gold reserves in the United States due to global wars.

As the Bretton Woods system became fully operational in 1958, most countries reestablished monetary stability with a return to the gold exchange standard. The International Monetary Fund, with fiscal prudence and guided transparency, helped countries adjust their interest rates, set tax policies, and regulate tariffs to boost their savings, productivity, and economic activity. In extreme circumstances, and only as a last resort, governments would reset their gold exchange rate with other nations. European countries, unlike today, held no national debt as they were required by the IMF to balance their budgets. The value of their currency would reflect the success—or failure—of their government and its economic leadership. It was not the amount of gold a country owned but how well a government managed its fiscal responsibilities made transparent through a global gold exchange standard. [24]

Currency Symbolism and Design

The U.S. dollar bill has gone through many design changes over the years. The last major redesign occurred in 1957 encouraged by religious public sentiment and support for the 1956 Act of Congress. The Act mandated inclusion of the new official motto “In God We Trust.” The maxim was used on Civil War greenbacks and periodically reappeared on coins and notes until officially legislated in 1957. Other changes have since been made to include security features to thwart counterfeiting.

Various cultures around the world attach either favorable or unfavorable folkloric connotations to the number 13. This number has been a positive recurring numeral and motif in the United States as it represented the 13 British colonies and inspired the design of the first flag. Thirteen colonies ratified the Declaration of Independence. On the one dollar bill there are 13 steps on the Pyramid, 13 letters in “E Pluribus Unum,” 13 letters in “ANNUIT COEPTIS,” (Favor our undertakings), 13 stars above the Eagle, 13 bars on the shield, 13 leaves on the olive branch, 13 olives, and 13 arrows. The design of the U.S. dollar represents the most emblematic note worldwide.[25, 26]

A proprietary blend of ink is used on the so-called paper money—a cloth composed of 75 percent cotton and 25 percent linen. The Bureau of Engraving and Printing prints approximately 16,650,000 one dollar bills each day, most of which replace worn older bills that are shredded. It is a huge operation as just 490 bills weigh one pound. Each of the twelve regional banks assesses their need for additional bills and directly requests them from the Bureau of Engraving and Printing. Federal Reserve notes, on average, remain in circulation for the following periods of time.[27] Generally, the higher the note value, the longer in circulation.

Denomination	$1	$5	$10	$20	$50	$100
Years in Circulation	5.8	5.5	4.5	7.9	8.5	15.0

Figure 12-7 *Years in circulation. Source: Federal Reserve Economic Department Public domain*

The front right of the bill has the ornate design of the Great Seal of the United States Treasury which shows both arms open with balanced scales representing justice. The key symbolizes its official authority with a chevron that displays the 13 stars representing the original states. To the left is the seal of the Federal Reserve with the location and letter for each of the 12 Federal Reserve District Banks. Each District Bank is independently incorporated with a nine-member board of directors appointed in staggered 14-year terms. Each District Bank can set its regional discount rate subject to the approval of the Board of Governors. The seven-member Board of Governors is appointed by the U.S. President with approval by the Senate. The FRB is held ultimately liable to the U.S. government based on the appointment by the President and Senate. The Board of Governors oversees the entire Federal Reserve System and its 12 District Reserve Banks. Included are 24 branch banks which serve to monitor, distribute, and provide financial services to the U.S. government and over 8,400 depository institutions regulated by the FDIC. [28, 29]

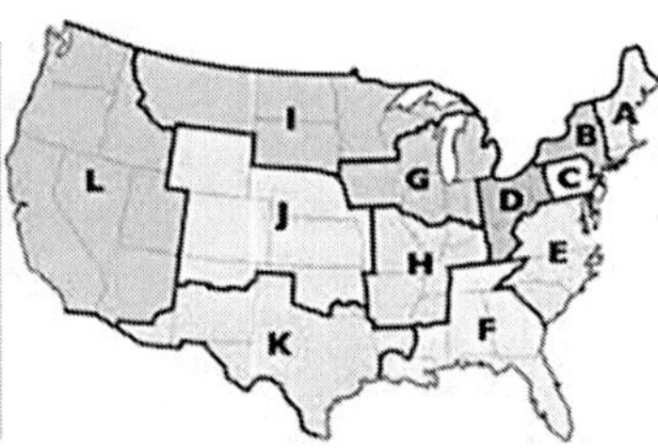

Figure 12-8 Left *District H St. Louis.* Figure 12-9 Center *12 District Reserve Banks.* Figure 12-10 Right *Great Seal of the United States Treasury. Public domain*

The reverse of The Great Seal on the left features a barren landscape dominated by an unfinished pyramid of 13 steps, topped by the "Eye of Providence" or "all-seeing eye of God" within a triangle. At the base of the pyramid are engraved the Roman numerals MDCCLXXVI (1776) for the starting date of American independence. At the top of the seal is the Latin phrase, ANNUIT COEPTIS for "Favor our Undertakings." At the bottom of the seal is a semicircular banner proclaiming "NOVUS ORDO SECLORUM" meaning "New Order of the Ages" in reference to the new American era. To the left of this seal, a string of 13 pearls extends toward the edge of the bill. [25]

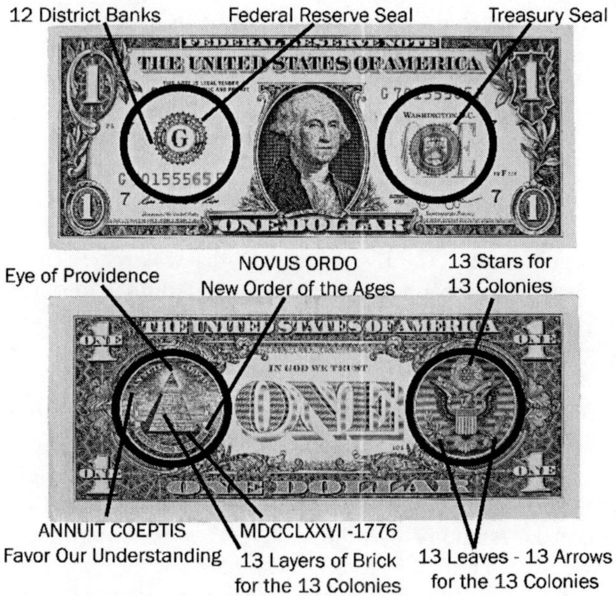

Figure 12-11 *Symbolism on the U.S. Bank Note—the world's most emblematic currency. Attribution: Jane Paquette at www.janessuncoastworks.com.*

The obverse of the seal on the right features the bald eagle as the national symbol of the United States. Above the eagle is a six-pointed star arranged in a radiant cluster of 13 stars to represent the 13 colonies. The eagle's breast is covered by a heraldic shield with the 13 stripes of the American flag. The eagle holds a ribbon in its beak which reads E PLURIBUS UNUM, a Latin phrase for "Out of many [states], one [nation]," a *de facto* motto of the United States (and the only one until 1956). The eagle holds 13 arrows in its left talon and, in its right, an olive branch with 13 leaves and 13 olives representing the powers of victory or peace. To the right of this seal, a string of 13 pearls extends toward the edge of the bill. [26]

The U.S. Mint tries to maintain a balance between public acceptance and the cost of currency production. Despite the government's efforts to promote their use, non-precious metal dollar coins have not been popular in the United States since the removal of gold and silver coins from circulation. The Government Accountability Office maintains that if the U.S. were to switch from a paper dollar to a dollar coin, taxpayers would save $4.4 billion over thirty years. Recent budgets passed by Congress have included provisions preventing the Treasury Department from spending any of its funds to redesign the one-dollar bill (largely because of potential financial impacts on the vending machine industry). There exist organizations specifically aimed at either preventing (Save the Greenback) or advocating (Coin Coalition) the complete elimination of the one-dollar bill in favor of a dollar coin.[30]

Attempts by the U.S. government to issue non-precious metal dollar coins have largely failed. The Eisenhower Dollar was issued from 1971 to 1978 and consisted of a copper-nickel clad metal similar to other coins in circulation. It was never very popular with the public due to its size and weight, and very few vending machines could accept it. Casinos favored it, but they now use tokens that approximate the size and weight of the Eisenhower Dollar which is now out of circulation. To celebrate women's suffrage (and perhaps appeal for their votes) the Democratic President Carter directed the U.S. Mint to produce Susan B. Anthony dollars from 1979 to 1981. They were authorized again in 1999 (by Democratic President Clinton). Susan B. Anthony was the first female to be portrayed on U.S. coinage in wide circulation. The coin was notoriously dubbed the "Carter Quarter" as it was similar to the existing quarter in color, size, and design and was often confused with it. It was not largely accepted and was soon discontinued.

Despite the failure of previous attempts to produce a dollar coin, the vending machine industry promoted the issuance of the Sacagawea Dollar. Over one billion of these coins, composed of copper clad in manganese brass, were mostly stocked by banks as the public mistook their size for quarters. The "Presidential $1 Coin Program" was another attempt at promoting the use of a dollar coin only to meet similar public resistance. By 2011, 1.4 billion uncirculated non-precious metal $1 coins were stockpiled in bank vaults, and the Presidential series was suspended with reduced production only for collectors.[30]

The issuance and design of the U.S. currency have gradually become more politicized and outside of the implicit control of the U.S. Mint.

Politicians openly pander to the public and yield to special interest groups but often find that the public rejects the design and use of the coinage. In 1987, the Canadian paper dollar bill was removed from circulation and replaced with a mandated gold-colored "Loonie" dollar coin (named after the Canadian Loon pictured on the coin). The nickname *loonie* became so popular among Canadians that the Canadian Royal Mint secured the intellectual property rights to it. The transition was smooth for Canadians who have now issued a popular "Toonie" or two-dollar coin. Both coins remain in widespread circulation and were accepted without controversy. Pointedly, the public's perception and acceptance of money largely rely on the emotional and cultural identity embellish by its design.

Figure 12-12 Left *The Eisenhower Dollar.* Figure 12-13 Center *Susan B. Anthony Dollar* Figure 12-14 Right *Canadian Loonie. Public domain*

The Nixon Shock: The End of the Gold Exchange System

The infamous "Nixon Shock" occurred on August 15, 1971, when, on the advice of politicians, he unilaterally invalidated the international convertibility of the U.S. dollar to gold. Republican President Richard Nixon favored less interventionist currency policies but faced massive financial debts of the Vietnam War, the costly entitlements for President Johnson's "War on Poverty," and for OPEC's increasing control over oil prices. In a failed attempt to stabilize inflation, Nixon imposed wage and price controls and added a 10 percent import surcharge fee on goods entering the United States.[31] Nonetheless, they resulted in higher unemployment and inflation which became known as "stagflation" (inflation without growth). Instead of adopting prudent fiscal policies to address these issues, he turned to the simple and expedient monetary solution of replacing the gold standard with a fiat currency. Nixon made famous a phrase first coined by economist Milton Friedman by stating, "*We are all Keynesians now.*" [32]

Niall Ferguson, in his book *The Ascent of Money*, expressed no remorse for the "Nixon Shock" and simply stated that countries could "*now choose their own monetary destiny apart from a global gold standard.*" [33] However, a new monetary system would need to be designed to stabilize world currencies and encourage global trade. A readjustment of the dollar's ratio to gold, along with more prudent fiscal policies, would have stabilized and solved most of the monetary problems—but then Nixon faced reelection. Despite Nixon's having said that closing the gold window would only be temporary, nearly 50 years later the window is still closed and currency and trade transactions between countries are by far more complicated. Floating currencies are not indicators of a free market but of the market's inevitable reaction to currency manipulation by governments and their elites .[34,35]

In 1973 the newly formed "Group of Seven" leading industrial countries, along with the International Monetary Fund, officially demonetized gold. IMF members were no longer required to hold gold reserves. Gold was officially just another commodity. The view of the monetary elites was that gold was dead and obsolete. Without a gold exchange standard, central banks found themselves more fiscally involved in the economic success or failure of their nation. Central banks were once confined to monetary adjustments based on a gold standard and bank reserve requirements, now central banks have become increasingly involved in fiscal policy issues typically reserved for government. The new and very different role of the FRB changed from that of simply stabilizing the currency. In January 2012, Congress passed a conflicting dual-mandate for the FRB to create maximum employment and moderate long-term interest rates, while controlling monetary stability.[36] Over time, the FRB has fundamentally transformed itself with more powers and higher expectations.

Gold, however, still insists on having a seat at the monetary table. Governments and their central banks largely maintain their gold (and silver) holdings as an implicit store of value and collateral. The U.S currently holds 8,133 tons of gold. The members of the Eurozone and European Central Bank hold 10,788 tons. China reports holdings of 1,788 tons, but estimates are closer to 4,000 tons, based on reliable data from Hong Kong exports and Chinese mining. Russia has 1,447 tons and has been acquiring over 200 tons per year. Mexico, Kazakhstan, and Vietnam, among other nations, have recently added to their gold reserves. However, between 1999 and 2002, the U.K. sold more than half of its gold at rock-bottom prices, and Canada proudly proclaims that it holds no gold whatsoever!

The purchasing power of gold has been preserved over a remarkably long period as the current spot price for gold hovers around a $1300 range in 2018. It is a market price considerably more than previously established under the gold exchange standard and an indication of the real monetary inflation of currencies by way of fiscal government policies.

The Operations of the Federal Reserve Banking System

The FRB officially acts as a privately held middleman between the U.S. Treasury and other sector institutions. The U.S. Constitution expressly prohibits the federal government or Treasury from directly circulating its own currency notes, but it can distribute and regulate them through private banks as was done in the free banking era. The U.S. Treasury is mainly responsible for collecting tax revenues through the Internal Revenue Service, overseeing the soundness of the nation's banking system through the Office of the Comptroller of the Currency (with oversight from its FDIC), and producing all currency, coinage and postage stamps through the U.S. Mint. The U.S. Mint exclusively sells to the privately held Federal Reserve Bank, coinage at face value and paper currency at an average printing cost of 5.0 cents per note in any denomination. In 2013 it sold 6.6 billion *notes* to the FRB. Federal Reserve *notes*, improperly called *dollars,* comprise some 99 percent of all U.S. currency in circulation. In 2016, it amounted to $1.46 trillion.[37]

The U.S. Mint distributes currency in 13 denominations from its four mint facilities (Philadelphia, Denver, San Francisco, West Point, and a depository at Fort Knox). These denominations include six coins (1¢, 5¢, 10¢, 25¢, 50¢ and $1) and seven bills ($1, $2, $5, $10, $20, $50, and $100). Public demand differs for each denomination. For example, there are an estimated 1.6 trillion pennies in circulation.

The Federal Reserve Bank issues, processes and distributes notes and coinage through its 28 cash offices to over 8,400 FDIC insured banks and thrift institutions. It forecasts currency demand and presents it to the U.S. Mint for production based on a 12-month rolling forecast of public demand. The Federal Reserve adjusts the domestic currency based on demand for goods and services, income levels, and alternate payment methods. Foreign demand for currency is adjusted by political and economic concerns associated with other currencies and exchanges. It is estimated that over two-thirds of U.S. currency is held abroad. While the Federal Reserve manages the domestic currency, the U.S. Treasury, through the Office of the Comptroller, manages all U.S. foreign-held currency.[38]

The Nugget

The history of the U.S. banking system has been one in which control of the money supply has vacillated between the U.S. Treasury and privately-owned financial institutions. The founders and framers of the U.S. Constitution envisioned the monetary system to be operated mainly by the private sector while maintaining the government's regulatory supervision over it. The central banks were initially designed to be middlemen or distributors of a stable regulated currency, which allowed the private markets to set demand for currency by way of interest rates. Over time, however, regulatory control and fiscal prudence have waxed and waned, while the central bank has grown significantly larger with increasing control over the monetary and fiscal responsibilities originally granted to it by Congress.

The creation of three central banking systems has not eliminated bank failures. Given today's modern information technology, the U.S. Treasury could well manage the currency and guide the financial markets, as was demonstrated during the long and productive history of the free banking era. It was an era when the currency was an obligation between private banks and their vigilant depositors—rather than an obligation of the U.S. Treasury and inattentive taxpayers.

CHAPTER THIRTEEN

GLOBALIZATION & THE PARADOX OF PROSPERITY

Keywords: Dutch Disease; Rule of 72; foreign direct investment; reserve currency; Forex; seigniorage

> "Compound interest is the eighth wonder of the world. He who understands it, earns it ... he who doesn't ... pays it."
>
> Albert Einstein, theoretical physicist

Globalization stems from the word to "globalize" which originally referred to the emergence of an international network of economic systems and has been used in an economic context since 1981. Theodore Levitt, a Harvard marketing professor, is credited with popularizing the term to explain how companies seek to rationalize their productivity. He defined it as the changes in technology and social behaviors that allow multinational companies to sell the same products worldwide—but conceded that companies had to balance deep-seated national cultural concerns with the general trend toward the embrace and efficiencies of global brands.

George Ritzer, a sociologist, argued that globalization has negative social and political repercussions resulting in cultural homogenization that he compared to fast-food restaurants—or global "McDonaldization." The concept of globalization has inspired competing definitions, interpretations, and debate. The academic literature commonly subdivides globalization into three major areas: economic globalization, cultural globalization, and political globalization.[1, 2]

Before the advent of chartered multinational corporations, many European monarchs, particularly the Portuguese and Spanish, maintained exclusive control over trade. The British East India Company, established in 1600, is considered the first multinational business organization that handed substantial control over to its shareholders and management. India's resentment toward the company's policies spilled over in 1806 with the Vellore Fort mutiny whereby over 100 British soldiers were killed. Hostility grew into the full-scale Indian Rebellion of 1857, directly aimed at the management of the British East India Company. [3]

The early history of multinational corporations is closely intertwined with the dark side of colonialism and exploitative mercantilism. Incentivized with government charters, these nascent companies were allowed unfettered expansion in international trade and exploitation. They undertook a direct role in formal colonization by creating and maintaining settler colonies and colonial trading posts such as the Hudson's Bay Company, the South Australia Company, and the London based Virginia Company. The British Royal African Company became the logistical component of the Atlantic slave trade, leading to more repugnance and animosity toward multinational corporations operating outside of home oversight. The company-owned colonies soon gave rise to foreign factories, ports, plantations, corporate levy of taxation, and even their own armies.[4]

The newly born international corporations created economic disparity between their home country and their colonies by simply exploiting colonial resources and labor, and then investing the profits in the home country, resulting in the enrichment of the colonizer and the impoverishment of the colonized. Intellectual colonization often followed with a view of inferiority toward those being colonized. Rebellions soon took place. Notably, the colonies of North America were reluctant to allow their profits to be repatriated back to Britain and, before the war for independence, maintained a higher standard of living than that of their contemporaries in England. The abusive powers of these pioneering corporations were made public during the 19th century, resulting in their corporate charters withdrawn and the state reasserting control and oversight over the companies and the colonies.

The state soon became directly embroiled in the complexities of colonialization, contributing to many local military disputes and eventual world wars. However, corporate control over colonial economic affairs persisted in many of the colonies. The European colonial charter companies were disbanded during the process of decolonization, with the final colonial corporation, the Mozambique Company, dissolved in 1972. However, the economic impact of corporate colonial exploitation has proven to be deep-seated and far-reaching with some asserting that its impact is among the chief causes of today's global income inequality among the formerly colonized countries. [4]

The Rise of a New Global Reserve Currency

Reserve currencies are not immune to history nor to change. Political and military dominance gave rise to the widely accepted gold and silver backed hard currencies of the Greek tetradrachm, the Roman aureus and denari, the Byzantine solidus and Arab dinar of the middle-ages, the Venetian ducat and the Florentine florin of the Renaissance, and the Dutch guilder and the French franc of the 17th century. The British pound dominated as a global reserve currency from the 1600s until the close of WWII. The advent of multinational corporations, however, spread a country's economic dominance along with the use of its currency—and the social and cultural hegemony that accompanied it. A reserve currency carries with it economic privileges but also social and cultural responsibilities.

Before the end of the World War II, and mindful of the how colonization and economic nationalism had contributed to its devastation, representatives from all 44 allied nations gathered for a conference at the Mount Washington Hotel in Bretton Woods, New Hampshire. The conference established the Bretton Woods system of monetary management which created the rules for commercial and financial relations among the United States, Canada, Western Europe, Australia, and Japan. The Soviet Union declined to sign the agreement, citing it as an instrument of capitalist Wall Street bankers.

The Bretton Woods system was the first example of a fully negotiated global monetary order intended to govern monetary relations among independent sovereign states. To address the lack of economic cooperation among the nations, the conference established the International Monetary Fund (IMF), and the International Bank for Reconstruction and Development (IBRD). The IMF was designed to bridge temporary imbalances of payments and prevent the competitive devaluation of the currencies based on the new gold standard. The IBRD was organized to finance reconstruction in Europe and is now part of the World Bank with member nations having voting shares. It currently offers loans to developing countries.[5]

The United States, which secured and controlled over two-thirds of the world's gold, insisted that all allied nations peg their currency to the U.S. dollar and adopt a monetary policy that maintained their external exchange rate within 1 percent of the dollar. The rate was set at 35 dollars per ounce of gold. The concept was not for countries to acquire gold—but for their governments to maintain sound monetary and fiscal policies so that their own currency remained within ± 1 percent of the exchange rate with the dollar.[6] The dollar became the dominant hard reserve currency commonly used in international transactions in which many commodities are priced. Natural gas, sugar, and coffee, for example, are commonly traded in dollars and oil in "petrodollars." Just because commodities are priced in dollars doesn't necessarily mean that a change in the price of the dollar changes the price of the commodity. Rather, the price of the commodity in dollars will change to reflect the change in the supply and demand of the commodity.

A reserve currency makes it easier to trade than a batch of different currencies each with its own interest rate, inflation rate, political, and cultural concerns. The privilege of an anchor currency or safe-haven currency is that people who live in a country that issues a reserve currency can purchase imports and borrow across borders more conveniently than people in other nations. This is because they do not need to exchange their currency in order to do so. It is the primary reason many countries peg their currencies to the dollar or some other regional reserve currency used in their international trade. Trade expands based on a common currency for an exchange transaction. The reserve currency is also accompanied by geopolitical and cultural prestige that further enhances the perceived value of that currency. The downside of a reserve currency is providing the security and ensuring the trust among those using it.

To further jumpstart the devastated global economy, President Harry Truman and Secretary of State George Marshall pressed the allies to create the General Agreement on Tariffs and Trade (GATT). Before this time, only bilateral agreements in reducing tariffs and quotas were made between nations by way of "most favored nation" status. GATT was charged with arranging numerous multilateral negotiations. By April of 1947, GATT negotiated 45,000 tariff concessions affecting $10 billion of trade—soon to be followed by eight rounds of successful large-scale multilateral reductions. GATT evolved into the World Trade Organization (WTO) in 1995 and is recognized as the world's most successful international organization in expanding global economic prosperity.

In 1947, the average tariff levels for the major GATT participants were about 22 percent of their GDP but were just 5 percent after the last round of large-scale reductions in 1999.[6] Economists attribute much of the tariff and quota reductions to the actions of GATT and the WTO. Today, WTO primarily adjudicates trade conflicts between nations as the easier reductions in post-war trade barriers have been largely abridged. The slashing of tariffs and other trade barriers after WWII brought unprecedented prosperity to millions of people worldwide.

The United States provided financial support to rebuild Europe and prevent the spread of communism. To speed lagging economic development in Europe, the United States provided direct support of 13 billion dollars under the Marshall Plan in 1948. The Marshall Plan's purpose was to remove trade barriers, modernize industry, and speed economic recovery for eighteen allied nations. The United States provided similar aid programs to Asia that were not part of the four-year duration of the Marshall Plan. The Soviet Union countered with their version of the Molotov Plan for the Eastern Block of nations with money raised from war reparations assessed mainly on Poland and Hungary.[7]

The return to a globally accepted and stable reserve currency backed by gold; the implementation of new international economic organizations; the direct financial aid of the Marshall Plan; the continued reduction of tariffs and quotas; along with the security of the United States Navy patrolling the commercial ocean lanes, provided a global boom in economic prosperity for those participating nations—and to the United States.

Foreign Direct Investment

By 1970, the second largest economy in the world was foreign direct investment (FDI) in Europe—by way of United States multinational corporations. [8] Currently, the proportion of dollars held outside of the United States, versus that held domestically, indicates the existence of a foreign-based dollar that mirrors an economy *twice* that of the U.S. domestic market.[9] U.S. businesses prospered with the outcome of the war and were the most capable to take advantage of the new global economic incentives. Exports from the United States were replaced with direct investment abroad, creating a simmering political and economic dilemma to this day.

FDI is characterized by controlling ownership of a business enterprise in one country by an entity based in another country. Investments in mining, agriculture, and manufacturing provide mostly positive long-term benefits to a country receiving FDI, while the purchase of real estate and packaged financial investment portfolios are often seen as short-term "hot money" used for speculation and may provide a negative impact to an economy. The awareness of such large-scale ownership of production and trade by the Americans became a major European concern in the late 1960s.

The French called the Bretton Woods system "America's exorbitant privilege" as it resulted in a lopsided financial system where non-U.S. citizens saw themselves supporting American living standards and subsidizing American multinationals. In 1965, in defiance of the economic alliance, President Charles de Gaulle announced his intention to exchange its U.S. dollar reserves, mainly obtained from the profits of U.S. multinational companies in France, for gold at the official exchange rate. Barry Eichengreen, a popular American economist, summarized: *"It costs only a few cents for the Bureau of Engraving and Printing to produce a $100 bill, but other countries had to pony up $100 of actual goods in order to obtain one."*[10] However, the United States was itself handcuffed to the gold standard and could not simply print more dollars without inflationary and other adverse domestic economic consequences.

United States currency significantly appreciated based on the demand by U.S. multinationals for dollars to convert their earnings from foreign operations to pay their home shareholders. The strong dollar made it harder for domestic companies to export, incentivized United States corporations to expand or move abroad, and gave rise to foreign company investments in the United States. U.S. multinationals were penalized with higher taxes and regulations *not* to bring their profits back home—so as *not* to further appreciate the dollar. The multinationals reacted by simply establishing off-shore dollar accounts, further exacerbating the problem.

The consequences resulted in a negative balance of payments, which moved the Federal Reserve to create monetary inflation causing the dollar to be seen as increasingly overvalued in the 1960s. The overly strong dollar may even have influenced the government to pursue the Vietnam War, and entitlement programs like the War on Poverty, simply to weaken the dollar and make it more competitive in international trade.[11]

In 1947, the compensation (profits, wages, salary, and bonuses) in the financial sector accounted for just 2.32 percent of U.S. GDP. Today it has grown to an estimated 9 percent of the U.S. GDP.[12] Meanwhile, the U.S. factory workforce diminished in size from nearly 40 percent in 1947 to just 8.5 percent today. The nation of manufacturers and small businesses has become a nation of financial managers, speculators, and real estate flippers.

The Rule of 72

Why, knowing the colonial history and inherent hegemony of multinational corporations, would a country accept FDI? The most obvious fact is that it is often very profitable to both the company and the host country if managed correctly. There are many classical economic theories to explain why and how companies and countries benefit from FDI. However, the "Rule of 72" is a simple financial method for estimating an investment's doubling time by which an investor is paid back for the use of their money.[13] It indicates the impact of compound interest and its benefits (espoused by Albert Einstein as the "eighth wonder of the world"). Although scientific calculators and spreadsheet programs have functions to find the accurate doubling-time of an investment, the rule is useful for easy mental calculations, and to illustrate the impact of the investment—particularly to suspicious nonbusiness government officials and adamant anti-capitalists.

An example of the rule of 72: invest $100 with compounding interest at a rate of 9 percent per annum, the rule of 72 simply divides 72 by 9 percent giving 8 years for the investment to be worth $200; an exact calculation shows ln (2)/ln (1+.09) = 8.0432 years. Other typical commercial examples: 72/20 percent would pay back in 3.6 years, and a 4% mortgage gives 72/4 percent or 18 years to payback. Gross profit margins on some computer chips today exceed 65%. This rule applies to exponential growth and is therefore used for compound interest as opposed to simple interest calculations.

New capital is created once the investment is paid back, strengthening the both currencies! Many well-managed companies can achieve payback in as little as three to seven years—providing the host country with substantial infrastructure, employment, new technology, and continued profits after the investment is paid off. Countries and local governments often extend tax incentives to attract FDI as the tax incentives themselves speed the payback period and the profitable returns to the host country.

In 1973 the world stockpiled $500 billion (in 2017 dollars) in foreign-exchange reserves, mostly from dollars earned by U.S. multinational corporations, and parked outside of the United States. Today two-thirds of total foreign reserves are denominated in dollars or an estimated $11 trillion.[14]

The Nixon Shock

On the 15th of August 1971, the United States unilaterally terminated the convertibility of the United States dollar to gold, ending the Bretton Woods monetary system. It was hoped that a new monetary system of floating currencies would stem the flow of the global demand for dollars, depreciate the dollar, smoothly reduce the trade deficit, lessen political resentment towards economic U.S. hegemony, and avoid a recession from the lack of domestic fiscal discipline. It allowed the U.S. to avoid a deep recession by *not* having to readjust its currency to parity with the gold standard. Many currencies became free-floating against the dollar such as the pound sterling, the French franc, and German mark. Other countries still today maintain a fixed exchange rate to the dollar, i.e., Saudi Arabia, or to another currency based on the relevance of its regional trade status. The instability of floating currencies has led to a mixed bag of currency depreciations, enormous speculation, central bank interventions, unrestricted and nontransparent government monetary and fiscal policies, and malinvestments in private capital. No longer bound by fixed exchange rates and the maintenance of the dollar's reserve status, the U.S. government's fiscal discipline further broke down.[15]

Countries could not agree to a formal revaluation of their currencies. The dollar plunged by a third during the 1970s setting the stage for stagflation (inflation with slow economic growth or stagnation). Petroleum prices inflated in step with that of the devalued dollar, inciting global instability and the rise of the OPEC oil cartel. The German mark appreciated significantly against other European nations after it was freed to float in May 1971. Japan's central bank significantly intervened in the foreign exchange market to prevent the yen from increasing in value. However, the large-scale intervention by Japan's central bank could not prevent the depreciation of U.S. dollar against the yen which floated between as little as 80 to as much as 120 yen to a dollar in just a few years.[15] European countries banded together to form their central bank and the euro currency. In 2015 the Chinese renminbi de-pegged from the U.S. dollar to become a free-floating and looming international reserve currency more commonly named the yuan.

Today, many central banks use money in their current account to adjust their currency within a range of a basket of major reserve currencies, as well as to balance their country's competing business interests. Multinational corporations largely exposed to international trade favor a weak currency to increase their book revenues and profits. Swings in currency alone often have a significant impact on reported earnings. However, domestically oriented companies generally prefer a strong currency to purchase cheaper foreign goods and post higher profits. The competing interests between national and business interests inflame ongoing trade disputes, currency wars, and domestic political divisions. The respected former president of the U.S. Federal Reserve, Paul Volcker, in 2011 expressed regret over the abandonment of Bretton Woods: *"Nobody's in charge... the Europeans couldn't live with the uncertainty and made their own currency, and now that's in trouble."*[16]

While free-floating national currencies *imply* market-driven adjustments based on supply and demand—they also carry risks and create uncertainties for international trade and investments. The volatility of a currency is difficult to assess without a hard measure like that of a gold standard, and partly the result of sophisticated financial markets that have flourished to help businesses hedge their risks. A free-floating monetary system leaves monetary managers free to guide their economic policies, but also leaves them free to be irresponsible—and, in some countries, they have been quick to take the opportunity.

The Balance of Trade Equation

Economists cite many factors that cause short-term trade surpluses or deficits which by themselves may be considered neither good nor bad. Economic globalists point out, for example, that a customer may purchase an item in a store by exchanging money for the purchased item. Who then is poorer if both parties get what they want: does one party run a surplus and the other a deficit? Nationalists argue that the underlying problem arises when the store exchanges one currency for that of another currency. Where does the customer earn the money to pay for the purchased items and what becomes of the value of the money accumulated by both parties over time?

A higher savings rate generally corresponds to a trade surplus, such as currently exists with Japan and Germany, while a country with a lower savings rate tends to run higher trade deficits, i.e., the United States. Savings are closely related to trade surpluses and provide the main source of physical investment used to produce fixed capital, such as factories and machinery that lead to higher wages based on increased productivity. By not using income from trade surpluses to buy consumer goods and services, it is possible for resources to be instead invested for economic growth. Japan and Germany maintain themselves as creditor nations with strong trade surpluses while the United States has become a debtor nation with persistent trade deficits.

Contrary to the assumption that persistent trade deficits are due to bad trade deals, trade deficits are likely due to the status of the dollar as the main global reserve currency. The dollar's continued status as a global reserve currency is as responsible as are bad trade agreements for persistent trade deficits. The high demand for dollars has tilted the pinball machine with odds against American exporters, workers, and taxpayers.

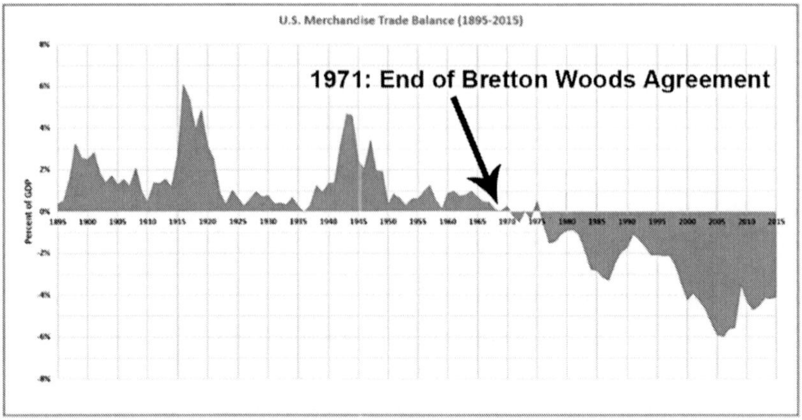

Figure 13-1. *The balance of trade is the difference between the monetary value of the flow of a nation's exports and imports over a given time. A positive trade balance or surplus indicates a country exports more than it imports, and conversely, a trade deficit or negative balance indicates it imports more than it exports. An abrupt change to the United States Balance of Trade occurred in 1971 with the unilateral withdrawal from the gold standard established with the Bretton Woods agreement. Source: Department of Foreign Trade*

In 1752, the Scottish philosopher David Hume reasoned that Great Britain could not permanently gain from exports because hoarding gold (i.e., pound sterling tied to the gold standard) would make gold more plentiful in England. Consequently, the prices of British goods would rise to make their exports less attractive and foreign goods more attractive to import. [17]

Milton Friedman, a Noble Prize-winning economic monetarist, underscored the views of Hume with a "worst-case scenario." It would be in the country's best interest if the profits from its exports *never* returned to the country of origin. The exporting country would be better off by exchanging the profits from exports for pieces of cheaply made paper. As Friedman put it, this would be the same result as if the exporting country burned the dollars it earned, never returning them to market circulation. [18]

The immense size and expansion of global companies have exasperated the dilemma of currency appreciation based on trade between countries. The Global 500 is an annual ranking by Fortune Magazine of the top 500 corporations worldwide as measured by revenue. Geographically, North America has 143 of such corporations (about 30 percent), Europe about 30 percent, followed by Asia—primarily Chinese companies, with about 40 percent of the total.[19] The S&P 500, the market that represents the 500 largest companies in the United States, receives more than 30 percent of their revenue from outside the U.S., while the Dow 30 companies get well over 50 percent. Multinational companies like Intel Corporation earn 80 percent of their revenue from outside the U.S., as do corporations like Exxon Mobil and McDonald's, each with 65 percent.[20] Those foreign earned dollars are under the scrutiny of the U.S. Treasury and outside of the control of the U.S. Federal Reserve System, leaving the dollar vulnerable to foreign currency manipulation on a grand scale by the central banks.

The Paradox of Prosperity

The paradox of prosperity (or paradox of plenty) is a monetary dilemma more commonly referred to as the "Dutch Disease." The term was first coined in a business magazine, *The Economist,* in 1977.[21] The economic paradox is based on a strong causal relationship between an increase in the development of one sector of an economy which affects an overall decline in other sectors. It was first diagnosed by noting a causal connection of a massive natural gas-field discovered in 1959 in the province of Groningen in the Netherlands —with that of the decline of the export-oriented Dutch manufacturing sector.

A large inflow of foreign revenues from the export of natural gas increased the value of the Dutch currency compared to the currencies of other nations. The result was that Holland's export-oriented productive sectors became more expensive for countries to buy and allowed for less expensive competitive imports to enter the country—undermining the existing home businesses. The revenues generated by natural gas sales abroad were primarily spent by the government on social entitlements. Eventually, the natural gas exports declined, and the recession left the country worse off than had it not discovered the gas-field at all.

This paradox challenges the theory underlying the economic principle of comparative advantage in international trade set forth by David Ricardo in 1817. That is, if two countries each produce a commodity and engage in free trade, then each country will export more and import less of the commodity it is more efficient at producing.[22] The assumption is that both countries would be better off engaging in international trade. Both Ricardo and Adam Smith did not consider currency appreciation and unfair monetary manipulation as they were living in a time of a stable gold exchange standard between nations.

Economists have since identified numerous examples of countries whose discoveries of various natural resources were exported in exchange for foreign currency causing general harm to other home industries. The IMF classifies 51 countries with extreme dependence on natural resource development. Evidence suggests they are cursed with low savings rates, lower productivity and growth performance, autocratic governments, and more corruption.[23] While the paradox was first attributed to the discoveries of natural resources like coffee, petroleum, diamonds, and metals, it is now recognized that *any* development that results in a large inflow of foreign currency, including FDI and foreign aid, may cause serious harm to other sectors of a nation's economy.[24]

Empirical evidence links the continued historical decline, stagnation, and lack of innovation in Spain's once globally dominant economy, to the large influx of silver from the Americas in the 1540s.[25] The influx of silver rendered their businesses globally uncompetitive due to their overly valued currency. Today the profits of Japanese companies take a substantial toll based on a stronger yen, as do those of other companies whose profits lead to an overly valued currency.[26]

The Asian financial crisis of 1997 carried with it all the symptoms of the Dutch disease and raised fears of a worldwide economic meltdown often referred to as the "Asian contagion." Asian countries offered high-interest rates attractive to foreign investors looking for a high rate of return. As a result, in the late 1980s and early 1990s the regional economies of Thailand, Malaysia, Indonesia, Singapore, and South Korea received a large inflow of foreign direct investment and experienced high growth rates of 8–12% GDP, which greatly increased the value of their currencies. The "Asian economic miracle" was widely acclaimed by financial institutions labeled the "Washington Consensus" which included the IMF, the World Bank, and the U.S. Treasury Department.[27]

The start of a global financial contagion began, however, when Thailand lacked enough foreign currency to support its currency peg to the U.S. dollar. The Thai baht was forced to float on the open exchange market, and foreign money and investment were quickly withdrawn. The short-term speculative foreign currency was dubbed "hot money." Thailand's stock market and asset prices collapsed, increasing its private debt, and the slumping currency crisis soon spread to inter-connected economies. On 11 August 1997, the IMF unveiled an initial rescue package for Thailand with more than $17 billion to help stamp out a crisis of its own making.[28]

Enormous amounts of financial aid and oversight were used to treat the disease, primarily with U.S. Treasuries stashed as collateral in the foreign countries' current accounts and in the reserves of large banks. Global markets resorted to currency "sterilization" which takes place when central banks aim to neutralize the impact of certain foreign exchange transactions, actions that Milton Freidman would consider the burning of dollars. In 1999, the backlash by developing countries against the Washington Consensus developed into an anti-globalization movement. [29, 30]

Natural resource wealth can be either a curse or a blessing depending on how the influx of foreign capital is used to support domestic industries in human capital formation, growth in productivity and wages, and economic openness. Four countries are cited as escaping the curse of the Dutch disease: Canada and Norway provide oversight of sovereign superfunds supported by their oil profits, Chile maintains regulatory governance over its copper and mineral resources, and Botswana guides reinvestments earned from its diamond production. Whereas Great Britain spent its taxes from North Sea oil to support public entitlements, the Norwegian government invested its taxes and profits into foreign direct investments. Their profits from returns in foreign currencies are used to keep their home currency stable, their businesses competitive, and supply the government with revenues for infrastructure improvements. The Norwegian oil fund currently has over $1 trillion (U.S.) in assets worth about $200,000 per Norwegian citizen.

These four countries provide government oversight of their key commodities and foreign sourced income. They support competition and prevent a concentration of ownership. They promote national transparency of how the influx of foreign capital is spent, and compensate export industries to improve their productivity or innovate into new competitive markets.[31, 32, 33] Their solution is proactive supervision and free market policies that keep their currency in balance with others and reduce undue harm to their economy.

The Plunge Protection Team to the Rescue

In response to series of abrupt currency swings and financial crises, the United States President Ronald Reagan signed an executive order on March 18, 1988, creating the President's Working Group on Financial Markets or simply the "Working Group," colloquially known as the "Plunge Protection Team." The Working Group is comprised of four of the most powerful people in global monetary policy: The President of the United States and the Chairpersons of the Security Exchange Commission, the Federal Reserve Board of Governors, and the Commodity Futures Trading Commission. The term "*Plunge Protection Team*" was originally used in the headline of an article in The Washington Post on February 23, 1997.[34] Attempts to create an international currency based on the IMF and its Special Drawing Rights have come to a standstill as central banks retain their sovereign hold over their currencies. Free trade, under a floating exchange rate system and the manipulation of the stock and financial markets, has become no more than a romantic fantasy.

Hard evidence suggests that the Working Group has directly intervened in global currency plunges like the market crash of Black Monday in 1987, the Mexican Peso Crisis of 1994, and the Asian Contagion of 1997, through buying stock market index futures contracts, either in cooperation with major banks or through trading desks at the U.S. Treasury.[34] The Working Group reacted to the global financial crisis of 2007-2008 by issuing trillions of dollars of "quantitative easing or QE," whereby a central bank buys its government's bonds or other financial assets in order to stimulate the economy and increase liquidity, thereby weakening the currency. The European, Japanese, and other central banks have also adopted this monetary policy, leading to sustained currency wars.[35] Many economists question whether the additional liquidity has filtered down to the worker and consumer and have called for a "QE for the people."[36]

There is suspicious evidence of the daily involvement of the Working Group in the stock market and other financial markets by way of the United States Federal Reserve through the United States Federal Open Market Committee (FOMC).[35] The FOMC controls the supply of credit to banks and the sale of U.S. Treasury securities, thereby increasing liquidity which directly affects the price of currencies both foreign and domestic.[35]

The FOMC can simply create more money and lend it at ultralow interest rates to those key financial institutions that it deems important. An approved bank can buy treasuries or cash at the central bank's "discount window" for .05 percent and loan it out to customers at 18+ percent interest on credit-cards, or use it as bank reserve collateral to make other types of loans. Currently, large U.S. corporations often resort to "stock buybacks" by borrowing money cheaply from large banks and buying back their shares on the stock market—once considered an illegal activity. Stock buybacks drive up the company's stock price without ever having to invest in the company or make a sale to a customer.[37]

The Forex

The foreign exchange market (or Forex) was formed during the 1970s as countries switched from the fixed exchange rate of the Bretton Woods system to market driven floating exchange rates. The Forex is a lightly regulated and decentralized system of large international banks and financial centers that buy, sell, and exchange currencies at current and determined prices for a profit. Forex does not set a currency's absolute value, as was done under the Bretton Woods gold standard, but rather determines its relative value by setting the market price of one currency with that of another, as currencies are always traded in pairs.

The larger banks often turn to a smaller number of "dealers," some insurance companies, and other interbank markets to complete the currency exchange. The public often sees currency traders or dealers in airports and international commerce centers. The decline in the acceptance of cryptocurrencies is largely due to the lack of controls by currency exchange dealers which are more open to computer fraud.

Speculation in the relative value of the currencies has led to a "carry trade" based on often wide differences in interbank rates, the interest rate between two currencies, as well as, central bank interventions. Over 5 trillion dollars are traded *daily* on the Forex in the form of hedges and bets using various financial products like options, swaps, forwards, and other derivatives. The largest volume of currency transactions occurs in London, while the most traded currency is the U.S. dollar with 88 percent daily share followed by the Euro (31 percent), the Japanese yen (22 percent), the pound sterling (13%) and so forth.[38]

Large corporations and sophisticated financiers typically secure conversion fees just hundredths of a percentage point off the interbank rates, however less sophisticated investors may pay more than a 3 to 5 percentage point spread based on interbank rate differences. Consider depositing $10,000 in a bank and the next day finding only $9,600 in the account minus the currency conversion fees made between several banks. A currency conversion fee of less than one percentage point can be made through trusted and regulated international money-transfer companies, such as, World First and the OFX Group. Published currency exchange rates posted online and in newspapers report the exchange rates *not* the fees charged.

A strong reserve currency needs a strong central bank for the simple—and perhaps only—task of ensuring monetary balance. Monetary balance comes from simply matching the supply and demand of a currency to achieve the desired outcome. Central banks need to recognize that they have total control over their currencies to fully manage them. They can employ any number of ways to increase the money supply to expand the economy, or decrease the money supply to slow it from overheating.

Currently, the amount of U.S. cash in worldwide circulation is 1.6 trillion dollars, of which two-thirds or $1.07 trillion circulates outside of the U.S. About $80 billion is held in depository institutions leaving $453 billion in the hands of U.S. domestic businesses and individuals.[9] Credit markets are shaped and generally mirror short-term cash.

The Federal Reserve System monitors and controls all domestic cash through its 12 regional districts—while the U.S. Treasury controls all cash outside of the United States. The establishment of dedicated U.S. regional central bank districts outside of the United States would bring much needed monetary control and transparency to the base money supply of both cash and credit markets. The wide disparities of currency distribution created by the differences in regional capital formation would best be addressed by giving more control to the regional bank districts over their base money supply as was done in the early formation of the Federal Reserve Bank. Regional monetary controls could adjust and balance credit markets and introduce competition among the local entities. Currently, both the Federal Reserve and the U.S. Treasury's involvement in the global and domestic currency markets is a one-size-fits-all solution to currency imbalances and growing regional monetary and social instability.

Today, the complexity of floating exchange rates distorts and corrupts currency markets with armies of financiers, bankers, economists, lawyers, bond dealers, foreign exchange specialists, managers of hedge funds, and derivatives managers all entrenched in the everyday transactions of a floating exchange currency market. The substantial size and decentralized financial operations have given rise to trade speculation, scandal, and a continuation of economic bubbles.[39, 40] Currency manipulation, particularly by central banks, remains a very real problem as carefully constructed trade deals between nations and businesses can be wiped out within days by the change of a few percentage points in the exchange rate or by a newly erected trade barrier.[41] This all begs the question: What is the U.S. dollar (or any currency) worth today? [42]

Epilogue

Western civilization evolved from an earlier period of simple trade and barter into today's unimaginable scale of worldwide economic prosperity. Western culture came to dominate much of the global economy through the cultivation and sophistication of capital and property ownership guided by an incentivized and educated labor force.

It is easy to observe that those countries and cultures with access to capital and property ownership are far better off than those with little or no access. The ancient Greeks introduced the notion of individual property ownership. The workers' labor, resulting in profits from private land ownership, evolved into capital. Capital took the early form of coinage, based on the rarity of precious metals, as it provides a simple way to count profits. Stored capital must be protected by a strong military, a responsive and uncorrupted government, and supportive social values and institutions. Capital has evolved from precious metals to paper, and then into complex options and derivatives—as capital reflects the changing values and needs of its culture.

Ancient philosophers and religious theologians have long debated how to treat the ownership of capital and property based on the evolving views of usury. Usury is defined as the illegal action or practice of lending money at unreasonably high rates of interest. A derogatory word for a usurer in current parlance is "loan shark." Long associated with moneylending, usury has had a sordid history and was much debated by philosophers and religious leaders from Plato to Jesus. Karl Marx not only struggled to explain interest but considered capital (and property ownership) as the main cause of alienation among labor and social relationships. The monetary interest of any kind is still forbidden by Islam as is full property ownership by an individual. History is replete with those who condemn simple interest as usurious. However, they could not possibly have imagined the social challenges of dealing with compound interest and the exchange of capital between independent national currencies. How capital should be treated is a continuing cultural saga.

Based on the value of labor, earned income is capital gained from employment, work, or through business activities. However, the treatment of capital formation and the gains from capital in the form of interest remain largely misunderstood. Henry George, a popular 19th-century American political economist and journalist, based his belief that people should own the value of their labor—but that the economic value derived from rents or profits on land (including natural resources) should be disbursed equally to all members of society. He coined the term "unearned income" or income gained through the passive ownership of land, capital assets, and capital gains. The most common forms of unearned income are interest income, such as interest earned on bank deposit accounts, loans, and capital gains based on any number of investments.

Henry George was a self-described capitalist who believed that the ownership of property and capital were the driving force behind human progress. The popularity of 19th century "Georgism" was the view that no tax should be applied to earned income on labor and wages, such as payroll taxes. That consumption and unearned income should be the sole source of taxation and used in support of public infrastructure for the benefit of all.[45] Some dismiss his ideas as radical, as the stored capital would lead to ever higher property prices. However, he posed the question as to how capital should be taxed, and how best to deal with currency appreciation as storage for capital. If capital goes to the wrong uses or does not flow at all, the economy will not operate efficiently, and economic growth will stagnate.

"Seigniorage" or the right of the lord *(seigneur)* to print money, is the revenue associated with the creation of money through routine debt monetization, or the expansion of the money supply during GDP growth while meeting yearly inflation targets.[45] Seigniorage is a convenient, and often unreported and misunderstood, public source of unearned income and revenue for many governments. It provides a government with increased purchasing power at the expense of the public's purchasing power—in essence, an *inflation tax* on the public.

Many in government consider new capital as theirs to spend, and others may consider it as a source of government corruption or mass usury. The transparent reporting of seigniorage by the central bank may help government leaders to understand persistent trade deficits and define the limits of public expenditures. Opaque government transactions allow for government corruption.

The Nugget

The dollar's status as a global reserve currency is in dire need of international monetary reform. The return to a hard currency as the source of good money is a cornerstone of good government, while soft money leads to corruption in government and social erosion. History suggests that stable exchange rates establish the most reliable and level playing field for free and fair world trade. The stability of exchange rates has historically been fostered by a fixed parity to gold as was successfully introduced some 2500 years ago. A fixed exchange rate, based on penalties to keep money stable and in parity to gold, holds governments liable for keeping their promises. Governments should never reach the point at which they are obligated to buy or sell gold by simply adjusting their base currency using the bank discount rate or open-market rates.

A currency fixed to gold doesn't solve all currency problems but is the least imperfect solution to avoid currency and trade wars. A gold standard links the value of paper currencies to the value of gold in much the same manner as quarters and dimes maintain a fixed relationship with dollar bills. Gold has not been a flawless foundation for a monetary system and has experienced its human frailties, but it has been the best system yet devised to ensure transparent government. The concept is not for governments to acquire gold—but for governments to maintain sound monetary and fiscal policies fixed to parity with gold.

The swing between soft money and back to hard currency has often occurred throughout history. Wars, social upheavals, and economic calamities have led to the distrust and suspension of a gold standard for short periods of history. However, the benefits of a gold-backed currency for trade and social stability have resurrected it numerous times over the past 2500 years.

Much of the population who lived under a previous gold standard ending in 1971 are near retirement, leaving later generations with no immediate incentive to recreate or reconsider the true benefits of the system. The advantages of hard money are unknown to those who have only an inkling of its success as an alternative to fiat currency. President Nixon suggested a return to the gold standard, and Congressman Jack Kemp had introduced the Gold Standard Act in 1984, but both attempts faced strong opposition. President Ronald Reagan created the "Gold Commission" with little time to initiate any action. Floating currencies could disappear just as suddenly as they appeared in 1971. Banks would simply return to managing their currencies through the supply of base money. The United States could easily reinstate the gold exchange system as the foundation of a new monetary system—if it could only get its fiscal house in order so as to prove its credence and trust.

Miguel de Cervantes Saavedra, the 16th-century author of Don Quixote de la Mancha, wrote: "*The gratification of wealth is not found in mere possession or on lavish expenditure, but in its wise application.*"

NOTES AND REFERENCES

Chapter One: The Bizarre World of Currencies

1. Ridley, M. (2010). *The rational optimist: How prosperity evolves*. London: Fourth Estate, pp. 55-58.
2. Friedman, M. (1991). *The island of stone money*. Hoover Institution, Stanford University.
3. Friedman, M. (1994). *Money mischief: Episodes in monetary history*. Houghton Mifflin Harcourt, p. 3.
4. Xinru, L. (2010). *The silk road in world history.* New York: Oxford University Press, p.11.
5. Einzig, P. (1949). Primitive money in its ethnological, historical, and economic aspects. Eyre & Spottiswoode, London, p.150.
6. Zeihan, P. (2014). *The accidental superpower: The next generation of American preeminence and the coming global disorder*. Twelve Pub, pp.29-35.
7. Edwards, E. (2017). Manilla or pen annular bracelet currency by Eric Edwards Collected Works. Retrieved from https://ericwedwards. wordpress.com /2013/11/07/manilla-or-penannular-bracelet-currency/
8. Meek, C. K. (1937). *Law and authority in a Nigerian tribe*. London, p.5.
9. Rees, A. (2000, April). Manillas. *Coin News*, pp. 46-47.
10. Senn, P.R. (1951). Cigarettes as currency. *The Journal of Finance,* 6, 329-332.
11. Wong, V. (2012). Cigarettes as the most stable international currency. Retrieved from https://www.bloomberg.com /news/articles/2012-03-04/
12. McHenry, C. (1992). In *The New Encyclopedia Britannica*. (15 Ed., p. 6). Chicago, IL: Encyclopedia Britannica.
13. Bullion, J.M. (2016). Metal spot prices. Retrieved from www.jmbullion.com
14. Rothkopf, D. (2012). *Power, Inc.: The epic rivalry between big business and government--and the reckoning that lies ahead.* Macmillan, p. 41.
15. History of copper currency in Sweden. (2017). Retrieved from www.wikipedia.org
16. Perlez J., & Johnson K. (2010, June 14). Behind gold's glitter: Torn lands and pointed questions. Retrieved from https://www.nytimes. com/2005/10/24/
17. Prior, E. (2013). How much gold is there in the world? Retrieved from www.bbc.news/magazine-21969100
18. Gold prices today. (2017). Retrieved from https://www.apmex.com /spotprices/gold-price
19. All the world's gold. (2017). Retrieved from www.numbersleuth. org/worlds-gold/
20. Gold supply. (2107). Retrieved from www.gold.org/supply-and-demand/

21. IMF (2015, December 1). *IMF executive board completes the 2015 review of SDR valuation.* Retrieved from http://www.imf.org/en/News/Articles /2015/09/14/01/49/pr15543.
22. M2 money stock. (2017). Federal Reserve Economic Data. Retrieved from https://fred.stlouisfed.org/series/M2
23. Kroll, G. M., & Robbins, R. H. (Eds.). 2008. *World in motion: The globalization and the environment reader*. Altamira Press, p.58.
24. Morteani, G., & Northover, J.P. (1994). *Prehistoric gold in Europe: mines, metallurgy, and manufacture*. New York: Springer-Verlag, p. 37.
25. Silver (2016). USGS. Retrieved from http://minerals.usgs.gov/minerals/ pubs/commodity/silver/
26. Konheim, A.G., (2015, June). Automated teller machines: Their history and authentication protocols. *Journal of Cryptographic Engineering* 6, 1, Retrieved from https://rd.springer.com/article/10.1007%2Fs13389-015-0104-
27. Dickler, J., (2008, July 31). Hidden credit card fees are costing you. Retrieved from http://money.cnn.com/2008/07/28/news/ credit_card_interchange/
28. Moore, D. & Rid, T. (2016). The darkness online. *Journal of Global Politics and Strategy* 58, 1, Retrieved from https://www.tandfonline.com/doi/full/ 10.1080/00396338.2016.1142085
29. *Statement of Jennifer Shasky Calvery,* (2013, November 19) *Director Financial Crimes Enforcement Network United States Department of the Treasury Before the United States Senate Committee on Banking, Housing, and Urban Affairs Subcommittee on National Security and International Trade and Finance Subcommittee on Economic Policy* (PDF). Financial Crimes Enforcement Network. Retrieved from www.fincen.gov.

Chapter Two: Civilizations & Cultures

1. Devlin, H. (2018, January 25). Oldest homo sapiens bones ever found shake foundations of the human story. Retrieved from https://www.theguardian. com/science/2018/jan/25/
2. Kennett, D.J. & Winterhalder, B. (2006). *Behavioral ecology and the transition to agriculture*. University of California Press.
3. Trigger, B.G. (2007). *Understanding early civilizations: A comparative study.* Cambridge University Press.
4. Wright, H. T. Rise of civilizations: Mesopotamia to Mesoamerica. *Archaeology* 42, 1. 46–48.
5. Haviland, W. A., et al. (2013). *The essence of anthropology* (3rd ed.). Belmont, California: Wadsworth, p. 104.
6. Maisels, C.K. (1999). *Early civilizations of the old world.* Routledge, p. 4.
7. Kuznetsov, P. F. (2006). The emergence of Bronze Age chariots in Eastern Europe. *Antiquity,* 80, 638–645.
8. The cuneiform writing system in ancient Mesopotamia: Emergence and evolution. (2017). Retrieved from https:// edsitement.neh.gov/
9. What was the economy of ancient Mesopotamia? (2017). Retrieved from www.reference.com

10. Hudson, M. (2000). How interest rates were set, 2500 BC-1000 AD. *Journal of the Economic and Social History of the Orient.* 132-161.
11. Wright, R. P. (2009). The ancient Indus: urbanism, economy, and society. Cambridge University Press.
12. Keightley, D. N. (1978). Sources of Shang history: The oracle-bone inscriptions of Bronze Age China. Berkeley: University of California Press.
13. Stark, M.T. (2006). *Archaeology of Asia.* Wiley-Blackwell, p. 84.
14. David, H. (2005, September 22). *Cast Chinese Coins*. Trafford Publish
15. Carmack, R. M.; Gasco, J. L. & Gossen, G. H. (1996). *The legacy of Mesoamerica, The history and culture of a native American civilization*. New Jersey: Prentice Hall.
16. Lewis, N. (2007). *Gold: The once and future money.* Agora Press.
17. Oldest city in the Americas *BBC News. (2001,* April 26) Retrieved fromhttp://news.bbc.co.uk/2/hi/science/ nature/1298460.stm
18. Mann, C. C. (2006). *1491: New revelations of the Americas before Columbus*. Vintage Books pp.199-221.
19. Croesus (n.d.). In *Ancient History Encyclopedia*, Retrieved from http://www.ancient.eu/croesus/
20. Graves, R. (2014). *Greek gods and heroes*. Rosetta Books.
21. Hunger, J. D., & Wheelen, T. L. (2003). *Essentials of strategic management*. New Jersey: Prentice Hall.
22. Acemoglu, D., & Robinson, J. A. (2013). *Why nations fail: The origins of power, prosperity, and poverty*. Crown Business.
23. Zeihan, P. (2014). *The accidental superpower: The next generation of American preeminence and the coming global disorder*. Twelve Pub.
24. Family Values. (2017). Retrieved from www.dictionary.com/browse/family-values.
25. The World Factbook. (2017). Retrieved from www.cia.gov/library/publications
26. International Monetary Fund Factsheet. (2017). Retrieved from www.imf. org/en/About/Factsheets/Sheets/2017
27. Population pyramids of the world from 1950 to 2100. (2017). Retrieved from http://www.populationpyramid.net/
28. Last, J.V. (2013). *What to expect when no one's expecting: America's coming demographic disaster*. Encounter Books.
29. Zuckerman, P. (2015, May 12). Christianity declining, secularism rising. *Psychology Today* Retrieved from https://www. psychologytoday. com/us/ blog/the-secular-life/201505/
30. Terpstra, V., Foley, J., & Sarathy, R. (2012). *International Marketing*. Naper Press, pp. 92-99.
31. Usury Laws for Your State. (2017). Retrieved from www.usurylaw.com
32. Samuelson, P. A. (1948). Foundations of economic analysis. *Science and Society* 13, 93-95.
33. Index of Economic Freedom Country Rankings. (2017). Retrieved from www.heritage.org
34. What is the difference between monetary and fiscal policy? In Investopedia. Retrieved from https://www.investopedia. com/ask/answers/100314

35. Dewey, J. (1944). *Democracy and education.* The Free Press, pp. 1-4.
36. Painter, J., & Jeffrey, A. (2009). *Political geography*. Sage.
37. Wilhelm, P. G. (2002). International validation of the corruption perceptions index: Implications for business ethics and entrepreneurship education. *Journal of Business Ethics*. Springer Netherlands. 35 (3), 177–189.
38. Comparing international R&D expenditures: Science and engineering indicators. (2014) National Science Foundation. Retrieved from www.nsf.gov/statistics
39. Ortega-Argiles, R.; Potters, L. & Vivarelli, M. (2011). R&D and productivity: testing sectoral peculiarities using micro data. *Empirical Economics*. 41 (3) pp. 81.

Chapter Three: Athena: Goddess of Wisdom & War

1. West, J. (2015, July 7). Teddy Roosevelt was obsessed with making the dollar look like the Greek drachma. Retrieved from https://www.motherjones.com /politics/2015/07/greek-drachma-euro-roosevelt/
2. Through the ages, Athenian owls. (2018). Retrieved from http://rg.ancients. info/owls/
3. D'Aulaires, E. & D'Aulaires, I. (1962). *Book of Greek myths.* Doubleday Books.
4. Nelson, E. D. & Nelson, A. (2005). *The complete idiot's guide to ancient Greece.* Alpha Press, p. 197.
5. Stanton, M. & Hyma, A. (1992). Streams of civilization: Earliest times to the discovery of the new world. Christian Liberty Press, p. 125.
6. J. Porteous, *The Nature of Coinage*. In *Coins: An illustrated survey, 650 BC to the present day*. Edited by M. Price, Hamlyn, London, 1980, pp. 9-12, presents an outline of the introduction of coinage in several locations in the world. S. Karwiese, p. 9, called Lydian Lion coins the "mother of all coinage."
7. Hanfmann, G. (1983). *Lydian culture and society.* In *Sardis from prehistoric to Roman times.* Harvard University Press, Cambridge, pp.67, 98.
8. Goldsborough, R. (2013). A Case of the World's Oldest Coin: Lydian Lion. Retrieved from http://rg.ancients. info/lion/article.html
9. Arrian, J.R. (1976). *The campaigns of Alexander.* Penguin Classics, p.65.
10. Freeman, P. (2011). *Alexander the Great*. Simon and Schuster, p. 320.
11. Yenne, B. (2010). *Alexander the Great: Lessons from history's undefeated general*. Palgrave McMillan. p. 159.
12. Hanson, V. D. (1998). *The landmark Thucydides: A comprehensive guide to the Peloponnesian war.* Ed. Strassler, R.B., Simon, and Schuster.
13. Ciocco, J. (2010). The development of ancient Greek naval warfare a study of the technical, social, historical, and political developments until the end of the Peloponnesian war. (Unpublished thesis). Rutgers University History Department
14. The Geopolitics of Greece: A Sea at Its Heart. (2011). Retrieved from http://geopolitics-gr.blogspot.com/2011/11

15. Durant, W. (1939). *The life of Greece: The story of civilization, Part II*. New York: Simon & Schuster
16. Guisepi, R. (1998). A vital legacy: A history of ancient Greece. Retrieved from http://history-world.org/greece%20legacy.htm

Chapter Four: Latifundia, Rome & the Economics behind the Roman Republic

1. Ferro, M. (2003). *The use and abuse of history: Or how the past is taught to children.* Routledge.
2. Pocock, J.G. (1976). Between Machiavelli and Hume: Gibbon as civic humanist and philosophical historian. *Daedalus* 105, 3,153–169.
3. The Editors of Encyclopedia Britannica: Latifunium (2017). Retrieved from https://www.britannica. com/ topic/latifundium
4. Petrusewicz, M. (1996). *Latifundium: Moral economy and material life in a European periphery*. Trans. Judith C. Green. Ann Arbor: University of Michigan Press.
5. Schneider, J. (1976). *Culture and political economy of western Sicily: Studies in social discontinuity,* Academic Press, p. 36.
6. Cato, M. P. (1966). *On Farming* (Vol. 17). Octagon Books.
7. Sokoloff, K. & Engerman, S. (2000). Institutions, factor endowments, and paths of development in the new world. *Journal of Economic Perspectives,* 14, 3.
8. Cornell, T. (1995). *The beginnings of Rome: Italy and Rome from the bronze age to the Punic Wars (c. 1000–264 BC).* Routledge.
9. The Editors of Encyclopedia Britannica (2018). Demographic and economic developments in Ancient Rome. Retrieved from https://kids.britannica. com/scholars/article/ancient-Rome/106272
10. The Editors of Encyclopedia Britannica. (2017). Lictor: Ancient Roman Official. Retrieved from https://www. britannica.com/topic/lictor
11. The Editors of Encyclopedia Britannica. (2017). Vestal Virgins. Retrieved from https://www.britannica. com/topic/Vestal-Virgins
12. Howgego, C. (2002). *Ancient history from coins*. Routledge, p. 36.
13. Roth, J., & Roth, J. P. (1999). *The logistics of the Roman army at war: 264 BC-AD 235* (Vol. 23). Brill.
14. Erdkamp, P. (Ed.). (2011). *A Companion to the Roman army*. John Wiley & Sons.
15. Sayles, W. G. (2003). *Ancient coin collecting* (Vol. 1). F+ W Media, Inc.
16. Livius, T., Weissenborn, W., & Müller, M. (1862). *Ab urbe condita* (i 41-48). Teubner.
17. Hornblower, S., Spawforth, A., & Eidinow, E. (2014). *The Oxford companion to classical civilization*. Oxford Companions.
18. Aicher, P.J. (2004). *Rome alive: A source-guide to the ancient city*. Bolchazy-Carducci Publishers, pp. 66-68.

19. Sullivan, G. H. (2009). *Not built in a day: Exploring the architecture of Rome.* Da Capo Press, pp. 33-37.
20. Crawford, M. H. (1985). *Coinage and money under the Roman republic.* Methuen & Co.
21. Weatherford, J. (1997). *The history of money.* Crown Publishers, Inc. New York, p.48.
22. Hammond, N.G.L. & Scullard, H.H. (Eds.) (1970). *The Oxford Classical Dictionary* Oxford: Oxford University Press.
23. The Editors of Encyclopedia Britannica. (2007). Aureus: Ancient Roman Money. Retrieved from https://www. britannica.com/topic/aureus
24. Shepard, R. (1993). *Ancient mining.* London: Elsevier Applied Science.
25. Religion in Carthage. (2104). Retrieved from https://www.revolvy.com /main/index.php?s=Religion%20in%20 Carthage
26. Mark, J.J. (2011). Scipio Africanus the Elder. Retrieved from https://www. ancient.eu/Scipio_Africanus_the_Elder/
27. The Editors of Encyclopedia Britannica. (2018). Demographic and economic developments in Ancient Rome. (2018). Retrieved from https://kids.britannica .com/scholars/article/ancient-Rome/106272
28. Schneider, J. (1976). *Culture and political economy of western Sicily: Studies in social discontinuity,* Academic Press
29. The history of ancient Rome. Victrix History Series. (2107). Retrieved from https://www.unrv.com/
30. Mining in ancient Greece and Rome. (2015). Retrieved from www.depositmag.com
31. Wilson, A. (2009). Approaches to quantifying Roman Trade. *Quantifying the Roman economy: Methods and problems.* 1, p. 217.
32. Rickman, G.E. (1980). The grain trade under the Roman Empire. *The American Academy in Rome*. 36, 264.
33. Oertel, F. (1939). The Economic life of the empire. *Cambridge Ancients History.* 12, 232-81. London, Cambridge University Press
34. Parker, A. J. (1992). *Ancient shipwrecks of the Mediterranean & the Roman provinces* (Vol. 580). Oxford: Tempus reparatum.
35. Historum: Ancient History. (2008). Retrieved from www.historum.com /ancient-history
36. Frier, B. W. (1999). Roman Demography. *Life, Death, and Entertainment in the Roman Empire*, 85-109. Population Tables 5 and pages 812-814, mortality rate page 788.
37. Evans, R. J. (1995). *Gaius Marius: a political biography.* (Doctoral dissertation)
38. Bartlett, B. (1994). How excessive government killed ancient Rome. *Cato Journal. 14,* 2, 287-303.
39. Elkington H.D. (1968). *The Development of mining lead in the Iberian Peninsula and Britain under the Roman Empire.* Durham University Library.

40. Plutarch (2017). *The parallel lives: The life of Julius Caesar.* Retrieved from http://penelope.uchicago.edu/ Thayer/E/Roman/Texts/Plutarch/Lives/Caesar*.html

Chapter Five: The Imperial Roman Empire

1. The Tribute Penny of Matthew 22.20-21. (2017). Retrieved from http://www.forumancientcoins.com/catalog/roman-and-greek-coins.asp?
2. Tameanko, M. (2009). Livia: The First Augusta of Rome. *Journal of Ancient Numismatics*Vol 1, Issue 4 Retrieved from http://coinproject.com/jan/ volume1/issue4/volume1-4-1.html
3. Frank, T. (1935). The financial crisis of 33 AD. *The American Journal of Philology.* 56, 4, 336-341.
4. Gruen, E. S. (2005). Augustus and the making of the Principate. In *The Cambridge Companion to the Age of Augustus (Cambridge Companions to the Ancient World)*. Ed. Karl Galinsky, 33–51. Cambridge University Press.
5. Mansfield, H.C. & Tarov, N. (1996). *Discourses on Livy*, trans. Chicago: University of Chicago Press. Originally published in 1531
6. Gibbon, E. (1898). *The History of the decline and fall of the Roman Empire (Vol. 5).* Methuen, p. 78.
7. The Editors of the Encyclopedia Britannica: Five Good Emperors of Rome. (2018). Retrieved from https://www.britannica.com/topic/Five-Good-Emperors
8. Ancient Coin Club of Los Angeles. (2015). Coins of the Five Good Emperors. Retrieved from http://www.accla.org/actaaccla/vgemperors.html
9. Rickman, G. E. (1980). The grain trade under the Roman Empire. *Memoirs of the American Academy in Rome.* 36, 261-275.
10. John, H. D., & Kopff, E. C. (1980). *The seaborne commerce of ancient Rome: Studies in archaeology and history* (Eds.). (Vol. 36). American Academy in Rome.
11. Frier, B.W. *Demography*. (2000). In A.K. Bowman, P. Garnsey, and D. Rathbone, Eds., *The Cambridge Ancient History XI: The High Empire, A.D. 70–192*. Cambridge University Press.
12. Lo Cascio, Elio. (2007). *The early Roman Empire: The state and the economy.* In W. Scheidel, I. Morris and R. Saller, Eds., *The Cambridge Economic History of the Greco-Roman World.* Cambridge University Press pp. 619-647.
13. Burnett, A. (1987). *Coinage in the Roman world.* London: Seaby.
14. Howgego, C. (1995). *Ancient history from coins*. London: Routledge
15. Roman Mints. (2018). Retrieved from http://www.tjbuggey.ancients.info/ mints.html
16. The Editors of Encyclopedia Britannica: Gresham's Law. (2018). Retrieved from https://www.britannica .com/topic/Greshams-law
17. What is quantitative easing? Bank of England. (2018). Retrieved from https://www.bankofengland. co.uk/monetary-policy/quantitative-easing
18. Forbes, S., & Ames, E. (2014). *How the destruction of the dollar threatens the global economy and what we can do about it*. McGraw Hill Professional.

19. Armstrong, M.A. (2018). Valerian I: The decline of the a*ntoninianus.* Retrieved from https://www. armstrongeconomics.com/research/monetary-history-of-the-world/roman-empire/chronology_-by_-emperor/end-of-severan-dynasty/valerian-i-253-260-ad/
20. Historia. (2017). The Roman imperial economy, hoarding, Gresham's Law and all that. Retrieved from https://www.forumancientcoins.com/historia/de-basement/economy.html
21. Mundell, R. (1998). Uses and Abuses of Gresham's Law in the history of money. *Zagreb Journal of Economics.* 2, 2, 3-38.
22. Brownworth, L. (2010). *Lost to the west: the forgotten Byzantine Empire that rescued western civilization.* Broadway Books, pp. 3-10.
23. Strotroan, B. (2018). Hyperinflation and tyranny in Diocletian's Rome. Retrieved from http:// bigfaithministries.com/hyperinflation-in-the-reign-of-diocletians-roman-tetrarchy-a-case-study-of-empire-building-and-subsequent-revolution/
24. Corcoran, S. (2000). The Empire of the Tetrarchs, imperial pronouncements, and government AD 284–324. Oxford University Press.
25. Peden, J.R. (2017). Mises daily article: Inflation and the fall of the Roman Empire. Retrieved from https://www.mises.org/library/inflation-and-fall-roman-empire

Chapter Six: The Middles Ages: Ascendance and Fusion of the Church and State

1. Brownworth, L. (2010). *Lost to the west: The forgotten Byzantine Empire that rescued western civilization.* Broadway Books, pp. 11-20.
2. Nightingale, R. (n.d.). The "sign" that changed the world. Retrieved from http://www.forumancientcoins.com /Articles/Constantine_Ch_Rho_files/Constantine_Ch_Rho.html
3. Odahl, C.M., (2004). *Constantine and the Christian Empire.* Routledge, pp. 160-180.
4. Zosimus. (2017). trans Ridley, R. *New History (Byzantina Australiensia 2).* Canberra.
5. Rosser, J. H. (2011). *Historical Dictionary of Byzantium.* Lanham, MA: Scarecrow, p. 2.
6. Laiou, A. E. & Morisson, C. (2007). *The Byzantine economy.* Cambridge: Cambridge University Press, pp. 6-13.
7. VanVoorst, J.F. (2012). *The Byzantine Empire.* Capstone, p. 14.
8. Grierson, P. (1999). *Byzantine coinage.* Washington, D.C.: Dumbarton Oaks, pp. 10-12.
9. Grabar, A. (1968). *Christian iconography: A study of its origins.* Taylor & Francis.
10. Lenski, N. (2006). *The reign of Constantine.* The Cambridge Companion to the Age of Constantine. New York: Cambridge University Press.

11. Pohlsander, H. A. (1995). *Helena: Empress and Saint.* Chicago: Ares Publishers.
12. Drijvers, J.W. (1992). *Helena Augusta: The Mother of Constantine the Great and her finding of the true cross.* Leiden & New York: Brill Publishers.
13. Firth, J. (2015). *Constantine the Great: The reorganization of the Empire and triumph of the Church.* Palatine Press.
14. Kousoulas, D.G. (2007). *The life and times of Constantine the Great.* Rutledge Books.
15. Hildebrand, S.M. (2011). *The Trinitarian theology of Basil of Caesarea.* The Catholic University of America Press.
16. Halsall, G. (2007). *Barbarian migrations and the Roman West.* Cambridge University Press, pp.376-400.
17. Baillie, M.G.L. (1994). Dendrochronology raises questions about the nature of the AD 536 Dust-Veil Event. *The Holocene* fig. 3, p. 215.
18. Brown, Peter (2003). *The rise of Western Christendom.* Blackwell, pp. 73-74.
19. Collins, D. (2008). Mapping the entrails: The practice of Greek Hepatoscopy. *American Journal of Philology,* 129, 319-345.
20. Heather, P. (2006). *The fall of the Roman Empire: A new history of Rome and the barbarians.* Oxford University Press, p. 378.
21. Evans, J.A. (2005). *The Emperor Justinian and the Byzantine Empire.* Westport, CT: Greenwood Press.
22. *St. Justinian the Emperor, the Orthodox Church in America.* (2017). Retrieved from https://oca.org/saints/lives /2017/11/14/103301-st-justinian-the-emperor
23. Ayer, J. C. ed. (1913). *A source book for ancient church history.* Mundus Publishing, pp. 538-540.
24. Ekonomou, A.J. (2007). *Byzantine Rome and the Greek Popes.* Lexington Books, p. 218.
25. Jolowicz, H. F. & Nicholas, B. (1972). *Historical introduction to the study of Roman law.* Cambridge University Press, p. 463.
26. Greatrex, G. (1997). The Nika riot: A reappraisal. *The Journal of Hellenic Studies.* 117, 60-86.
27. Snell, M. (2017). The Nika revolt: Violent uprising in early Medieval Byzantium. Retrieved from www.thoughtco. com/the-nika-revolt-1788557

Chapter Seven: The Middle Ages: The Beginning of the End

1. Alchon, S.A. (2003). *A pest in the land: New world epidemics in a global perspective.* University of New Mexico Press, p. 21
2. Maas, M. (2005).*The Cambridge companion to the age of Justinian.* Cambridge University Press, pp. 70-71.
3. Ska, J. L. (2006). *Introduction to reading the Pentateuch.* Eisenbrauns, pp. 227-228, 260.
4. Kaadan, A.N. & Angrini, M. (2013-2014). Was the plague disease a motivating or an inhibiting factor in the early Muslim community?

International Society for the History of Islamic Medicine. 107-114. Retrieved from http://www.academia.edu/11294412/

5. Canduci, A. (2010). *Triumph & tragedy: The rise and fall of Rome's immortal emperors.* Pier 9.
6. Lewis, J.J. (2017, March 25). Irene of Athens: Controversial Byzantine Empress. Retrieved from https://www.thoughtco.com/irene-of-athens-p2-3529666
7. Besançon, A. (2009). *The forbidden image: An intellectual history of iconoclasm*. University of Chicago Press
8. Heck, G.W. (1999). Gold mining in Arabia and the rise of the Islamic state. *Journal of the Economic and Social History of the Orient*. 42, 3, 364-395.
9. Kazhdan, A., ed. (1991). *The Oxford Dictionary of Byzantium*. New York and Oxford: Oxford University Press, p. 1448.
10. Brownworth, L. (2009). *Lost to the West: The forgotten Byzantine Empire that rescued Western Civilization.* Crown Publishers.
11. McKitterick, R. (2008). *Charlemagne: The formation of a European identity*. Cambridge, UK: Cambridge University Press.
12. Redish, A. (2006). *Bimetallism: An economic and historical analysis.* Cambridge University Press.
13. Heather, P. (2014). *The restoration of Rome: Barbarian Popes and imperial pretenders*. Oxford University Press
14. Kidd, B. J. (2013). *Churches of Eastern Christendom.* Routledge, pp. 208-213.
15. Grierson, P. (1999). *Byzantine coinage*. Washington, DC: Dumbarton Oaks, 964-965.
16. Head, C. (1977). *Imperial twilight: the Palaeologus dynasty and the decline of Byzantium.* Nelson-Hall, p. 168.
17. Brownworth, L. (2009). *Lost to the West: The forgotten Byzantine Empire that rescued Western Civilization.* Crown Publishers.
18. Asbridge, T. (2012). *The Crusades: The war for the Holy Land.* Simon & Schuster.
19. Riley-Smith, J. ed. (2001). *The Oxford History of the Crusades.* Oxford University Press
20. Brownworth, L. (2009). *Lost to the West: The forgotten Byzantine Empire that rescued Western Civilization.* Crown Publishers.

Chapter Eight: The Dawn of Banking and Capitalism

1. Ralls, K. (2007). *Knights Templar Encyclopedia*. Career Press, p. 28.
2. Benson, M. (2005). *Inside secret societies*. Kensington Publishing Corp, p. 90.
3. Barber, M. (1995). *The new knighthood: A history of the Order of the Temple*. Cambridge: Cambridge University Press
4. Watson, P. (2005). *Ideas*. London: Weidenfeld & Nicolson, p. 373.
5. Breay, C. (2010). *Magna Carta: Manuscripts and myths*. London. UK: The British Library.

6. Brand, P. (2007). Henry II and the creation of the English common law. In Harper-Bill, C. & Vincent (Eds.) *Henry II: New Interpretations* by, N. Woodbridge UK, Boydell Press, p. 216.
7. Ralls, K. (2007). The essential guide to the people, places, events, and symbols of the Order of the Temple. In *Knights Templar Encyclopedia* New Page Books.
8. The Temple Church, London, Official Site. (n.d.). Retrieved from http://www.templechurch.com/
9. Martin, S. (2004). *The Knights Templar: The history & myths of the legendary military order*. New York: Thunder's Mouth Press.
10. Hartston, W. (2007). *The encyclopedia of useless information*. Sourcebook, Inc.
11. Menache, S. (2002). *Clement V.* Cambridge University Press, p. 253.
12. Miner, S.W. (1787). *The impact of Masonry on the constitutional convention.* Retrieved from http://www. masonicworld.com/education/articles/htm
13. Lombardo, E. (2018). *Enrico Dandolo.* Retrieved from www.britannica.com /biography/Enrico-Dandolo.
14. Madden, T.F. (2008). *Enrico Dandolo and the rise of Venice*. JHU Press, p. 110.
15. Allen, L. (2011). *Global financial system 1750-2000*. Reaction Books, p. 128.
16. Temporal Punishment and Suffering. (n.d.). Retrieved from http://www.catholic-forum.com/members/catholictracts /tract117.html
17. McLaughlin, M. (1994). *Consorting with saints: Prayer for the dead in early Medieval France.* Cornell University Press, p. 18.
18. Duffy, E. (1997). *Saints & sinners: A history of the Popes.* New Haven CT USA: Yale University Press.
19. Soyer, A. (1977). *The Pantropheon or a history of food and its preparation in ancient times.* Wisbech, Paddington Press, p. 172.
20. List of cathedrals. (n.d.). Retrieved from https://en.wikipedia.org/wiki/Lists_of_cathedrals
21. Ganss, H. G. (1912). *Johann Tetzel*. In Herbermann, C. (Ed.) Catholic Encyclopedia. New York: Robert Appleton Company, 14, 540.
22. Weber, M. (2002). *The Protestant ethic and the spirit of capitalism.* (P. Baehr, & G.C. Wells, Trans.). Penguin Books.
23. Burke, P., (1998). *The European Renaissance: Centre and peripheries.* Wiley-Blackwell.
24. Perry, M. (2012). *Sources of the Western Tradition Volume II: From the Renaissance to the present.* Cengage Learning.
25. Stark, R. (2005). *The victory of reason: How Christianity led to freedom, capitalism, and Western success.* Random House, NY, p. 56.
26. Lewis, G. (1999). Braudel, Fernand, In *The Encyclopedia of Historians and Historical Writing*, Boyd, K. (Ed). Chicago: FitzRoy Dearborn, p. 114.
27. Walsh, M. (2003). *The conclave: A sometimes secret and occasionally bloody history of papal elections*. Rowman & Littlefield.
28. The Editors of the Encyclopedia Britannica. (n.d.). *Ducat Venetian Coin.* Retrieved from www.britannica.com/ topic/ducat.

29. Herlihy, D. et al. (n.d.) *Florentine Renaissance Resources: Online Catasto of 1427-29.* [online database]. Retrieved from http://cds.library.brown.edu/projects/catasto/overview.html
30. The Economist. (1999, December 23). *Those Medici.* Retrieved from https://www.economist.com/node/347333
31. de Roover, R.A. (1948). *The Medici Bank: Its organization, management, and decline*. New York University Press.
32. de Roover, R. (1966). *The rise and decline of the Medici Bank 1397-1494.* W.W. Norton & Company, p. 6.
33. Lee, G. A. (1977). The coming of age of double entry: The Giovanni Farolfi ledger of 1299-1300. *Accounting Historians Journal*. 4, 2, 79–95.
34. Soll, J. (2014). *The reckoning: Financial accountability and the rise and fall of nations*. Basic Books

Chapter Nine: The Origins of Modern Currency and the Dutch Golden Age

1. Schama, S. (1987). *The embarrassment of riches: An interpretation of Dutch culture in the Golden Age,* New York: Alfred Knopf.
2. Appelbaum, D.M. (2012, May 24). *The miracle of the Dutch Republic.* Retrieved from http://www. dianamuirappelbaum.com /?p=583#. WxAs70
3. De Vries, J. (1976). *The economy of Europe in an age of crisis, 1600-1750.* Cambridge: Cambridge University Press.
4. de la Court, P. (n.d.) *The True Interest and Political Maxims of the Republic of Holland* [1662] Online. Retrieved from http://www1.umassd.edu/euro/resources/dutchrep/19.pdf
5. Harreld, D.J. (2004, August 12). The Dutch Economy in the 'Golden Age' (16th-17th Centuries). E.H. Net Encyclopedia, Whaples, R. (Ed.) Retrieved from http://eh.net/encyclopedia/the-dutch-economy-in-the-golden-age-16th-17th-centuries/
6. De Vries, J. & Van der Woude. (1997) *The first modern economy: Success, failure, and perseverance of the Dutch economy, 1500-1815.* Cambridge: Cambridge University Press, pp. 430-435.
7. Black, S. (2014, December 1). This was the most valuable company in history. Retrieved from www.sovereignman. com/trends/when-adjusted-for-inflation-its-highest-market-capitalization-would-be-worth-over-7-trillion-today.
8. Goetzmann, W.N. & Rouwenhorst, G. (Eds.) (2005). *The origins of value—The financial innovations that created modern capital markets.* Oxford University Press.
9. Quinn, S. & Roberds, W. (2006). An economic explanation of the early Bank of Amsterdam, Debasement, Bills of Exchange, and the emergence of the first Central Bank. Federal Reserve Bank of Atlanta, FRB of Atlanta Working Paper. Retrieved from https://www.frbatlanta.org/-/media/Documents/research/publications/wp/2006/wp0613.pdf

10. de Roover, R.A. (1948). *The Medici Bank: Its organization, management, and decline*. New York University Press, p. 24.
11. Rabinowitz, J. J. (May 1956). The origin of the negotiable promissory note. *University of Pennsylvania Law Review*. 104, 7, 927–939.
12. Ames, Glenn J. (2008). *The Globe Encompassed: The Age of European Discovery, 1500–1700*.
13. De Vries, J. & Van der Woude. (1997) *The first modern economy: Success, failure, and perseverance of the Dutch economy, 1500-1815*. Cambridge: Cambridge University Press, p. 69.
14. Dash, M. (2011). *Tulipomania: The story of the world's most coveted flower & the extraordinary passions it aroused*. Hachette UK.
15. Shiller, R. J. (2005). *Irrational Exuberance*. Princeton: Princeton University Press, pp. 247-248.
16. de la Vega, J. (2013). *Confusion de confusiones*. Martino Publishing, Mansfield Centre, CT
17. The Bank of Amsterdam. (2012, August 5). Retrieved from https://wiki.mises.org/wiki/Bank_of_Amsterdam
18. Epstein, S. R. & Prak, M. (Editors). (2008). *Guilds, innovation, and the European economy, 1400–1800*. Cambridge University Press

Chapter Ten: The United Kingdom and the Wizard of the Gold Standard

1. Westfall, R.S. (2007). *Isaac Newton*. Cambridge University Press.
2. Newton, I. (1717). Sir Isaac Newton's Report on the Gold and Silver Coin in 1717. *The Numismatic Chronicle and Journal of the Numismatic Society*. (April 1848–January 1849), 11, 181-185.
3. Odlyzko, A. (2018, May 16). Newton's financial misadventure in the South Sea Bubble. Retrieved from http://www.dtc.umn.edu/~odlyzko/doc/mania13.pdf
4. Keynes, S. *Offa*. In *The Blackwell Encyclopaedia of Anglo-Saxon England*. Oxford, Blackwell Publishing, p. 340.
5. Bordo, M. D., & Rockoff, H. (1996). The gold standard as a 'good housekeeping seal of approval.' *The Journal of Economic History*, *56*, 2, 389-428.
6. Narron, J. & Skeie, D. (2013, September 30). The not so great re-coinage of 1696. Retrieved from http://libertystreeteconomics.newyorkfed.org/2013/09
7. Odlyzko, A. (2018, May 16). Newton's financial misadventure in the South Sea Bubble. Retrieved from http://www.dtc.umn.edu/~odlyzko/doc/mania13.pdf
8. The Old Currency Exchange. (2015, August 20). Financial Crisis (1667) avoided by Charles II, via London Goldsmiths' Loans. Retrieved from https://oldcurrencyexchange.com/2015/08/20
9. Kindleberger, C. P. (2007). *A financial history of Western Europe*. Routledge.

10. Bank of England. (2016, September 13). Banknotes. Retrieved from https://www.bankofengland.co.uk/about/history
11. Carrington, C. (1950). *The British overseas: Exploits of a nation of shopkeepers.* Cambridge, England: Cambridge University Press, p. 217.
12. Frumkin, M. (1945, March). The Origin of Patents. *Journal of the Patent Office Society.* XXVII, 3, 143-155.
13. Leaffer, M. (1990). [Book Review]. *Inventing the industrial revolution: The English patent system, 1660-1800.* Article by Maurer, MacLeod, Christine (1988). *Inventing the industrial revolution: The English patent system, 1660-1800.* Cambridge: Cambridge University Press
14. Intellectual Property Office. (2012, February 7). History of patents. Retrieved from http://webarchive.nationalarchives.gov.uk/20120207081502/
15. Davies, K. G. (1999). *The Royal African Company.* Routledge/Thoemmes Press, p. 106.
16. Zook, G. F. (1919). The company of royal adventurers trading into Africa. *The Journal of Negro History* 4, 2, 134–231.
17. Challis, C.E. (1992) *A new history of the Royal Mint.* Cambridge University Press, p. 244-248.
18. Marsh, M.A. (1996). *Benedetto Pistrucci: Principal engraver and chief medalist of the Royal Mint, 1783-1855.* Michael A. Marsh Publications.
19. Ferguson, N. (1998). *The world's banker: The history of the house of Rothschild.* London
20. Bordo, M. D. (2008). Gold standard. *The Concise Encyclopedia of Economics.* Library of Economics and Liberty.
21. Bordo, M. D., & Rockoff, H. (1996). The gold standard as a 'good housekeeping seal of approval.' *The Journal of Economic History,* 56, 2, 389-428.

Chapter Eleven: The American Experience: A Currency and Culture in Transition: Part I

1. Pauketat, T. R. (1994). *The ascent of chiefs: Cahokia and Mississippian politics in native North America.* University of Alabama Press.
2. Bell, J. (2013). *Empire, religion, and revolution in early Virginia, 1607–1786.* Macmillan.
3. Simanaitis, D. (2016, March 02). Hiawatha Belt. Retrieved from https://simanaitissays.com/2016/03/02/the-haudenosaunee-builders-of-a-house/
4. Flynn, D. & Giráldez, A. (1995). Born with a "silver spoon": The origin of world trade in 1571. *Journal of World History,* 6, 2, 201-221.
5. Walton, T. R. (1994). *The Spanish treasure fleets.* Pineapple Press.
6. Marx, R. (1968). *The treasure fleets of the Spanish Main.* World Pub. Co.
7. Origin of dollar sign is traced to Mexico. (1930, February). *Popular Science.* 116, 2, 59. Retrieved from

https://books.google.com/books?id=4ykDAAAAMBAJ&printsec=frontcover&source=gbs_ge_summary_r&cad=0#v=onepage&q&f=false
8. Nussbaum, A. (1957). *A history of the dollar.* New York: Columbia University Press, p. 56.
9. Thaler Siver Coin. (2011, December 11). *Coin Talk.* Retrieved from https://www.cointalk.com/threads/1520-silver-count-schlick-thaler-aka-joachimsthaler.196558/
10. Newman, E.P. (2008). *The early paper money of America.* 5th edition. Iola, Wisconsin: Krause Publications.
11. Wright, R. E. (2008). *One nation under debt: Hamilton, Jefferson, and the history of what we owe.* New York: McGraw-Hill.
12. Carson, C. (1983, July 1). The Constitution and paper money. Retrieved from https://fee.org/articles/the-constitution-and-paper-money/
13. Rappleye, C. (2010). *Robert Morris: Financier of the American Revolution.* New York: Simon & Schuster.
14. McGinty, J.C. (2016, June 17). End the $100 bill? Uncle Sam says no. *Wall Street Journal*, A2, 18-19. Retrieved from https://www.wsj.com/articles/end-the-100-bill-uncle-sam-says-no-1466155982
15. Wood, L. (2018, April 4). 30 things you never knew about $100 bill. Retrieved fromhttps://www.gobankingrates. com/making-money/economy/100-dollar-bill-facts/#8
16. Nussbaum, A. (1937, November). The law of the dollar. *Columbia Law Review*, 37, 7, 1057-1091.
17. Stack's Bowers Galleries sets world record with the sale of 1794 silver dollar for $10,016,875. (2013, January 25). Retrieved from https://www.prnewswire.com/news-releases/stacks-bowers-galleries-sets-world-record-with-sale-of-1794-silver-dollar-for-10016875-188316191.html
18. Brands, H. W. (2005). *Andrew Jackson: His life and times.* Anchor.
19. Remini, R.V. (1967). *Andrew Jackson and the bank war: A study in the growth of presidential power.* W.W. Norton & Company.
20. Selgin, G.A. (1988). *The theory of free banking: Money supply under competitive note issue. Lanham, MD/: Rowman & Littlefield.* Retrieved from http://oll.libertyfund.org/titles/selgin-the-theory-of-free-banking-money-supply-under-competitive-note-issue
21. Rothbard, M. (2002). *A history of money and banking in the United States: The colonial era to World War II.* Rothbard Publishing.
22. Strum, H. (1994). Rhode Island and the Embargo of 1807. *Rhode Island History,* 52, 2, 58-67.
23. Irwin, D.A. (2008, November). Antebellum tariff politics: Regional coalitions and shifting economic interests. *Journal of Law and Economics,* 51, 715–42.
24. Martin, D.A. (1977). The changing role of foreign money in the United States, 1782–1857. *Journal of Economic History*. 4, 1009–1027.
25. Bateman, F. & Weiss, T. (1981). *A deplorable scarcity: The failure of industrialization in the slave economy.* Univ. of North Carolina Press.
26. Williamson, S. H. & Cain, L.P. (2018). *Measuring slavery in 2016 dollars.* MeasuringWorth. Retrieved from www. measuringworth.com/slavery.php

27. Grooms, R. (1997). *Dixie's censored subject: Black slaveholders.* Retrieved from http://thebirdman.org /Index/Others/Others-Doc-Blacks/+Doc-Blacks-Slavery&Reparations/BlackSlaveownersInTheConfederacy.htm
28. Freeman, D.S. (1934). *R. E. Lee, a biography.* Charles Scribner's Sons.
29. Phillips, U.B. (1905). The economic cost of slaveholding in the cotton belt. *Political Science Quarterly,* 20, 2, 257–275.
30. Conrad, A.H. & Meyer, J. R. (1958). The economics of slavery in the Ante Bellum South. *Journal of Political Economy,* 66, 2, 95–130.
31. Neal, L. (1994). *The international library of macroeconomic and financial history Volume 1.* Edward Elgar Publishing.
32. Rawls, J.J. & Orsi, R.J. (Eds.) (1999). *A golden state: Mining and economic development in gold rush California.* California History Sesquicentennial Series. University of California Press, p. 61.
33. Mint Act of 1873, Public law 42-131, U.S. Statutes at Large 17 Stat. 424
34. Kazin, M. (2006). *A godly hero: The life of William Jennings Bryan.* New York: Alfred A. Knopf.
35. Van Allen, L.C. & Mallis, A. G. (1991). *Comprehensive catalog and encyclopedia of Morgan & peace dollars.* Virginia Beach, DLRC Press.
36. Zerbe, F. (1920, October). Commemorate peace with a coin for circulation. *The Numismatist.* 443–444. Retrieved from http://dictionary.sensagent.com/Peace%20Dollar/en-en/

Chapter Twelve: The American Experience: Part II

1. Parthemos, J. (1987). The Federal Reserve Act of 1913 in the stream of U.S. monetary history, *FRB Richmond Economic Review.* 74, 4, 19-28. Retrieved from https://papers.ssrn.com/sol3/cf_dev/AbsByAuth.cfm?per_id=1876488
2. Johnson, R.T. (1999). Historical beginnings... The Federal Reserve System. Monograph Federal Reserve Bank of Boston. Retrieved from https://ideas.repec.org/b/fip/fedbmo/1999htfr.html
3. Bryan, D. (2012, September 30). The banking crisis–from Detroit's collapse to Roosevelt's bank holiday. Retrieved from https://www.americanhistoryusa.com/1933-banking-crisis-detroit-collapse-roosevelt-bank-holiday/
4. PBS. (2003, May 8). Frontline: The Wall Street fix: Mr. Weill goes to Washington: The long demise of Glass–Steagall. Retrieved from https://www.pbs.org/wgbh/pages/frontline/shows/wallstreet/weill/
5. Tracy, R. (2018, March 26). Regulators split on how to police banks. *The Wall Street Journal*. B7.
6. Stiglitz, J.E. (2009, January). Capitalist fools (PDF). *Vanity Fair.* Retrieved from https://www.vanityfair.com/news/2009/01/stiglitz200901-2
7. Lewis, N. (2007). *Gold: The once and future money.* Wiley, p. 191.
8. Bogart, D. & Ludlow, E. (1919). Kinley, D. (Ed.) *Direct and indirect costs of the Great World War* (2nd Ed.). Vancouver: Oxford University Press.
9. Kimble, J. (2006). *Mobilizing the home front: War bonds and domestic propaganda.* Dallas: Texas A&M University Press.
10. Lee, H. (1920). *Liberty bonds: A handbook.* London: Higginson & Co.

11. Key Facts of U.S. Foundations. (2014 Edition). Retrieved from http://foundationcenter.org/gainknowledge/research/keyfacts2014/pdfs/Key_Facts_on_US_Foundations_2014.pdf\
12. Battiston, S.P. (2017, May 12). File: Retrieved from https://upload.wikimedia.org/wikipedia/commons/7/79/USAHistorical_Marginal_Tax_Rate_for_Highest_and_Lowest_Income_Earners.svg 12
13. Kolb, E. (2012). *The Weimar Republic*. (P.S. Falla, Trans). Routledge, p. 92.
14. Cable and Associated Press (1924, November 15). Americans with marks out of luck: *Los Angeles Times.* 1.
15. Burns, K. (2012). The dust bowl, episode 1: The great plow-up. Retrieved from http://www.kenburns.com/films/dust-bowl/
16. McMahon, T. (2018). Inflation and CPI consumer price index 1920-1929. Retrieved from https://inflationdata.com/articles/inflation-consumer-price-index-decade-commentary/inflation-cpi-consumer-price-index-1920-1929/
17. A Reichsbanknote (5 Trillion Marks 1923) *National Numismatic Collection, National Museum of American History.* Retrieved from https://en.wikipedia.org/wiki/German_Papiermark.
18. 5 Million Mark coin Weinmer Republic Germany 1923. (2018, June 15). Retrieved from https://www.ebay.com/itm/1923-Germany-Westphalia-5-Million-Mark-Gilt-Bronze-Coin-NGC-MS-66-Lamb-579-10/391957528590.
19. Carr, D. (2018). FDR's 1933 gold confiscation was a bailout of the Federal Reserve Bank. Retrieved from http://www.moonlightmint.com/bailout.htm
20. Hoarding of gold. (1933, April 6). *The New York Times.*7 Retrieved from https://www.nytimes.com/1933/04/06/archives/text-of-presidents-gold-hoarding-order.html
21. Treasury Direct: Beginnings of the savings bond program. (2018). Retrieved from www.savingsbonds.gov.
22. D'Arista, J. (2009). The evolving international monetary system. *Cambridge Journal of Economics*, 33, 633–652.
23. Pickford, S. (2018). Britain's big bailout. (1976, December 16). Retrieved from https://www.chathamhouse.org/publications/twt/britain-s-big-bailout-december-15-1976
24. Mason, E.S. & Asher, R.E. (1973). *The World Bank since Bretton Woods: The origins, policies, operations and impact of the International Bank for Reconstruction.* Washington DC: Brookings Institution, p. 29.
25. Kids' Corner – a One Dollar Lesson' www.jestkidding.com Retrieved August 2016 http://jestkidding.com/about/privacy-and-use-statement/
26. U.S. Currency. How money is made. (2018). Bureau of Engraving and Printing. Retrieved from https://www.bep.gov/uscurrency/howmoneyismade.html
27. How long is the life span of U.S. paper money? ((2018). Retrieved from https://www.federalreserve.gov/faqs/how-long-is-the-life-span-of-us-paper-money.htm
28. 12 U.S.C. § 225a Title 12 of the United States Code (outlines the roles of banks and the banking system)

29. Wolin, N. S. (2011, December 13). Reducing the surplus dollar coin inventory—saving taxpayer dollars. Treasury Notes. Retrieved from https://www.treasury.gov/connect/blog/
30. Yeoman, R.S. (2016). *A guide book of United States coins (69th Ed.)*. Atlanta, GA: Whitman Publishing, LLC, pp. 364-368.
31. Kollen-Ghizoni, S. (1971, August). Nixon ends convertibility of U.S. dollars to gold and announces wage/price controls. Federal Reserve History. Retrieved from https://www.federalreservehistory.org/essays/gold_convertibility_ends
32. The economy. "We are all Keynesians now." (1965, December 31). *Time.* Cover. Retrieved from http://www.bradford-delong.com/1965/12/time-the-economy-we-are-all-keynesians-now.html
33. Ferguson, N. (2008). *The ascent of money.* Penguin Press, p. 58.
34. Lewis, N. (2007). *Gold: The once and future money.* Wiley, p. 15.
35. The Federal Reserve's dual mandate. (2018, June 6). Federal Reserve Bank of Chicago. Retrieved from https://www.chicagofed.org/research/dual-mandate/dual-mandate
36. Purposes and functions. (2018). Retrieved from https://www.federalreserve.gov/aboutthefed/pf.htm
37. Banking and the financial system. (2018). Retrieved from www.federalreserve.gov/paymentsystems
38. How much U.S. currency is in circulation? (2018). Retrieved form https://www.federalreserve.gov/faqs/currency_12773.htm

Chapter Thirteen: Globalization and the Paradox of Prosperity

1. Babones, S. (2007). *Studying globalization: Methodological issues*. Oxford: Blackwell Publishers. pp. 144-161.
2. Ritzer, G. (2004). The McDonaldization of society. *Newbury Park.*
3. Fremont-Barnes, G. (2014). *The Indian Mutiny 1857–58.* Bloomsbury Publishing.
4. Painter, J. & Jeffrey, A. (2009). *Political Geography: An introduction to space and power.* London: Sage.
5. Goldstein, J.L., Rivers, D. & Tomz, M. (2007). Institutions in international relations: Understanding the effects of the GATT and the WTO on world trade. *International Organization.* 6, 1, 37–67.
6. Brown, C. P. & Irwin, D. A. (2016). *The GATT's starting point: Tariff levels circa 1947.* The World Bank.
7. De Long, J. B., & Eichengreen, B. (1991). *The Marshall Plan: History's most successful structural adjustment program* (No. w3899). National Bureau of Economic Research.
8. Maneschi, A. (1998). *Comparative advantage in international trade: A historical perspective*. Edward Elgar Publishing.

9. McGinty, J. C. (2018, July 7-8). Cash flow or cash stash? How money moves. *Wall Street Journal*, A2.
10. Eichengreen, B. (2011). *Exorbitant privilege: The rise and fall of the dollar and the future of the International Monetary System.* Oxford University Press.
11. Blanchard (2000), op. cit., Ch. 9, pp. 172–173, and Ch. 23, pp. 447–450.
12. Blinder, A. S., Loh, A. W., & Solow, R. M. (Eds.). (2013). *Rethinking the financial crisis*. Russell Sage Foundation.
13. What is the "Rule of 72" Investopedia 2018. Retrieved from https://www.investopedia.com/terms/r/ruleof72.asp
14. Rushton, S. (2018, March 29). Monetary reform would rebalance trade. Wall Street Journal, A17.
15. Garber, P. M. (1993). The collapse of the Bretton Woods fixed exchange rate system. In *A Retrospective on the Bretton Woods system: Lessons for international monetary reform*. University of Chicago Press. Pp. 461-494.
16. Lowenstein, R. (2011, August 4). The Nixon Shock. Bloomberg BusinessWeek Magazine. Retrieved from https://www.bloomberg.com/news/articles/2011-08-04/the-nixon-shock
17. Hume, D. (1907). Essays: Moral, political, and literary (Vol. 1). Longmans, Green, and Company.
18. Friedman, M., & Friedman, R. (1990). Free to choose: A personal statement. Houghton Mifflin Harcourt.
19. Visualize the Global 500 (2018). Retrieved from 2018 http://fortune.com/global500/visualizations/?
20. Wursthorn, M. (July 2, 2018). Dow slips back into the red for the year. *Wall Street Journal*, B2.
21. The Dutch Disease. (November 26, 1977). *The Economist*, pp. 82–83.
22. Maneschi, A. (1998). Comparative advantage in international trade: A historical perspective. Cheltenham: Elgar.
23. Venables, A. J. (2016, February). Using natural resources for development: Why has it proven so difficult? *Journal of Economic Perspectives*. 30, 1, 161–184.
24. Ebrahim-zadeh, C. (2003, March). Back to Basics–Dutch Disease: Too much wealth managed unwisely. *Finance and Development*, IMF. Retrieved from http://www.imf.org/external/pubs/ft/fandd/2003/03/ebra.htm
25. Drelichman, M. (2005). The curse of Moctezuma: American silver and the Dutch disease. *Explorations in Economic History*. 42, 3, 349–80.
26. Fujikawa, M. (2016, May 17). Stronger yen takes a toll on Japanese companies' profits. *Wall Street Journal*, B5.
27. Yamazawa, I. (1998, September). The Asian economic crisis and Japan. *The Developing Economies*. 36, 3, 332–351.
28. Blustein, P. (2001). *The Chastening: Inside the crisis that rocked the global financial system and humbled the IMF.* New York: Public Affairs.
29. Delhaise P. F. (1998). *Asia in crisis: The implosion of the banking and finance systems*. John Wiley & Sons.
30. Kaufman, G.G., Krueger, T.H. & Hunter, W.C. (1999). *The Asian financial crisis: Origins, implications, and solutions*. Springer

31. Four countries that beat the resource curse. Global Risk Insights (2014, April) Retrieved from https://globalriskinsights.com /2014/04/ four-countries-that-beat-the-resource-curse/
32. Havranek, T., Horvath, R., & Zeynalov, A. (2016, December). Natural resources and economic growth: A meta-analysis. *World Development*. 88, 134–151.
33. Kurtz, M. J. & Brooks, S. M. (2011, March 15). Conditioning the "resource curse": Globalization, human capital, and growth in oil-rich nations. *Comparative Political Studies*. 44, 6, 747-770.
34. Fromson, B. (1997, February 23). "Plunge Protection Team." *The Washington Post*. H01
35. Phillips, K. (2008). *Bad money: Reckless finance, failed politics, and the global crisis of American capitalism*. Viking.
36. Kaletsky, A. (2012, August 1). How about quantitative easing for the people? *Reuters Blogs*. Retrieved from http://blogs.reuters.com/anatole-kaletsky/ 2012/08/01/
37. Wursthorn, M. (2018, July 9). Stock Prices defy surge in buybacks. *Wall Street Journal*, A1.
38. Triennial Central Bank Survey Foreign exchange turnover in April 2016" (PDF). Triennial Central Bank Survey. Basel, Switzerland: Bank for International Settlements. p. 7. Retrieved from https://www.bis.org/publ/ rpfx16fx.pdf
39. Foreign exchange market. (2018). Retrieved from https://www.revolvy.com/ topic/Foreign% 20exchange%20market
40. Blackstone, B. (2017, August 3). Swiss puzzle: How to spend $750 Billion. *Wall Street Journal*, B12.
41. Shelton, J. (2009). *Money Meltdown*. Simon and Schuster.
42. Dulaney, C. & Insebashvili, I. (2017, November 10). What's a dollar worth? Depends whom you ask. *Wall Street Journal*, B12.
43. Lehrman, L. (2013). *Money, Gold & History*. TLI Books.
44. George, H. (1879). *Progress and Poverty: An inquiry into the cause of industrial depressions, and of increase of want with increase of wealth. The Remedy*. K. Paul, Trench & Company.
45. Arnott, R. J. & Stiglitz, J.E. (November 1979). Aggregate land rents, Expenditure on public goods, and optimal city size. *Quarterly Journal of Economics*. 93, 4, 471–500.
46. Neumann, Manfred J.M. (1992, March 1). Seigniorage in the United States: How much does the U.S. government make from money production? (PDF). Federal Reserve Bank of St. Louis. 74, 2. Retrieved from https://research.stlouisfed.org/ publications/ review/1992/03/01/

INDEX

R

S

T

U